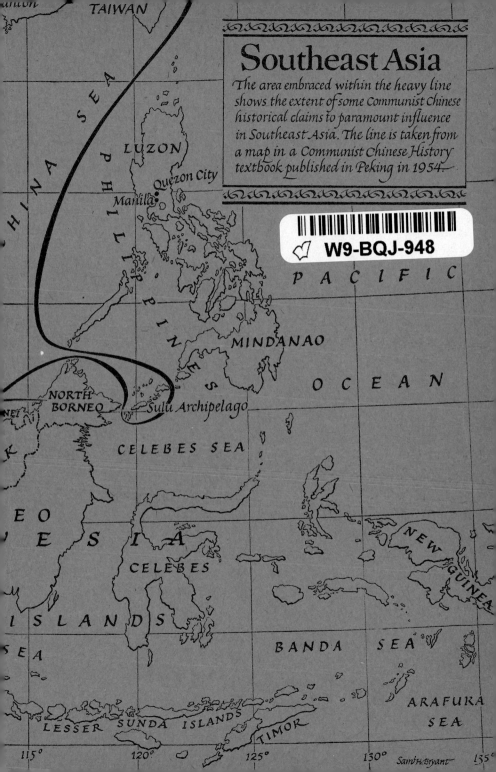

Southeast Asia

The area embraced within the heavy line shows the extent of some Communist Chinese historical claims to paramount influence in Southeast Asia. The line is taken from a map in a Communist Chinese History textbook published in Peking in 1954.

W9-BQJ-948

TAIWAN

CHINA SEA

LUZON

Quezon City

Manila

PHILIPPINES

PACIFIC OCEAN

MINDANAO

NORTH BORNEO

Sulu Archipelago

CELEBES SEA

NEW GUINEA

ESIA

CELEBES

ISLANDS

BANDA SEA

ARAFURA SEA

LESSER SUNDA ISLANDS

TIMOR

115°   120°   125°   130°   155°

Sam'H.Bryant

꧁꧂

Southeast Asia:
Problems of
United States Policy

꧁꧂

Southeast Asia: Problems of United States Policy

EDITED BY

WILLIAM HENDERSON

THE M.I.T. PRESS

MASSACHUSETTS INSTITUTE OF TECHNOLOGY

CAMBRIDGE, MASSACHUSETTS

To J. P. *with Thanks*

FOREWORD

THE PAPERS PRINTED IN THIS
book were presented at a Conference on United States
Policy in Southeast Asia sponsored jointly by The Asia Society and The Association for Asian Studies and held at
Asia House in New York in May 1963. The scholarly quality
of the papers and their enlightening contribution to the
formation of United States policy in the area prompted us
to encourage their publication. Neither The Asia Society nor
The Association for Asian Studies takes any responsibility,
however, for the views expressed in the papers, as neither
organization expresses views on political or economic questions.

AUGUST MAFFRY

Chairman of the Executive Committee
The Asia Society

INTRODUCTION

U NITED STATES POLICY IS STILL
groping for the means and concepts to come to grips effectively with the deep-seated problems rending the fabric of Southeast Asian life. More than most other regions of the world, Southeast Asia has been the target of almost uninterrupted Communist expansion and subversion since the end of World War II. Despite strenuous efforts, United States policy has not succeeded in permanently blunting this onward thrust. During the past decade North Vietnam has been lost, the Western position in Laos gravely weakened, and South Vietnam subjected to all-out assault by Vietcong guerilla forces, while elsewhere in Southeast Asia the Communists have also made serious inroads. Quite apart from the Communist threat, moreover, although affording a climate within which it flourishes, acute problems of political instability, economic backwardness, and social unrest continue to plague the region.

The last year or two have witnessed a series of major turning points in the long-continued crisis of Southeast

Asian politics. Negotiation of a precarious and highly controversial "settlement" of the civil war in Laos, which has not settled anything; intensification of the fighting in South Vietnam, and a greatly increased United States commitment to that struggle; apparent solution of the seemingly intractable dispute between Indonesia and the Netherlands over West New Guinea; the profound shock of Communist China's aggression against India; and formation of the new Federation of Malaysia are some of the most important recent developments in the rapidly changing environment of Southeast Asia. The United States has played a major part in most of these events. If anything, our role throughout the region has broadened and deepened with each passing year, and the outlook is for an ever growing involvement in the period ahead. But at the same time, thoughtful voices are increasingly heard in this country—in Congress, the press, the academic community, and among the public at large—that question the American role in Southeast Asia, the extent of our already vast commitments there, indeed, the basic wisdom of our present course in this once remote area of the world.

In view of all this, The Asia Society, headed by Paul C. Sherbert, Executive Director, and the Southeast Asia Committee of The Association for Asian Studies, under the chairmanship of Professor John F. Cady of Ohio University, undertook jointly to sponsor a conference to reappraise the whole pattern of United States policy in Southeast Asia. Approximately thirty of this country's leading experts on Southeast Asian affairs subsequently met, May 10–11, 1963, at Asia House in New York for two days of searching and fruitful discussion covering the range of our Southeast Asian policy.

In preparation for these deliberations, a series of papers was specially commissioned dealing with various aspects of the problem, with particular attention to the Southeast Asian environment within which United States policy must operate and to the various instrumentalities available to

American policy in the region. The quality of these essays was such that it was decided to make them available, through publication, to a wider audience. The essays are presented here as revised in the light of discussion at the conference. In addition, the editor of the volume has added a brief concluding chapter setting forth some reflections on the course of United States policy in Southeast Asia.

The several contributors include:

John M. Allison, Associate Director, Overseas Operations Program, University of Hawaii, and former United States Ambassador to Japan, Indonesia, and Czechoslovakia;

John F. Cady, Professor of History, Ohio University;

Russell H. Fifield, Professor of Political Science, University of Michigan;

Clifford Geertz, Associate Professor of Anthropology, University of Chicago;

William Henderson, Adviser on International Affairs, Socony Mobil Oil Company, Inc., and former Associate Executive Director, Council on Foreign Relations, Inc.;

Amos A. Jordan, Colonel, United States Army, Professor of Social Sciences, United States Military Academy;

Lionel Landry, former United States Information Service Director in Burma and Indonesia;

Paul M. A. Linebarger, Professor of Asiatic Politics, School of Advanced International Studies, Johns Hopkins University;

Genevieve C. Linebarger, Consultant, Foreign Policy Research Institute, University of Pennsylvania;

Roger M. Smith, Fellow, Southeast Asia Program, Cornell University;

Frank N. Trager, Professor of International Affairs, New York University;

Charles Wolf, Jr., Senior Economist, The RAND Corporation;

David Wurfel, Assistant Professor of Political Science, University of Missouri.

As the reader will quickly realize, the authors do not always agree among themselves on various important points of Southeast Asian history, politics, and economics or on many aspects of United States policy toward the region. No effort has been made to enforce an artificial consistency of views, and the several essays reflect simply the convictions of the individual authors. Nor was any attempt made at the Asia House conference to reach a consensus among the participants on outstanding questions of United States policy toward Southeast Asia. The discussions themselves were privileged. The editor is alone responsible for the concluding chapter, although he acknowledges his debt for many ideas to his colleagues contributing to this volume, and to the other conference participants.

WILLIAM HENDERSON

TABLE OF CONTENTS

1

THE HISTORICAL BACKGROUND
OF UNITED STATES POLICY
IN SOUTHEAST ASIA

෯෯෯෯෯

JOHN F. CADY

MAJOR PERIODS OF SOUTHEAST ASIAN HISTORY

The long history of the political and cultural development
of Southeast Asia's peoples provides the essential context
for understanding their contemporary viewpoints and aspirations. The most persistent factor in this history, which
dates from ancient times, derives from the location of the
region between the two great states of India on the one side
and China on the other. Tongking and the Annam littoral
were integral parts of China down to the end of the Tang
dynasty in the early 900's A.D., and modern Vietnam still
carries the imprint of Confucian culture. Other peoples of
Southeast Asia, with the exception of the Filipinos, absorbed
an enormous increment of acculturation from India during
the period of Han China's decline and disappearance. Areas
of Indianization emerged first in the narrow regions of the
Malayan isthmus, where a number of portage routes de-

1

veloped after A.D. 200 to facilitate commercial exchange between the Bay of Bengal and the South China Sea. Indianized trading centers also grew up adjacent to the Mekong River delta, in southern Sumatra, eastern Borneo, and western Java, all designed to service ships on the China trade.

The initial period of political and cultural adaptations of Indian tradition modulated in time toward the so-called classical age of Southeast Asian history, which developed in various localities from the ninth to the thirteenth centuries. It witnessed the flowering of talents and capacities of leading indigenous peoples, such as the Javanese, Khmers, Mons, Burmans, and Chams, under the stimulation of intimate contacts with India. Sumatran Srivijaya ruled for six centuries a great commercial empire dominating the shores of both the Malacca and Sunda Straits. The great monuments of the period include Javanese Borobudur, Cambodian Angkor, and Burman Pagan.

A major transition occurred during the course of the 1200's with the accelerated movement of Shan or Thai peoples southward from the borders of China's Yunnan province, and with the repeated Mongol-Chinese incursions into Southeast Asia sponsored by Kublai Khan. Mongol forces overran Tongking, destroyed Pagan, twice attacked Annam, invaded eastern Java, and threaded the Malacca Strait. They exacted subservience from many countries of Southeast Asia and afforded moral support to selected vassals, in particular the emerging Shan state of Sukhotai.

The third period of Southeast Asian history, dating from around 1300, saw the projection of a politically charged Muslim faith emanating from India into northern Sumatran ports, along the shores bordering the Malacca Strait, and through the sea routes leading eastward to the spice islands. Two great centers of power and influence developed in this period at Siamese Ayuthia and Muslim Malacca, founded in 1350 and 1404 respectively (the latter under Chinese patronage). Javan Kediri and Majapahit constituted, in turn, the principal political authorities to the east, and each main-

2

tained important commercial and political connections in the Moluccas. This third period came to an end during the 1500's, which witnessed the Portuguese capture of Malacca and the arrival of the Spanish in the Philippine archipelago, hitherto outside the main currents of Southeast Asian affairs.

The early modern period spanned more than two hundred years following the arrival of the Dutch and English around 1600. During these centuries the alien European impact was limited for the most part to the sea lanes and to devising new patterns of commerce. European control proper was confined to the shores of the Malacca Strait, Java, the spice islands, and the upper islands of the Philippine archipelago. Several mainland countries experienced the daring exploits of private European adventurers, who operated either as captives or as mercenaries in the service of local rulers. The leading state of the early modern period was Siam, although it was twice seriously challenged by a reunited Burma, from 1550 to 1581 and from 1750 to the 1790's. Cambodia suffered complete eclipse from pressures exerted by the Siamese from the west and by the Vietnamese (conquerors of Champa) from the east. Burman destruction of Siam's capital, Ayuthia, in 1767 left an indelible and embittered memory among the Siamese, although Siam itself recovered quickly from the disaster. The development and control of seaborne commerce between Asian ports was the key to Dutch predominance throughout the late seventeenth and much of the eighteenth centuries. The Dutch also developed in Java an important new world source for coffee and an Asian source for sugar. After the 1780's British-Indian traders took over the commercial hegemony previously enjoyed by the Dutch in the swing around the corner of Southeast Asia from Indian ports to China. Under British control, Southeast Asia trade developed further within a world context.

A fifth period of Southeast Asian history, covering slightly more than a century from around 1830 to the outbreak of World War II, saw the reduction of the entire region (with the exception of the central nucleus of Siam) to colonial

3

status under various Western powers. The later phase of colonialism was characterized by intensive capital investment and by consequent phenomenal increases in productivity, trade, and population in all of the more progressive economic areas. The process began in 1830 with inauguration in Java of the Dutch system of forced cultivation of products demanded by world markets. This program was expanded both in Java and the outer islands on more liberal economic terms after 1870, when opening of the Suez Canal afforded all of Southeast Asia more direct access to European markets. British private enterprise in Burma accomplished a similar economic transformation, with emphasis on rice cultivation, teakwood extraction, plus mining and oil. Tin and rubber production in British Malaya came in the twentieth century, as did American stimulation of hemp, sugar, and vegetable oils in the Philippines. French mercantilist development of the economic potential of Cochinchina and Tongking was also a twentieth-century phenomenon. Siam alone managed to escape colonial subjection but lost control over tariff and taxation policies, as well as legal jurisdiction over alien Western residents. In addition, it had to sacrifice extensive territorial holdings, mainly to French Indochina.

The remarkable increases in population in the colonial investment period, attributable to better health conditions and to increased output and opportunities for employment, were not accompanied by any general increase in per capita income. The indigenous peoples had to compete with Asian immigrants, mainly Indian and Chinese, who fitted in between the dominant Western elements and the native population at almost every focal point of economic advance. Chinese came to dominate local trade, to provide the service functions and skilled crafts at virtually every port and urban center except in Burma, where Indians performed such roles, and in Tongking, where the industry of the Vietnamese matched that of the Chinese. The general increase of population precluded any possibility of Southeast Asia returning to its precolonial subsistence or narrowly regional economy without concern for the wider channels of world trade.

Because the technological and marketing advantages enjoyed by Western business interests in Southeast Asia derived from colonial control over government administration, police and courts, taxation, and commercial regulations, the Europeans were loath to jeopardize their economic stake by encouragement of politically minded nationalists among the indigenous population. Except in the Philippines, virtually no preparations were made in colonial Southeast Asia prior to 1920 for popular experience in self-government or for educational training at the professional or university levels. Some constitutional concessions were made in British Burma during the interwar decades, but Dutch moves toward self-government in the Indies were extremely cautious, and the French continued to run the economically developed areas of Indochina as a closed mercantilist reserve.

By 1940, the Philippines alone had been promised full independence; Burma was in its third year of fairly autonomous government under the 1935 constitution; the Netherlands had flatly rejected moderate Indonesian proposals for self-rule; while the harried, short-lived cabinets of France were apparently incapable of conceiving reform measures. The Malay states had developed a plural society in which hereditary sultans shared a modicum of political power with the British, while an elite apolitical class of Chinese entrepreneurs at Singapore and Kuala Lumpur thrived inordinately. Most of the labor was done by Chinese and Indian coolies, who together more than equaled the native Malay population.

Nationalist anticolonial agitation throughout Southeast Asia was, prior to World War II, generally uncoordinated and subject to police restraints wherever articulate. But the apparent prospect of continued colonial rule for several more decades was abruptly transformed by the outbreak of World War II and by Japanese conquest and occupation of the whole region. This event inaugurated a sixth and final period of Southeast Asian history, marked by recession of the Western tide and the recovery of political independence.

ASPECTS OF THE HISTORICAL HERITAGE

At this point it may be useful to review salient aspects of Southeast Asia's historical heritage from the precolonial and colonial periods. These considerations can perhaps best be described country by country.

INDONESIA

The dominant tradition in Indonesian history relates to the political and cultural hegemony of populous central and eastern Java. Here were developed from the early centuries of our era extensive hydraulic systems for rice cultivation, a series of impressive religious and dynastic monuments such as Borobudur, considerable seaborne trade, and the highest levels of Indonesian social, cultural, and artistic expression. The Nusantara imperialist tradition currently associated with the Majapahit dynasty of the 1300's, although greatly overplayed, tends to reinforce the primacy of Java in a contemporary Indonesian empire including the outer islands, West New Guinea (West Irian), and prospectively, elements of North Borneo.

A contrary Indonesian tradition of political fragmentation derives in part from traditional outer-island resistance to Javanese control, especially strong in areas of Sumatra and Celebes. Present-day centrifugal tendencies also reflect ideological differences between proponents within Java of an essentially secular state as opposed to a full spectrum of Muslim parties, varying from reformist modernists to obscurantist traditionalists. President Sukarno's postwar advocacy of centralized direction or "guided democracy," utilizing ultranationalist army support and the large, disciplined Communist party, is currently designed to bridge existing political rifts and to exploit and sustain the fervor of revolutionary zeal. The problem of relations with the several million resident Chinese in Java and Sumatra carries over from the colonial period to complicate the difficult task of restoring economic production in a nation that must cope with embarrassing population pressures.

THAILAND

Siam's escape from colonial domination, a fact that sets it apart from all other countries of Southeast Asia, entailed both advantages and disadvantages. The former relate to the preservation of Siam's basic social and cultural traditions, including the uninterrupted acceptance of the symbols of governmental authority. When Siam's revolutionary modernizers in 1932 set aside the traditional absolutism of the king and established a façade of constitutional rule, the authority of the Bangkok government and the effectiveness of the permanent bureaucracy were not seriously impaired by the change. Nor have the subsequent periodic somersaults of successive military factions unduly disturbed the stability of the state. Traditional patterns of bureaucratic and village control on the countryside have tended to resist the erosion of Bangkok's modernization trends. Although the clannishness and economic power of the resident Chinese community raised perennial difficulties, no other serious problems developed in noncolonial Siam such as land alienation or the excessive growth of Western economic influence. Siam has also remained free from the xenophobia that characterized most of its neighbors. The country has habitually adjusted its foreign orientation toward the dominant outside influence operating in the area (Japan during the war and currently the United States). Bangkok's traditional relationship of vassalage to China, which persisted into the nineteenth century, has now long since been repudiated, a factor which rankles currently in Peking. Friction with

China has been aggravated by Siam's endeavors since the 1930's to assimilate culturally its 3 or 4 million resident Chinese, who may some day openly seek protection from a strong China.

Siam has longstanding frontier problems with Cambodia and Laos. From approximately 1430, when Siamese pressure forced Cambodia to abandon its capital at Angkor, the princes of the once extensive Khmer state continued until 1863 to be vassal to Ayuthia or to Bangkok, and often simultaneously vassal to Vietnam as well. The only historical exception was the brief period from 1560 to around 1590, when Burman invasions of Siam made possible a temporary revival of Cambodian rule at Angkor. French policy succeeded in recovering the frontier provinces of Battambang and Siemreap for Cambodia as late as 1907 by negotiation with Siam. French separatist movements engineered by Consul Pavie from 1890 to 1907 also resulted in the alienation from Siam of substantial territories currently incorporated in independent Laos. Today these and other considerations influence Bangkok to regard Laos, with some reason, as an artificial state, and also as an area whose control in friendly hands is essential to Thailand's security. Thailand may also recall a similar centuries-old status as suzerain over most of the petty sultans of the Malay peninsula, a connection that was finally terminated by the British between 1874 and 1909. But here ethnic, religious, and language barriers are involved which make this southern frontier issue less urgent than Thai irredentist claims along the borders of Cambodia and Laos.

A final potential border problem relates to the long and bitter tradition of Siamese rivalry with Burma, which might conceivably revive. Burma's Tenasserim coast was for several centuries (from 1300 to 1560 and from 1590 to 1760) a part of Siam. If the restive Shan states of Burma's eastern plateau area should eventually attempt to secede from Burma, their only recourse would be to associate, albeit reluctantly, with their distant Siamese kinsmen living to the east and south. Thailand's current hostility to Communist China and its close association with the United States are also regarded by informed Burmese as dangerously provocative.

BURMA

Associated with Burma's tradition of hostility to Siam was the widely entertained, if not always justified, self-image of the Burmans as exemplars of military might. Under able leadership, Burman armies on repeated occasions invaded both Siam and upper Laos, as well as Manipur, Assam, and Chittagong on the Indian frontier. Burman forces also repelled repeated invasion attempts from China in Ming and Manchu times. Burma's military prestige declined dismally following the British conquest and occupation of coastal Tenasserim province in 1825, and completely collapsed in 1885. It was partly revived during General Aung San's time in the 1940's, and it has reasserted itself in the authoritarian military regimes of General Ne Win in 1959 and 1960, and again since 1962, even though they have lacked the traditional cover of service to a Buddhist-oriented divine monarchy. Another tradition associated with Burman political pre-eminence has been dominance over subordinate ethnic groups in Burma such as the Shans, Mons, Karens, Kachins, Chins, and Arakanese. This issue is still closely intertwined with Burman nationalism and ethnic pride.

As a result of its subservience to British India from 1885 to 1937, when Indian immigrants had the run of the country, Burma is much more anti-Indian than anti-Chinese, despite the country's cultural affinities with India. On numerous occasions in its history, Burma's rulers sent tribute missions to China to maintain friendly relations and to seek Chinese authentication of royal titles. Burma readily recognized Red China in 1950 and has sought to negotiate with it since. These attempts to develop neighborly relations demonstrate

Burma's concern to avoid becoming again a battleground between international giants. Although Burma withdrew from the British Commonwealth in 1948, the Burmese people generally hold Britain and the British in fairly high respect, and westernized leaders feel apologetic about their inability thus far to operate successfully a proper parliamentary system of government. Burma's postwar economic development programs have faltered badly, due mainly to cultural maladjustment and palsied leadership. But the country is not overpopulated, as are Tongking and Java, and it can maintain indefinitely the essential means of livelihood despite an ineffective administration.

VIETNAM

Vietnam's thousand years of subjection to China (to A.D. 939) contributed at least three important historical traditions. One is an instinctive hostility, found in Tongking especially, toward any prospect of reannexation to China. The memory of repeated Chinese invasions by Mongol armies in the 1200's, and later by Ming and Manchu forces, reinforce this feeling. The occupation of northern Indochina by looting Chinese forces down to the 16th parallel after World War II constituted a fresh reminder of what Chinese domination would probably mean. A more positive result of long association with China is the cultural sophistication of the Vietnamese and their unusually disciplined industry. Except in formerly Khmer-inhabited sections of Cochinchina and as an economic stratum subordinate to the French in the Saigon-Cholon area, Chinese immigrants and traders have not found much to attract them to Vietnam, partly because the two peoples are so much alike. Finally, the traditional pattern of government, administration, and imperial authority in Vietnam was based on Confucian principles relating to the mandate of heaven rather than on symbols of divine kingship derived from India. Reverence for ancestral spirits and other factors that contribute to social and political cohesion within Vietnam owe much to the long-continued Chinese connection.

Annamese traditions in Vietnam also include a deep-seated historical rivalry between north and south. Prior to 1470, the north Vietnamese fought as today against the Chams and Khmers to the south; some sixty years of chronic feuding marred north-south Vietnamese relations during the middle 1600's; and the Nguyen dynasty's eventual victory around 1800, with the help of French volunteers, culminated a century of north-south conflict and twenty-five years of constant civil war. Partly because of the inhospitable terrain and climate of the cordillera which parallels the Annamese coast, and the hostility of the tribal peoples inhabiting the upland regions, the Vietnamese never moved laterally westward into the Mekong Valley in any large numbers. Their generally antagonistic relations in modern times with the Khmers of the Mekong delta and of Cambodia proper have been those of conqueror, displacer, and suzerain.

CAMBODIA

The Khmers accepted French rule after 1863 partly because it afforded them protection against the neighboring Siamese and Vietnamese, to both of whom vassal homage had long been paid. The French interfered little with Cambodia's traditional governmental system, its culture or economy, but contributed correspondingly little in the way of improvements. After World War II, Khmer fears of the possible consequence of French withdrawal, which would leave Cambodia exposed to historical aggressors on both flanks, tended in 1945–1946 to overshadow anti-French nationalist feeling expressed in the postwar Khmer Issarak (Free Cambodia) movement. Today the population still accords virtually automatic recognition of authentic princely leadership to the person of Norodom Sihanouk, and their sheltered Buddhist culture has been little affected by the acids of modernity.

LAOS

As previously indicated, the Lao peoples on both banks of the middle Mekong Valley constituted in precolonial times a projection of Siam's influence culturally, linguistically, commercially, and politically. Of the three main parts of the Lao country, Champassac in the south was in precolonial times normally an integral part of Siam; the middle area centering at Vientiane was usually a close vassal; and the northern kingdom of Luang Prabang was only semi-independent. Despite these close relations, the Lao did not relish Siamese control, and they accepted French protection partly to escape it.

The Lao peoples shared much less in common with the Vietnamese, from whom they were insulated by the intervening mountainous watershed inhabited by half-savage tribal peoples. The vigorous if poverty-stricken hill folk usually viewed Lao and Vietnamese with impartial hostility if not contempt, and the upland country which they inhabited was so unattractive and difficult as to preclude historically any serious intrusions by more developed neighbors. How far Red China may seek to exploit access to Laos remains to be seen. There appears to be no record of any Chinese invasion southward down the Mekong Valley during two thousand years of frontier contacts. By contrast, Chinese armies repeatedly invaded both Burma and Tongking-Annam. The principal threats to Laotian freedom historically have come from Buddhist neighbors, the Burmans and Siamese, peoples whose culture is very similar to the Lao.

MALAYA

Until the advent of Muslim Malacca in the early 1400's and the presence of the Portuguese at the same city from 1511, it was the upper half of the Malayan peninsula that had been important historically in connection with the trans-isthmian portage trade from the Bay of Bengal to the Gulf of Siam. Prior to the assertion of Siamese suzerainty over the territory, dating from the fourteenth century, control of the lower peninsula was contested by rival island-centered rulers, frequently from lower Sumatra, sometimes from Java, or from Acheh at the northern tip of Sumatra. The British founded the Straits Settlements during the 1820's, but interfered little with the peninsular sultanates until the period from 1874 to 1909. Malayan cultural traditions are Hindu-Muslim, and the same is superficially true of the coastal states of North Borneo, which came under British control during the middle of the nineteenth century. A particularly noteworthy development in British Malaya and Singapore was the predominant economic role achieved by descendants of alien Chinese immigrant stock, who today make up 78 per cent of the population of Singapore and nearly 40 per cent of the people of Malaya proper.

Three historical factors have conditioned the outlook of leaders of the postwar Federation of Malaya. The first is the inherited and generally accepted authority of the sultans themselves, who appear destined to play a continuing role behind a façade of democratic governmental forms. The second is concern that the Chinese population of the Federation not expand its predominant economic power into the political sphere as well. Malays hold the balance of political power, but Chinese are also generously represented. To avoid the possibility that Chinese Singapore might decide to join hands with Communist China, Federation and Singapore authorities decided in 1962 to incorporate the entrepôt into the Federation, with provision for Singapore's exercise of substantial autonomy. The third factor relates to the potential danger that Malaya's 7 million inhabitants, relatively prosperous from tin, rubber, and fruit production, may face from the 100 million Indonesians who live nearby. This concern influenced both Kuala Lumpur and Singapore to acquiesce in the continued presence of British armed forces within the Federation and in 1962 to invite the British possessions of North Borneo, including oil-rich Brunei, to join in a larger Malaysian Federation. The Philippines registered counterclaims to parts of North Borneo based on vague Spanish claims; while Indonesia, under the Nusantara tradition, encouraged local rebellion against the Sultan of Brunei in 1962–1963 and threatened military action against the entire North Borneo coast. Now successfully established in cooperation with British naval, air, and ground forces, the new Federation of Malaysia will constitute a barrier to Indonesian imperial aspirations and to the possible extension of Chinese Communist control into the Indies. American policymakers cannot avoid a strong interest in the situation.

THE PHILIPPINES

Although Philippine–United States relations are disturbed periodically by aid demands made upon Washington, by questions of trade relations with the United States, and by problems attending American access to military bases, the authorities at Manila are generally too keenly aware of the need for security assistance to quarrel with the continued presence of American power in the islands. The principal threat to the Philippines comes from Red China, with potential dangers from a possibly resurgent Japan to the north and an imperialist-minded Indonesia to the south. Cultural traditions date mainly from Spanish times, while governmental and economic characteristics of the island state reflect the influence of four decades of American occupation. Almost alone in Southeast Asia, the Philippines operates a democratic government as the accepted pattern of authority, even though its functioning is far from perfect. The country provides an indispensable ideological and military anchor of American policy in Southeast Asia. If Filipino claims along the Sulu shores of North Borneo can be satisfied by negotiation with Malaysia, a cohesive pro-Western regional alliance held together by mutual security interests might be forged between the Philippines, Thailand, and the newly established Malaysian Federation.

WORLD WAR II AND AFTER

SIAM–UNITED STATES RELATIONS DURING WORLD WAR II

Siam was the only Southeast Asian country with which the United States maintained regular diplomatic relations prior to World War II. Relations were particularly cordial during the 1920's, when an American adviser to the foreign office supervised the renegotiation of Siam's array of unequal treaties. Leading Thai manipulators of the 1932 revolution, while paying lip service to democratic aspirations, eventually decided, after witnessing the ascending star of Japan in East Asia, to cultivate Tokyo's support in preference to that of the United States or Great Britain. The likely prospect of the liquidation of French Indochina after 1940 afforded a tempting opportunity for Siam to recover territories lost to France between 1893 and 1907. Bangkok occupied two French-held enclaves on the right bank of the upper Mekong River in 1940, and later accepted Japanese "mediation" of additional claims to extensive segments of Laos along the same valley, plus three Cambodian provinces adjacent to Siam. Other territories in northern Malaya and along the Shan States border with Burma were added by Siam with Japanese approval during the course of World War II. Siam's expansionist moves were all opposed by Washington as patently tailored to profit from Japan's aggressive posture. American influence at Bangkok reached a low point in 1942, when Phibun's government, responding to further Japanese instigation, declared war on both the United States and Great Britain.

America's mild reaction to Phibun's declaration of war was conditioned in part by the refusal of the astute Thai ambassador at Washington, Prince Seni Promoj, to deliver the declaration on the ground that it was unrepresentative of Siamese opinion and therefore of dubious validity. By co-operating with Promoj and the emerging Free Thai move-ment (headed by Phibun's rival Pridi), Washington was able in time to establish useful intelligence contacts reaching into Bangkok itself. When the war in the Pacific began to turn against Japan in mid-1944, a changing of the guard at Bangkok (Pridi for Phibun) brought leaders of the secret Free Thai movement to power, thus strengthening plans for Siamese-American cooperation in future wartime oper-ations.

How useful this connection might have proved in the event of an attempted Allied military conquest of Siam was never to be tested, but because of it Washington felt justi-fied in vetoing punitive aspects of Great Britain's proposed peace treaty with Siam after the war. Bangkok's declaration of war was ignored, and Siam's entry into the United Na-tions was facilitated by Washington. The United States in-sisted, nevertheless, that all territorial gains realized by Siam under the aegis of Japan be surrendered, and in addition that rice supplies be provided cheaply to meet Southeast Asian needs in the immediate postwar period.

WARTIME BURMA

United States wartime policy toward Japanese-occupied Burma involved two disparate considerations. The first re-lated to the periodic abortive requests made by President Roosevelt to Prime Minister Churchill for an explicit promise to the Burmese peoples on the postwar status of Burma that would give them a clear stake in an Allied victory. But-tressing the Prime Minister's uniformly negative reaction to the American requests was the British assumption that the very presence of Japanese occupation forces, including ac-tivities of the brutal Japanese secret police, would of itself create a lively demand for their removal. The second factor was connected more directly with American concern to re-establish effective overland contact with Chungking than with Burmese affairs *per se*. It related to General Stilwell's impatience with Lord Mountbatten because of the latter's unwillingness to mount an early Burma campaign. American Office of Strategic Services (OSS) detachments operated in northern Burma and subsequently in the Akyab area. Tentative preparations were even made for possible American civil administration in remote areas of Burma. As events developed, the reconquest of Burma in 1945 was predominantly a British affair, with American air power playing a minor role.

Although local British efforts to ignore the political importance of General Aung San nearly brought overt rebellion in early 1946, this approach was overruled in time by Prime Minister Attlee, and Burma moved toward independence without resort to violence. A generous settlement of the American Lend-Lease account provided Burma, among other things, with an adequate supply of motor vehicles for nearly a decade and more than ample funds for the Fulbright exchange program. Burma did not constitute a serious concern of United States policy until Communist and other rebellions developed after 1948. It was the subsequent failure of American officials to prevent the flow of arms from Formosa to the disorderly Kuomintang refugee troops in eastern Burma in 1951–1953 that precipitated Burma's first abrupt shift away from cordial relations with Washington. They have never been entirely restored. Burmese generally entertained no desire to become enmeshed in America's quarrel with Red China.

INDONESIA

The Dutch were understandably impatient at the tardy American response to appeals, following Japan's surrender, for ships to transport American-trained Dutch marines from the United States to Indonesia, and Dutch male internees

sible the deep penetration of Ho's Communist-nationalist intelligence apparatus during the ensuing months, with active American liaison and support.

By August 1945, Ho's influence extended across the northern districts of Tongking and down to the delta provinces. He was understandably in high favor with the OSS agents who first arrived at Hanoi shortly after the Japanese surrender. At that time, Roosevelt's ill-defined objective to avoid the re-establishment of French colonial rule had still not been either fully approved or rescinded by the Department of State. Exactly what Roosevelt had in mind was not known, and he was now dead. With the new President's attention riveted on Europe, Greece, and Iran, the resulting policy deadlock was not resolved. Meanwhile returning French forces moved ahead aggressively until events in Vietnam overtook Washington's faltering initiative. Nationalist pleas for sympathy and support fell on deaf ears, and Washington's eventual recognition of French sovereignty followed the path of least resistance.

France recovered fairly effective military and governmental control over the southern half of Indochina by late 1945 in collaboration with the occupying British forces of General Gracey. The north was resecured by negotiations with Nationalist China in February and March 1946. In deference to nationalist sentiment, France promised Ho Chi Minh that Vietnam would be united, and that it would constitute a self-governing unit within the projected Indochinese Federation, which was to be part of the new French Union. Insisting that the problem was a purely domestic matter, and recognizing Ho Chi Minh by implication as an authentic nationalist spokesman, Paris challenged sharply any presumption of American interest in the situation. Subsequent negotiations with Ho at Fontainbleau in mid-1946 came to nothing, partly because the French governor at Saigon, Admiral d'Argenlieu, repudiated an earlier pledge to include Cochinchina, where French interests centered, within the new Vietnamese state. They failed also partly because the French left's bid for political power in France, upon which Ho had counted, fell short of its goal. Relations deteriorated steadily following Ho's return to Hanoi in September, and by December 1946 civil war had broken out. Thereafter the French faced the dreary prospect of indefinite involvement in a costly and exhausting guerilla war, waged throughout Vietnam but mainly in Tongking. Genuine Vietnamese nationalist sentiment swung increasingly to the side of the Communist leadership of Ho Chi Minh.

THE BAO DAI EXPERIMENT

The bankruptcy of French policy in postwar Indochina was somewhat less apparent than that of the Dutch in Indonesia because it seemed to have a real chance of succeeding. Failure stemmed in the end from the combined effects of political confusion within France itself, the inability of French opinion to face political realities in Vietnam, and above all the excessive influence exerted on the spot by unregenerate French colonials in Cochinchina, including the equivocal actions of Governor d'Argenlieu in particular. By siding with the French, the United States compromised its reputation as a friend of political freedom not only among the Vietnamese but also in suspicious Burma and Indonesia as well. Washington kept hold of the hand of French colonialism as it disappeared down the drain.

As early as September 1947, the French recognized the need to develop a counterattraction to the Communist-led nationalists of the Vietminh by making overtures to ex-Emperor Bao Dai, then resident in Hongkong. United States spokesmen also made simultaneous representations to Bao Dai to the effect that American support for nationalist objectives would perhaps be more readily available on behalf of a non-Communist Vietnamese regime. Bao Dai thereupon began a cat-and-mouse game which lasted more than two years, during which the indolent but very shrewd former ruler persuaded the French authorities to make repeated concessions in favor of both Vietnamese unity and self-government, while drawing Washington more deeply into the affair. Generous French paper concessions made in June 1948 were not promptly and fully implemented. It was not until 1949, after the arrival of victorious Communist Chinese forces along the northern borders of Tongking forced the French hand, that unequivocal commitments to Bao Dai were finally made. But French promises were by that date far too late and too much distrusted to attract Vietnamese nationalist sentiment, except within the most extreme anti-Communist circles. Even so the Elysée accords of March 8, 1949, with Bao Dai were not ratified by Paris for more than ten months.

American military aid to French colonial forces, authorized under the Mutual Defense Assistance Act of 1949, was ostensibly given as part of the world struggle against communism. Actually it was extended entirely on French terms, and the United States thus became involved in financing an essentially colonial struggle against both Vietnamese nationalist and Communist opponents. The French would not permit American representatives to maintain direct relations with any of the associated "independent" states of the Indochinese Federation; all aid had to be delivered exclusively to the French. When it became apparent locally after May 1950 that only those Vietnamese loyal to the French connection could hold office at Saigon, the United States came to share in large measure the distrust and unpopularity of the French within a widening circle of Southeast Asian opinion that extended southward as far as Java and westward into Burma and India.

CAMBODIA AND LAOS

Meanwhile French postwar relations with Laos and Cambodia were following a familiar pattern of divide and rule through the manipulation of rival princely factions. The Japanese-installed Khmer Issarak (Free Cambodia) regime

22

under Son Ngoc Thanh in Cambodia was easily displaced by General Leclerc in October 1945. Approximately half of Son Ngoc Thanh's anti-French followers subsequently turned to brigandage or to collaboration with the Vietminh. The "autonomy" subsequently granted to King Norodom Sihanouk's Cambodian government in January 1946 left the French substantially in control of the country. Following the French withdrawal in 1954–1955, the activities of political agitators forced Sihanouk to abdicate as king and enter actively into the political arena. Thereafter the specter of Cambodia caught in the traditional pincers of neighboring enemies, Vietnam and Siam, came to dominate the political horizon at Phnompenh.

The postwar situation in Laos was somewhat more complicated than in Cambodia. Here rival elite groups vied for control of the country. Prince Boun Oum of Champassac promptly welcomed the French return in the south, but the presence until June 1946 of looting Chinese occupation armies in the north, an area long since abandoned by the Japanese whose surrender the Chinese were supposed to take, encouraged growth of the heterogenous Lao Issara (Free Lao) movement at Vientiane. The movement was led by the disgruntled and ambitious Prince Phetsarath, whom the Francophile King Sisavang Vong had dismissed as viceroy in October 1945. When reoccupying French forces eventually began to move northward up the Mekong Valley in early 1946, the Lao Issara, which had previously declared the king deposed, and which had by this time developed connections with Vietminh, tried in vain to engineer Sisavang Vong's return as constitutional monarch. In face of the French advance to Vientiane by late April, and to Luang Prabang by May, Lao Issara partisans fled to Siam. Following formal French recognition of the unity and autonomy of Laos, a constituent assembly was convened in early 1947, and a constitution drafted under which a national assembly was duly elected the following November. King Sisavang Vong was recognized as ruler of an "independent" Laos within the Indochinese Federation and the French Union, but final negotiations regarding the precise status of Laos were postponed for nearly two years.

The settlement eventually concluded in July 1949 conferred on Laos considerably less than full sovereignty. But it was nevertheless sufficiently generous to satisfy the requirements of most of the exiled Lao Issara leaders, who for the most part promptly returned to Vientiane and resumed active participation in politics. Prince Phetsarath continued to sulk in Bangkok, however, while the more intransigent Prince Souphanouvong fled to North Vietnam, where he formed the nucleus of a new Liberation Committee in cooperation with the Vietminh. Not until collapse of the French military campaign at nearby Dienbienphu in 1954 did Souphanouvong's renamed Pathet Lao movement take on sufficient political importance to warrant serious American concern.

Thereafter the Pathet Lao faction profited from the Francophile reputation of its rivals in Laotian politics, from the allegedly pro-Siamese policy of the United States in the area, and from the deep-seated hostility of the hill tribes generally toward the long dominant Lao of the Mekong Valley. American military assistance to the decidedly non-belligerent royal Laotian army served mainly to line the pockets of well-placed officials. Cambodia's Prince Sihanouk strongly opposed American intervention in Laos following the collapse of France, in part because it allegedly encouraged the extension of Vietminh influence into the area. Sihanouk himself extended diplomatic recognition to both the Vietminh and to the Chinese Communist regime at Peking. The United States finally opted for the dubious consolation prize of a theoretically neutral Laos in 1962, content to concentrate its military efforts on saving the faltering regime of President Ngo Dinh Diem in South Vietnam.

Ngo Dinh Diem had come to power in South Vietnam following the collapse of French power in Indochina in 1954 and the partition of the country at the Geneva Conference in July of that year. For three years his government made considerable progress in consolidating its hold on the south. But thereafter conditions began to deteriorate with the renewal of guerilla warfare fomented by the Vietminh. Historical factors bearing on the subsequent crises in South Vietnam include the long tradition of north-south rivalry within Vietnam and the widespread desire to unify the country. The personalism of Ngo Dinh Diem's administration, with its nepotism and Catholic partisanship, and its denial of free elections, apparently carried in time far less nationalist appeal throughout South Vietnam than the Communist regime of Ho Chi Minh in the north. The Hanoi government was concerned not to become a satellite of Red China, and Ho Chi Minh, in deference to Moscow's wishes, was willing after Dienbienphu not to take full advantage of its opportunities to intervene in Laos, while becoming involved a few years later in the guerilla struggle directed against the American-supported Ngo Dinh Diem regime at Saigon.

CONCLUSION

More than enough has been indicated to demonstrate that a great variety of historical factors traditionally present in Southeast Asia have already vitiated and will continue to render ineffective any American policy based exclusively on the dichotomy resulting from cold war psychology. Political assumptions and premises that seem almost axiomatic from the Western point of view often prove to be highly irrelevant when examined from the perspective of Southeast Asia itself. Hence the need arises to view both American policy and the Communist threat through Southeast Asian eyes, however difficult and sometimes painful this process may be for us. We must understand, too, that Southeast Asians may sharply differentiate between Soviet interests and policies and those of Red China.

Psychological factors relating to indigenous political rivalries, and also to suspicion of outsiders, enter the picture especially in the problem of modernizing the newly independent countries to meet the demands of economic development. In few countries does the westernized minority capable of participating in the modernizing process exceed 10 per cent of the population. In regions long ruled indirectly by colonial powers, such as the outer islands of Indonesia, the former Unfederated Malay States, Burma's Shan States, British Borneo, Cambodia, and Laos, the traditional social and cultural patterns are still largely intact. In more modernized areas, the elite itself is often divided between the somewhat better educated but politically emasculated upper classes, and the youthful half-educated nationalists who have managed to seize control as revolutionized situations have developed, for example, in Burma, Indonesia, and North Vietnam. Faltering efforts at political and economic modernization are everywhere handicapped by the inertia of traditional habits and value judgments, as well as by continued erosion of the credentials of the best elements drawn from colonial or traditional elites. The old order tends to lose its own potential for stability, while at the same time it constitutes a roadblock to development of a westernized system, which is itself only half-digested as yet. Obviously the ordering of the problems of Southeast Asia is not to be accomplished by any arbitrary application of American economic and military assistance, which on occasion serves simply to aggravate basic difficulties. An effective American policy must take adequate account of the historical factors.

2

SOME ASPECTS OF THE "VALUE"

OF SOUTHEAST ASIA

TO THE UNITED STATES

☙☆☙☆☙☆☙

CHARLES WOLF, JR.

INTRODUCTION

How important is Southeast Asia to the United States? [1] The same question can also be legitimately raised concerning the other major international trouble spots that rank high among current and potential United States foreign policy problems: Cuba, Berlin, Taiwan—indeed, Western Europe, as well. The view put forward in this essay is that, although the question is unanswerable in a strict sense, some useful remarks can be made to clarify the question and help to distinguish between more and less unsatisfactory answers to it.

The essay is mainly concerned with describing an analyti-

[1] Any views expressed in this essay are those of the author. They should not be interpreted as reflecting the views of The RAND Corporation or the official opinion or policy of any of its governmental or private research sponsors.

cal framework for considering the question of a country's or region's value to the United States, illustrating this framework with respect to Southeast Asia in particular, and suggesting at least some personal impressions as to what these illustrations add up to from the standpoint of Southeast Asia's importance to the United States. Finally, I shall consider very briefly the relevance of this discussion to basic United States objectives in Southeast Asia: what we should be, and I think are, trying to accomplish there, to the extent that United States policy is able to influence the situation.

Let me begin by clarifying some terms and concepts that will be referred to later.[2] The first concept concerns the distinction between the *direct* and *indirect* value of a country or region to the United States. By direct value is meant those aspects that can be immediately related to United States interests. By indirect value is meant those aspects of a particular country's value that relate to *other* countries which, in turn, are of direct value to the United States.

The second point concerns a distinction between value to the United States and value to the Soviet Union or to Communist China. Particular countries or regions may well differ in their cardinal and ordinal values to the United States, the Soviet Union, and to China; this essay is mainly concerned with relating value to *United States* interests.

The third point concerns the obvious distinction between the value of a particular area in connection with local wars and its value in various central war contingencies. A further distinction can be made between the value of an area to the United States in connection with wars involving China and wars involving the Soviet Union, or with both Communist powers.

[2] The main theoretical framework summarized in this essay draws on a previously published paper. See Wolf, Charles Jr. "Some Aspects of the 'Value' of Less-developed Countries to the United States," *World Politics*, Vol. 15, No. 4, July 1963, pp. 623–635. The referenced paper, as its title indicates, is focused on the less-developed countries, generally, whereas the present essay applies the same approach specifically to Southeast Asia.

Finally, there is a distinction between values, or components of value, that can be *quantified,* and those components that, at best, can only be *qualified.* The components of value that can be quantified are those for which an alternative cost can be estimated, or at least those aspects for which the concept of alternative cost has meaning. *Where it is possible to estimate the cost of achieving some given and constant consequence or outcome in two different ways, the value of one way can be considered, as an upper bound, to be defined by the cost of obtaining the same result in the alternative way.*

For some aspects of the value of an area, this notion of alternative costs can be usefully applied in order to give a rough indication of the magnitude of the quantifiable components of a country's value. The approach has merit for and is applicable to both the military and economic components of value.

However, for other components of value, this approach does not make sense. When we discuss the political, psychological, and ideological components of an area's value to the United States, alternative cost does not help very much. For these aspects of value, we simply have to rely on opinions, discussion, and judgments. Moreover, these qualitative aspects of value may well dominate those that can be quantified. This does not imply that we should refrain from trying to identify the relevant numbers wherever we can. Nor does it mean that all ways of expressing the qualitative components of a country's value to the United States are equally clear, comprehensive, and useful. One can be qualitative in better and worse ways, just as one can be quantitative in better and worse ways.

SOME QUANTITATIVE COMPONENTS OF "VALUE"

Let us first consider those aspects of the value of other countries which can be approached quantitatively. My aim here is to give some idea of a method that might be employed, as well as a rough indication of some of the numbers that might enter this work. Incidentally, when I use the adjective "large" or "substantial" to characterize my conjectures about these numbers, I will have in mind five-year costs that are, say, over $1 billion, while "small" will mean that my guess is that the figure would be below this threshold. (I want to emphasize the words "conjecture" and "guess" in the preceding sentence.)

MILITARY ASPECTS OF VALUE

The military value of a country or area can be upper-bounded by assuming the "loss" of the particular area, formulating a number of different war scenarios, and then asking what costs the United States would have to incur to make its expected outcome in these contingencies equivalent to its expected outcome without the loss of the country or area concerned. In this context the term "loss" is used in a complete and unsophisticated sense to mean simply the inclusion of the country within the Communist bloc so that the bloc is enabled to derive whatever military benefits the area might confer on it. In making this purposely extreme assumption, the implication is not that such a "loss" is the *only*, or even the *most likely*, alternative to an existing relationship between the United States and the particular country. The implication is simply that the assumption of "loss," in this complete sense, provides a useful means for upper-bounding the military components of that country's value to the United States.

Let us illustrate this notion of value more concretely. To pick a hypothetical but not implausible case, consider a scenario involving an attempt by North Vietnam, China, or the Soviet Union to accelerate the buildup within South Vietnam and Thailand of a capability for waging guerilla war against the present governments in those countries. Now, assume the "loss" of *Laos* in the sense in which I am using that term. Given this assumption, we could then estimate the military "value" of Laos by examining several different kinds of "costs" that would have to be incurred in order to maintain an equivalent *counter*guerilla capability in Vietnam and Thailand after this assumed "loss." One kind of cost would be that associated with maintaining enough additional surveillance along the 700-mile common border between Laos and Thialand and the 200-mile common border between Laos and South Vietnam, so that the support or build-up of guerilla manpower, training, supplies, and equipment would be as difficult (i.e., as costly) for the Communists as it would have been *without* the loss of Laos.

As an alternative, or supplement, to these surveillance costs, we could attempt to estimate the increase in Thai and Vietnamese paramilitary, civil-guard-type forces, which would be necessary to restrain the level of guerilla, insurrectionist incidents to some "acceptable" maximum, even allowing for some increase in the flow of guerilla manpower and supplies across the common Thai and South Vietnamese borders with Laos.

To take another example, consider a scenario involving a direct invasion of Thailand or of South Vietnam by a Vietcong or combined Chinese-Vietcong force of consequential size. In this scenario, the value of Laos might be estimated by calculating the increase in Thai and Vietnamese forces that would be required to gain the same defensive time and hold the same military infrastructures to enable intervention by friendly, e.g., United States, forces on the assumption that the loss of Laos would mean that tactical warning would begin at the time Red forces crossed the Mekong or crossed the Annamese cordillera from Laos, rather than at the time they crossed the borders from China proper or from North Vietnam into Laos.

Note that in both of these crude scenarios the value of Laos is related to contingencies involving countries other than Laos itself. It is in this sense that the "stack of cards" or "dominoes" analogy, which has sometimes been applied to the countries of Southeast Asia, makes a certain amount of sense. A "loss" of Laos increases the vulnerability of environing countries; stated in another way, such a loss requires that additional costs be incurred if the vulnerability of environing countries is to be held constant.

I might express a personal judgment that both types of contingencies would require large expenditures by the United States and the free world in order to maintain equivalent expected outcomes after the loss of Laos. Perhaps these two scenarios are really just a roundabout way of making a very obvious point: the military vulnerability of one or more countries in a particular area, for example, Thailand and South Vietnam, can depend significantly on the military and political status and orientation of a neighboring country, in this case Laos. In this sense, the defense of South Vietnam or Thailand is very closely related to the problem of defending Laos. To put it slightly differently, we can consider the *value* or importance of Laos to be upperbounded by what we and our Thai and Vietnamese allies would have to pay in order to offset the increase in their vulnerability following the "loss" of Laos.

The same kind of analytical approach can be used to consider the question of the military value of all Southeast Asia including, say, Thailand, Burma, Vietnam, Malaya, and Indonesia, taken together. In this case, it might be more appropriate to consider scenarios that involved countries adjacent to this group of Southeast Asian countries, like the Philippines, India, Taiwan, and Australia.

For contingencies involving threats to island countries like the Philippines, Taiwan, or Australia, the costs of maintaining equivalent military effectiveness, given the loss of all Southeast Asia, would probably not be exorbitant (although apparently the Philippines tends to view the military uncertainties that have been created by the accession of North Borneo to Malayan sovereignty as more dangerous than this suggests). In fact, countries that are entirely littoral may, by that fact, already be exposed to infiltration or invasion in ways that are little affected by the loss of other mainland areas. If Indonesia were to be lost, along with the mainland, the Philippines is probably right in its implicit assessment that some additional costs would be required to keep infiltration into Mindanao and the Sulu archipelago within bounds, but in general I would think that such incremental costs would be relatively modest. On the other hand, for countries like India and Pakistan whose common land borders with Communist countries would be extended by the loss of Southeast Asia, the incremental costs of maintaining equivalent defensibility might well be appreciable.

Again, as in the scenarios relating to the influence of Laos on the costs of defending Thailand and Vietnam, the value of all of Southeast Asia from the military point of view relates mainly to limited, nonnuclear conflicts in such adjacent areas as India, Australia, Taiwan, Pakistan, and the Philippines. In other words, if one contemplates the expansion of militant Chinese communism into Southeast Asia, either directly or through indigenous proxies in the Southeast Asian countries, the cost of compensating for this expansion by an offsetting buildup of military capabilities in the adjacent countries, as well as of United States theater capabilities to intervene in these adjacent areas, would be substantial.

On the other hand, if one considers various central war contingencies involving nuclear conflict, whether of a countercity, counterforce, or some other variety of controlled response pattern between the United States and the Soviet Union, or the United States and Communist China, the value or importance of Southeast Asia is likely to be quite minor. Such value as the area might conceivably have in these contingencies would presumably relate primarily to central war targets that might be assigned to air force units based in or staging through the area. Since reaching these targets from other areas, or through the use of other weapons systems not having such basing requirements, would probably not entail heavy incremental costs, the value of

Southeast Asia in central war is likely to be of minor signifi-cance.

Presumably a perception of this fact lies behind such views as that expressed in the recent report on Vietnam and Southeast Asia by a Senate group headed by Senator Mansfield. In effect, the Mansfield group tentatively con-cluded that perhaps the military significance of Southeast Asia had been exaggerated, and that "a thorough assessment of our own overall security requirements . . ." might very well show that "an orderly curtailment of [United States] programs and missions [in Southeast Asia] need not pose a significant increase in the threat to our national security." [3]

While this view makes good sense if we think of national security interests in relation to *major nuclear* conflicts, it would be a mistake to conclude that the military value of Southeast Asia in all the relevant military contingencies, including nonnuclear conflicts in adjacent areas, is small. The United States is a world power with military commit-ments, allies, and interests in areas remote from its strategic bases at home and abroad. As such we must be concerned with the effect of major changes in the political and military orientation of areas like Southeast Asia on the defensibility of adjacent areas. We must, for example, be concerned with the effect of a change in the status of Laos on the costs of defending and securing Thailand and South Vietnam; and we must be concerned with the effect on the defense of India and Australia, as well as on the whole balance of forces in the Far East, of a "loss" of Southeast Asia, or of a change in the status of a major portion of the area such as Indonesia.

ECONOMIC ASPECTS OF VALUE

The economic aspects of an area's value to the United States can be divided into several components: principally,

[3] Senators Mansfield, A. S. Mike; Boggs, J. Caleb; Pell, Claiborne; and Smith, Benjamin A., *Viet Nam and Southeast Asia*, 88th Con-gress, 1st Session, Washington, D.C., 1963, p. 19–20.

the value of investments owned by American residents in the area, and the net value of (or "gains" from) trade with the area. As in the case of military aspects of value, the economic components can be approached in terms of the foregone benefits (or opportunity costs) of the hypothetically "lost" investments, imports, and exports.[4] It should be noted, however, that "loss" in a military context does not necessarily imply "loss" in an economic sense. A country might become a part of the Communist bloc, or even a Communist military base, and still continue to trade with the free world. Conversely, a country might expropriate foreign assets and forego trading with the United States, while still refusing to permit Communist military installations on its territory.

A. The value of American *investments* in a particular area is the discounted value of the income stream associated with them. Stripped of jargon, the point is that the value of an asset is the earnings that are expected to be derived from it. The more distant in time the earnings are expected to accrue, the less they are worth in the present; that is, future earnings must be discounted to give them a present value, and the sum of these discounted present values is the value of the asset.

[4] Harry Benda has called my attention to the fact that there is another aspect of value which might be taken into account, namely denial to the Communists of the economic benefits that they might realize from exercising control of Southeast Asia. Denial of control imposes on them "costs" in the sense of these foregone benefits, and these "costs" might be considered an additional "value" to the United States.

With two qualifications, his point is well taken: (a) Southeast Asia's potential economic "benefits" to the Communist bloc or, more specifically, to China must be interpreted in the sense of *net* benefits, i.e., the *difference* between the increased resources that control of the area might make available and the *costs* of maintaining control. It would not be correct, for example, to assume that if Southeast Asia became Communist, its present exports of rice would simply become available to China at no cost. (b) Although denial of benefits to an adversary is certainly a "value" to us, we cannot assume that a dollar of benefits denied to him is equivalent to a dollar of benefits realized by us. The question of an area's "value" is *not* subject to a "zero-sum" answer. An area's "value" to the United States is not necessarily equal to the "value" denied the Chinese.

Though the concept is clear, measurement is quite difficult because of the uncertainty connected with the income stream, and with the appropriate discount rate to use in calculating present value. However, as a practical matter, a number might be attached to this component of Southeast Asia's value by taking the average income received in the last four or five years from United States investments in the area as a basis for estimating the income stream over, say, a twenty-year useful life and calculating present values by using three or four alternative, but plausible, discount rates. Alternatively, and still more simply, this component of value might be quantified by making an adjustment—i.e., upwards—in the book value of American assets in Southeast Asia (and perhaps supplementing this estimate with a further upward adjustment in the book value of similar assets, both direct and portfolio, of Western Europe and Japan in these areas). As an indication of the orders of magnitude that are involved here, the following figures on United States private direct investments in 1959 in all of Asia, compared with other areas, are of interest:[5]

Latin America	$ 8.2 billion
Europe	5.3 billion
Africa	.8 billion
Asia (excluding the Middle East)	1.0 billion
The Middle East	1.2 billion
Canada	10.2 billion
Other	3.0 billion
TOTAL	$29.7 billion

Of the Asian total, $210 million represented direct investments in Japan. India, Pakistan, and Ceylon accounted for $178 million, leaving only slightly more than $600 million for the Southeast Asian countries of which over 60 per cent was accounted for by the Philippines.

[5] *U.S. Business Investments in Foreign Countries,* United States Department of Commerce, Washington, D.C., 1960, p. 92.

These figures are, of course, understated because they reflect book value, rather than present or market value. They are also understated, from the standpoint of the "value" problem, because they do not include, for example, the value of European investments in, say, the Far East and the Middle East, which are frequently greater than those of the United States, yet which are of indirect value to the United States. Anyhow, they give some indication of the general orders of magnitude that are involved. Obviously, in Southeast Asia, as a *part* of the relatively small Asian total, the value of American investments is minor, indeed.

B. The value of a country or area as a source of United States *imports* is *not* equivalent to the total value of imports from that area. Imports obviously have to be paid for, and the loss of imports from an area also means that the payment is saved. In a rough sense, the net value of gains from United States imports from a particular area can be approximated by the *difference* between what we currently pay for these imports and what we would have to pay if the imports were to be bought from the *next-best* source.

In the case of Southeast Asia, we can roughly approximate the value of United States imports in this sense by considering what, if any, effect there would be on the prices of rubber, tin, and copra, for example, if, in the extreme case, Southeast Asia were to orient its trade entirely toward the Communist bloc (a circumstance which, as previously noted, would not necessarily follow from an absorption of Southeast Asia into the Communist bloc). Although Southeast Asia is a major world supplier of each of these commodities, we would have to examine fairly carefully the elasticity of their supply from other countries in order to get some notion of the effect on prices that would result from a change in Southeast Asia's status. Without having attempted any such examination, I would hazard the guess that the net value of Southeast Asia's imports (roughly estimated as the increase in prices that would result from the loss of trade there, multiplied by the quantity of current imports by the United States from Southeast Asia) would be minor in comparison, for example, with the total magnitude of United States imports from Southeast Asia. To give some very rough idea of the orders of magnitude, total *world* imports by the United States, Canada, Western Europe, and Japan were about $72 billion in 1957 and about $65 billion in 1958. Of these totals, about $4.5 billion in each year was provided from the *entire* area of South and Southeast Asia, including India, Pakistan, and Ceylon, as well as Singapore, Malaya, Indonesia, the Philippines, Thailand, Burma, Vietnam, and Cambodia.[6]

C. The value of a particular area or country as a market for United States *exports* is *not* properly construed as the total value of the exports themselves. In general, such exports have an alternative, though less favorable, outlet so that in fact the net value or gains from exporting to Southeast Asia can be approximated by the expected *fall* in United States export prices that would result from such a shift in market outlet, multiplied by the quantity of present exports to Southeast Asia. Again, as previously noted, a change in the political orientation of Southeast Asia toward the Communist bloc does not necessarily imply a loss of the area as an export market for the United States.

To get some idea of what the value of Southeast Asia as an export market is, in this sense, would require examination of the elasticity of demand in other markets. Without such an examination, I would nevertheless hazard the guess that Southeast Asia's value as an export market for the United States and its major allies would be minor in the case of the United States but major for some of our European allies. To give some rough idea of the orders of magnitude, exports by the United States, Canada, Western Europe, and Japan to *all*

---

[6] *Economic Survey of Asia and the Far East* (Bangkok: Economic Commission for Asia and the Far East, 1959); and *Direction of International Trade* (New York, 1959).

of South and Southeast Asia amounted to $7.6 billion in 1957 and $5.8 billion in 1958, out of their total global exports of $70 billion and $67 billion, respectively.

POLITICAL AND PSYCHOLOGICAL ASPECTS OF VALUE

As previously mentioned, some, and perhaps most, important aspects of value in this context are nonquantitative. This does not mean that a serious attempt to fill in the numbers should not be made, where possible. But it does mean that the qualitative aspects must be borne prominently in mind before reaching conclusions on the basis of the economic and military components alone.

The first major qualitative consideration arises from the political-psychological interdependencies among countries and areas. Some interdependencies (for example, those I have referred to between Laos on the one hand, and Vietnam and Thailand on the other) can be identified in military and/or economic terms, costed, and compensated for, or simply accepted. But there are others, relating more to attitudes which can be described in terms of such phrases as "wave of the future," or "march of history," or "inevitable trend," that cannot be readily compensated for or accepted. Even though measures may be attempted to compensate for the apparent military and economic consequences of a particular country's loss, it is more difficult to find ways to compensate for the effect of even a dimly perceived notion of trend on the loyalties and confidence of other people and countries. While this applies particularly to the underdeveloped areas, it extends beyond them. We would be wrong to think that the "loss" of a country like India might not have nearly as profound a psychological impact on the United Kingdom and Western Europe as, for example, the loss of Laos would have on confidence and loyalties in Thailand and South Vietnam, or as the loss of South Korea might have on Japan.

Secretary Rusk has made this point: "If you don't pay

attention to the periphery, the periphery changes, and the first thing you know, the periphery is the center." Even if a periphery includes more than one area (or one country), there is an important truth in the Secretary's words.

If we try to consider the effect of the loss of Southeast Asia in particular, or of other Asian areas, on the mood and character of American society, the connections become more dubious and tenuous, and certainly more difficult to measure. Unlike the effect of a "loss" of Western Europe, or even Japan, results of a collapse of Southeast Asia might be minor. On the other hand, the effect on Western Europe and Japan themselves of such a detachment of Southeast Asia might be very substantial, and a progressive erosion of the free world a genuine possibility. One effect of such a specter would certainly be to raise the United States defense budget and to lower somewhat our real national product as well as its rate of growth. Notwithstanding some prophets of gloom, a 20 per cent or a 50 per cent, or even a 100 per cent, increase in the size of our defense budget would not "bankrupt" the United States, nor would a 2 per cent annual rate of growth in national product, rather than a 5 per cent growth rate, mean national doom. However, it is probably fair to say that substantially increased defense budgets maintained over a protracted period, if associated with a relatively slow rate of growth in the economy, would be likely to have significant effects on the character and quality of American society domestically: on the extent of bureaucracy, on the control of information, and on the sense of tension and vigilance in daily living.

Such a progressive erosion is, fortunately, farfetched, though not so farfetched as to be fantastic. Under such circumstances, it might ultimately become extremely difficult for us to determine where the Iron Curtain began and where it ended. A progressive reduction in the area of the world in which we could freely travel would significantly curtail our freedom, quite apart from the effect of such insulation on the quality of domestic society in the United

States. In effect, under such extreme contingencies, the Iron Curtain would become something around *us*, rather than around the Soviet bloc.

Finally, a world of such a piecemeal and sequential erosion could demoralize new generations of Americans to the extent that they would affiliate with, rather than oppose, the trend. An inward-directed and withdrawn America might increasingly generate its own domestic opponents, as well as an increasing disposition to overturn it from within. It is all too easy to become gloomily apocalyptic about these matters if one lets one's imagination run wild. But if we posit a world in which the countries whose value we are assessing are in fact the rest of the free world, the John Birch Society might come to have a genuine mission in life . . . and an increasingly difficult one at that!

UNITED STATES OBJECTIVES IN UNDERDEVELOPED COUNTRIES: CONCLUDING REMARKS

In brief, the previous discussion has made the following main points:

a. The military value of Southeast Asia in regard to credible nonnuclear conflicts in adjacent areas is probably large, but its military value in regard to nuclear wars among the major powers is probably negligible.

b. The economic value of Southeast Asia to the United States is probably small; to American allies in Western Europe and Japan, the economic value is more substantial.

c. The political-psychological value of the area to the United States is hard to estimate, but at least it seems very likely that its *indirect* political-psychological importance, from the standpoint of effects on Western Europe, Japan, and other areas, and the effect of these in turn on attitudes and expectations in the United States, may very well be large.

In the light of these points, particularly point *a,* it seems to me that much of the discussion in recent years of United States objectives in Southeast Asia has been unrealistic. Part of this discussion, for example, has focused on whether it should be an objective of United States policy to support allies or "neutrals" or both. Part of the accompanying dialogue, in which American specialists on Asia have been particularly active, has been concerned with explaining how "neutralism" and "nonalignment" are understandable and sensible policies for Asian countries to follow. Actually, our interest is in a secure and independent Southeast Asia. Its importance to us in the event of major wars with China or the Soviet Union, or for general deterrence purposes, is negligible. Instead, we are concerned for its defense and its progress as an area whose independence from Soviet or Chinese Communist influence or control is secure. To say that a country in the area wants to be, or should be, "nonaligned" with us in these objectives, is in effect to say it does not or should not want to support its own defense and independence.[7]

In Southeast Asia threats facing the area are *both* military and social-economic, both internal and external. We would do well to remember that whatever the administrative inadequacies of civilian governments in Laos in the past and in South Vietnam as well, the main successes of the Pathet Lao and of the Vietcong, respectively, have come about because of the relatively ineffective *military* capabilities of the government forces that were arrayed against them. Moreover, as the recent Chinese military probes in Ladakh and the northeast frontier demonstrated in India, domestic economic development cannot compensate for an invitingly weak military posture.[8] Indeed, I would be inclined to say

[7] I am indebted for this point to a number of discussions with my colleague, Albert Wohlstetter.

[8] See Wolf, Charles Jr., "Defense and Development in Less-Developed Countries," *Operations Research,* November–December 1962, p. 837.

that the military threat, both internal and external, to Southeast Asian countries, as well as to other less-developed countries on the Asian periphery, may very well intensify as and if they have more success than they have had so far in meeting the vast problems of economic and social improvement which face them. I would tend to support the proposition that the intensification of Vietcong guerilla activities in South Vietnam since 1960 came about partly *because* of the marked economic and political improvements accomplished during the period from 1955 to 1960 by the Ngo Dinh Diem regime, which raised the ante that the Communist countries were willing to stake on efforts to disrupt that regime.

What does this imply with respect to the question of United States objectives in Southeast Asia? I think it implies that Southeast Asia is of substantial, though certainly not infinite, value to us, and that our aim in these countries should be to help them provide, or otherwise to obtain, a judicious balance between the capabilities and competences needed to meet both the internal and external, and both the military and nonmilitary, threats which they face: both the military threats of armed guerillas and of invasions of various levels of violence, and the nonmilitary threats of internal stagnation, frustration, and hopelessness. There is no easy or formulary way of finding this judicious balance. Moreover, it is at best a dynamic balance. What may be adequate economic or military performance levels at one time may become seriously inadequate at another time.

This does not give us a precise answer to the question, but it suggests where to look for answers and where not to look for answers. It suggests that we keep our sights and our aims on the balance between military and political-economic capabilities available or becoming available *in* these countries and, in the case of military capabilities, available for deployment *into* these countries. And it suggests that a formal declaration that a country is "neutralist," "allied," "committed," or "uncommitted," or that it will or will not receive aid from the Soviet bloc, may be less important to United States objectives in Southeast Asia than what countries *do* with respect to the improvement of their individual and collaborative defense capabilities and their economic development performance.

3

THE SOCIAL-CULTURAL CONTEXT OF POLICY IN SOUTHEAST ASIA

CLIFFORD GEERTZ

I

As Ernest R. May has recently pointed out, the formulation of a country's foreign policy rests simultaneously on two quite different sorts of considerations: (a) deliberate, self-conscious, as we say "rational," means-end calculations of the usual risks and possibilities sort; and (b) unquestioned, commonly unstated, and sometimes even unrecognized canonical axioms derived from historical experience. And, as he also points out, it is usually the latter element which, though it draws less attention, causes more difficulty.[1] In human endeavor generally it is what we take for granted—and so blithely assume everyone else takes for granted as well—that most often trips us up. Mistakes in strategy can, unless fatal, be corrected, for they are anyway recognizable as mistakes. But misconceptions of the very nature of the game being played, the battle being fought, tend to be, if

[1] May, E. R., "The Nature of Foreign Policy: The Calculated Versus the Axiomatic," *Daedalus*, Vol. 91, Fall 1962, pp. 653–667.

not incorrigible, certainly very difficult to alter, for we are not even aware that we are in error; or if we do vaguely sense that we are, we are not certain what kind of error it is and where precisely it lies. Like the color blind, we adjust our judgments to fit the defects of our perception. It is only when some fairly drastic failure occurs—such as a red light thought by virtue of its reversed position to be a green one —that we sense that something somewhere is seriously amiss, that we have been proceeding under some false assumptions about how things are, in fact, ordered.

As with foreign policy in general, so with United States policy toward Southeast Asia in particular; and I want to deal with the problem of the social-cultural context of policy in Southeast Asia from precisely this angle. More concretely, it is my impression that a very great deal of American policy toward Southeast Asia proceeds under an unconscious assumption, an unrecognized axiom, derived from the diplomatic history of nineteenth- and twentieth-century Europe— an assumption which is radically inappropriate to that melange of languages, cultures, religions, and races crammed in between India, China, and the Pacific, and which consequently leaves us prey to a series of unpleasant and baffling surprises of the sort that ensue when one at length begins to suspect that it is not the relative position of traffic lights which is crucial after all, but something else that one is not even equipped to see. This is the notion that there is an identity, or at least a very close internal relationship, between a state and a nation, a country and a people, a polity and a culture.

Though it is, actually, not so long that we have been doing it, we are quite used by now to thinking of states as expressions of cultures. The Germans, French, British, Hungarians, Spanish, Russians, even, rather oddly, the Swiss and the Belgians are to us both a people and a country, and the one by virtue of the other. Patriotism in the sense of civil loyalty to the state and in the sense of a primordial loyalty to a cultural tradition is not differentiated. Every people gets the government it deserves, and every government is thus but the public expression of the genius of a people. The Habsburgs discovered they were a German monarchy only shortly before they expired, and no one would have dreamed of confusing the Ottoman state with any people whatsoever, but to our eyes, more clouded than we like to think by the doctrines of romantic nationalism, the variously colored patches on the European map are both political and ethnographic units. A nation is at once a sovereign state and a cultural community. We conceive ourselves as interacting not just with the French government but with the French; not just the Italian government but the Italians.

Whatever validity this axiomatic identification of state and nation may or may not have with respect to Europe, for Southeast Asia it is seriously misleading. In all the countries of the region, with the partial exception of Thailand, the relation between government and the society of which it is the government is quite different from what we are used to from recent European history, or even from our traumatic encounter with gentilic Japan. The government, despite the rhetoric of radical nationalism in which it phrases its alarms and ambitions, is not so much the political expression of a culture as a kind of extraordinary committee for the conduct of foreign policy, an *ad hoc* commission for economic planning, and a self-conscious symbol of a social consensus which does not in fact exist. The cultural and the political exist almost in different planes, not unrelated, to be sure, but not very fully transposable either—as anyone who tries to remember whether a Burman is a Burmese speaker or a citizen of the Union of Burma, or figure out exactly what a Laotian is, is made, perhaps at least subliminally, aware.

There are a number of reasons for this state of affairs, but perhaps the most important is what Lauriston Sharp in his presidential address to The Association for Asian Studies last year called the broken history of the region's cultural development.[2] Unlike China or India, there is not discernible in Southeast Asia any more or less continuous Great Tradition giving it a distinct and definite character, no "major cultural stream flowing steadily out of a distant past" to imbue it with a specific ethos. Instead there is a sequence of extraordinarily disparate external influences and maddeningly diverse internal developments which has left the region a many-splendored thing indeed:

> Discontinuities, cultural fault lines, borders between ways of behaving confront us everywhere as we move across Southeast Asia, the one part of the globe where we find represented in small space all four of the only great surviving human traditions which singly or in combination may influence and inform our behavior for generations to come: the Sinic, Indic, Islamic and North Atlantic. But these too are cross-cut by complex and intricate divisions: Buddhists and Catholics, Moslems and kafirs; traditionalist and modernist; communist and capitalist; urban elites westernized in varying degrees and still illiterate rural masses; industrial sectors and agricultural sectors. And if we move vertically rather than horizontally, we encounter in the divisions between hill and valley peoples an ethnic stratification such as is rarely found elsewhere, the despair of cultural cartographers.[3]

This is not to say that many of these same discontinuities do not exist in India and China—or Europe—as well. But in Southeast Asia they have been arranged by the mere accidents of a wayward history and an irregular geography into such a crosscutting pattern of incompatibles as to make very difficult the crystallization of homogeneous cultural communities that are large enough and clearly bounded enough to support viable national states. China, and especially India, are marked by great local variation and internal

[2] Sharp, L., "Cultural Continuities and Discontinuities in Southeast Asia," *The Journal of Asian Studies*, Vol. 22, November 1962, pp. 3–11.

[3] *Ibid.*, p. 5.

discontinuity, but yet they sum, by virtue of the Sinitic and Indic Great Traditions and certain widely shared social institutions, to enough of a single cultural community that one can at least plausibly represent state and nation as inwardly conjoined. But over the greater part of Southeast Asia this sort of congruence between polity and community is, Thailand aside, difficult to arrange. If the political unit is large enough to be viable as a modern state—as Burma, Malaya, Indonesia, or the Philippines—it is culturally, racially, linguistically, and/or religiously very heterogeneous. If it is small enough to be reasonably homogeneous in such matters —as Cambodia, Vietnam, and to a lesser extent, Laos—its ability to subsist as an independent political entity in the modern world is extremely problematic. The comparison ought not to be pushed too far, for these are other times and other peoples, but Southeast Asia today seems to face much the same dilemma Southeast Europe faced around 1914: a choice between "national" units too large for cultural realities or too small for political ones.[4]

This whole problem is made more severe by the steadily accelerating importance in this century of the sovereign state as a positive instrument for the realization of collective aims. All the new states of Southeast Asia, save again Thailand, are, of course, ex-colonies, and colonial governments, like the aristocratic governments of premodern Europe in whose image they were fashioned, were not activating governments but equilibrating ones. The terms are not the best, but what I mean is that where colonial governments stood outside the societies they ruled and acted upon them arbitrarily, unevenly, and unsystematically (no one ever saw them as an expression of the culture of their subjects either), the governments of the new states are located in the midst of the societies they rule, and, as they develop, act upon

[4] The incongruence of cultural and political units is, of course, a general problem in the "new states" of Asia and Africa. For an over-all review, see Geertz, C., "The Integrative Revolution," in Geertz, C., ed., *Old Societies and New States* (New York: The Free Press of Glencoe, 1963).

them in a progressively more continuous, comprehensive, and purposeful manner. It is not that colonial government had no aims, but that its aims were external to those of the peoples over which it ruled, and thus, for all the severity of the economic demands made upon the population, positive political demands were minor or even virtually absent. The colonial government needed "law and order" or "rust en orde" in their bailiwicks, and so were quite abrupt with subversion. But they did not need, perhaps did not even want, more than a minimal degree of civic enthusiasm. They were not attempting, as the governments of even the most ineffectual of the new states are attempting, to mobilize the entire society into a massive attack upon the problems of ignorance and poverty. They were not trying to mobilize the entire society at all. Though, by the end, they all had their welfare programs and their wistful dreams of a progressive Orient that would justify their stewardship in the eyes of history, as governments they were not really going anywhere. They had policies but not plans, objectives but not ambitions.

The governments of the new states are, however, nothing if not ambitious. That their performances do not even approach their aspirations is true, but beside the point. The point is that they have the aspirations and that they worry the masses to realize them. The transfer of sovereignty—so far as Southeast Asia is concerned, one might even say the creation of sovereignty—has changed the whole nature of the state. From an administrative device necessary to maintain order, facilitate foreign trade, and improve the natives, it has become a political device designed to mobilize collective resources for collective goals. Today, instead of a set of directionless proxy governments dominating not countries but mere locations on the map, we have in Southeast Asia a set of grimly purposeful popular regimes concerned not just to cope with their peoples but to shape them. Infused with what Edward Shils has called "the will to be modern," they are absorbed with the grand strategy of national advance.[5]

Decolonization has thus led to even greater tension between the cultural and political planes, for with the growth of a positive state the conflict that the diverse pulls which the two sorts of loyalties exert becomes extremely acute. The state now wants, needs, expects, and demands much more from its citizens than mere abstinence from subversion and a seemly docility. It begins to touch their lives at almost every point rather than just those few which happen to be of importance to some distant power. And it impresses upon them the twentieth-century truism that the possibilities for social reform and material progress they so intensely desire rest upon their being enclosed in a reasonably large, powerful, well-ordered polity which can protect its interests internationally and carry forward its plans domestically. Yet, at the same time, it is the specific and immediate bonds of ethnic affiliation, even at times those of tribe, family, dialect, or locality that, except (perhaps) for a few cosmopolites, seem the more real to them, seem to form the very substance of their existence as identifiable individuals. The achievement of independence in Southeast Asia has brought into full relief the incongruity inherent in the superimposition of what de Jouvenel has called the powerhouse state upon a society crisscrossed by Professor Sharp's cultural fault lines.[6]

[5] Shils, E., "Political Development in the New States," in two parts: *Comparative Studies in Society and History,* Vol. 2, No. 3, April 1960, pp. 265–292 (Part 1), and Vol. 2, No. 4, July 1960, pp. 379–411 (Part 2). There is a fatal ambiguity in English concerning the word "nation" which means, according to Webster's, both (*a*) "A people connected by supposed ties of blood generally manifested by community of language, religion, customs, etc."; and (*b*) "The body of inhabitants of a country united under a single independent government; a state." In the sequel, I shall use "state" for the second meaning and nation (or nationality) for the first alone. Unfortunately, no proper adjectival form for state exists, and so "national" (and "nationalism") will have to do double duty, with the hope that the context will make clear whether the political or primordial sense is meant.

[6] de Jouvenel, B., *On Power* (Boston: Beacon Press, 1962).

Freedom has posed an awkward riddle: is the "self" in "self-rule" an ethnic or a political self?

So far as the new states themselves are concerned, they have mainly attempted to straddle the question rather than answer it. There is really little else they could have done. To have denied the political relevance of culture altogether would have cut the ground out from under the nationalist ideology by which their struggles for independence were justified. What could "Burma for the Burmese" or "Malaya for the Malayans" then mean? But to have accepted the ethnic or primordial definition of "self" as central would have been to lay themselves open to internal dismemberment, next to neocolonialism their most pervasive fear. Indeed, the separatist movements of the Ambonese in Indonesia or the Karens in Burma were based, ideologically, on just such an argument. The new states were caught on the horns of a dilemma. They had to give enough cultural or ethnic content to the "self" in "self-rule" to legitimate their freedom and yet not so much as to endanger their integrity. The solution, not always entirely successful, has been to insist, with a stridency that betrays an underlying incertitude, that for every new state there is a corresponding ethnic entity—Burmese, Indonesian, Filipino, or whatever.[7] National identity could be defined neither in political terms (for there was no indigenous political unit or record of governmental performance to which it could be referred) nor in terms of genuine ethnic divisions (because then nationalist movements and colonial regimes would not coincide), but rather had to be defined, so to speak, oppositionally: Shans were Burmese, West New Guinea Papuans were Indonesians, and Mindanao Moros were Filipinos,

[7] The sharpness of the communal division in Malaya made the complete submergence of the non-European population into a single pseudo-ethnic entity even more difficult than usual, so that one finds a prior lumping of language, religious, and racial groups into a tri-ethnic division of "Malays," "Chinese," and "Indians." See Freedman, M., "The Growth of a Plural Society in Malaya," *Pacific Affairs*, Vol. 33, June 1960, pp. 158–167.

because they were ruled by the rulers of Burma, the East Indies, and the Philippine Islands. For the initial phases of national consolidation this kind of ideological ethnogenesis has been, as I say, no doubt essential. But it is not essential —it is in fact mischievous—that we should accept it as an accurate picture of either political or cultural reality in Southeast Asia.

It is mischievous in the first place because the continued viability of the new Southeast Asian states, both domestically and internationally, depends upon their being able over the next few decades to shift the grounds of their legitimacy from the diffuse ties of an imagined ethnic unity to the more specific ones of an effective political integration; and, as one's self-image is always in such great part a reflex of how others seem to see one, our acceptance of the one-state, one-people myth merely strengthens for a time an image of national identity that, however essential it has proved to be in the immediate past, will soon prove unworkable. It is mischievous in the second place because it leads us to misinterpret the actual flow of events in Southeast Asia and to make grossly inappropriate responses to them —much as on the personal level an uncritical acceptance of others' illusions about themselves as simple fact is harmful to them, to our relationship to them, and thus ultimately to ourselves.

II

The failing power of a myth of cultural unity to provide the motivating force for national self-assertion in Southeast Asia is already becoming apparent. In Burma, the second military take-over seems in great part to amount to a realization, in certain circles anyway, that the country's future rests not on the acceleration of the Burmanizing policies of U Nu, which were evidently stimulating minority discontent rather more than they were moderating it, but on the creation of a governmental apparatus capable of administrative efficiency and political vigor. As in the new states generally, army

CLIFFORD GEERTZ

take-over has been less the result of ideological militarism
than of a nearly total failure of civilian leadership to produce the sort of self-legitimizing body politic a modern
state, and particularly a multiethnic modern state, demands.[8] In Indonesia, the myth has been clung to in face
of its rapidly ebbing strength, with the result that the country, unable to face the reality of its own diversity, is plagued
with both ethnic disaffection and political incapacity, all
cloaked in a miasma of one-state, one-people ideologizing.
In Malaya and the Philippines, the transition to a more civil
form of politics is, for the moment, proceeding more easily:
in the first case because the depth of communal divisions
is so great that notions of a single nationality, though es-
poused, have never been terribly convincing; in the second
because of the somewhat greater cultural homogeneity and
an early inculcation, by the colonial power, of a purely
political approach to the problems of "national" integration.
In the countries of former French Indochina, partition has
retarded the decline of ethnic nationalism because it has
made the new separate states less culturally heterogeneous
at the cost of rendering them less politically viable. And in
Thailand, the myth of cultural unity is not a myth, and
neither radical nationalism nor civil politics seem yet to
have broken the hold of an essentially premodern pattern
of government.

The main cause of the fading power of cultural nationalism—whether in the form of U Nu's ecumenical Buddhism,
Sukarno's village populism, or Ngo Dinh Diem's puritan
Confucianism—to direct and animate the political process,
has been, again, the steadily increasing demands made upon
the state as a positive instrument, both in terms of domestic
planning and international maneuver, since the achievement

[8] For a general discussion of the relation between military intervention in government and the weakness of civilian political institutions in the new states, see Janowitz, M., *The Military in the Political Development of New Nations: A Comparative Analysis* (Chicago:
University of Chicago Press, in press).

54

of independence.[9] Saddled internally with social and economic conditions ranging from the difficult to the desperate, and projected externally into a regional balance of power whose major characteristics are lability and lack of definition, the new states are finding the claims of nationalism founded on quasi ethnicity to be a less and less effective political weapon than it was for the attack on an alien colonial government. This is not to say that this discovery (which is more sensed than understood, and then not very surely) is leading to a decline in the intensity of this variety of nationalism; in Indonesia, potentially the great power of the region, it is having just the opposite effect. It is merely to say that, accepted or resisted, the movement from a cultural (or ethnic) to a political (or civil) definition of the national self is perhaps the most fundamental development on the contemporary Southeast Asian scene and a development that an axiomatic identification of state and nation completely obscures.

As we are concerned with American foreign policy in Southeast Asia, let me ignore the domestic dimensions of this gathering sea change and concentrate on its international aspects alone.[10] There is rather little we can do, except worry, about the former in any case; and it is with respect to the latter, with problems falling into the realm of international affairs—the West New Guinea, or Irian, dispute; the formation of a Malaysian Federation; the relations among the severed parts of former French Indochina —that the inadequacies of quasi-ethnic nationalism are at the moment being most clearly revealed.

The New Guinea dispute, now brought, one hopes against hope, to a stable resolution, is in fact something of a model

[9] For a discussion of the vicissitudes of homemade "national philosophies" in Southeast Asia, see Pauker, G., "Political Doctrines and Practical Politics in Southeast Asia," *Pacific Affairs*, Vol. 35, Spring 1962, pp. 3–10.
[10] For a discussion of ethnic diversity and domestic politics in Indonesia, Malaya, and Burma, see Geertz, *op. cit.*

case in point. The thoroughgoing confusion of political and cultural issues by all parties concerned was perhaps the outstanding characteristic of the whole controversy. The entire dispute was discussed as though the problem were one in forensic anthropology: i.e., whether or not those two imaginary ethnic entities "Papuans" and "Indonesians" were racially, linguistically, and culturally related or not and *therefore* ought to be politically joined or not. (The distinction between the various sorts of ethnological relationship was hardly grasped, and the methods by which such questions are scientifically approached not grasped at all.) The result was international high comedy. On the one hand, we had an ex-colonial power arguing for an ethnic concept of governmental legitimacy—i.e., "national" self-determination—that scarcely a decade and a half earlier it had bitterly opposed to the point of open warfare (and that it still would not care to apply to Surinam and Curaçao). On the other hand, we had a passionately nationalist new state arguing for a purely political concept of legitimacy which its most revered ideological slogan—"one people, one country, one language"—expressly rejects, and occasionally trying, if a bit sheepishly, to save the ideology by inventing some "non-Western" anthropology. And in between them, we had a "neutral" Western power—ourselves—agreeing morally with one side, forwarding the aims of the other, and ending up feeling not that it had performed a rather skillful job of diplomatic brokerage, but that it had somehow played the coward and sacrificed principle to expediency.[11] Clearly,

[11] It is perhaps somewhat unwarranted to attribute sentiments to the State Department officials who played active roles in the negotiations. My judgment is rather more based on the absolutely universal dismay with which the American Establishment, as reflected in the bewigged press (*The New York Times* being perhaps the outstanding example), in certain rather apologetic public statements by shamefaced liberal diplomats, and in my own discussions with knowledgeable university people, viewed the New Guinea settlement, regarding it as an abject surrender to "Indonesian colonialism." The fact that, so far as I know, the United States government has never attempted to defend or even explain its actions suggests to me at least that

something was seriously wrong with the whole framework within which the dispute progressed. Played by these rules, those of Wilson, Mazzini, and de Valera, the game had no solution.

The absurdities which result from the consistent application of the one-state, one-people form of thought to the New Guinea dispute should have been apparent to anyone who thought the matter through with any persistence at all. If "Papuans" were to be held politically unassimilable to Indonesia on ethnic grounds as such, then should northern Halmahera, which is also "Papuan" linguistically, "racially," and, so far as we know, culturally, be detached from Indonesia as well?[12] (And why, in fact, was not this area excluded from the original transfer of sovereignty as West New Guinea itself?) In fact, if one based the argument, as most did, simply on racial grounds, or what they took to be racial grounds, should not the more negroid, but Malayo-Polynesian-speaking groups of East Indonesia generally also be detached? Nor would such issues be avoided if the problem were cast in purely cultural terms; for, of course, a great many of the peoples of the Lesser Sundas and the Moluccas have much closer ethnological affiliations with the Melanesian culture sphere than with the Malaysian. (Even the Sumatran islands of Nias and Mentawei have been so char-

---

this general feeling that we behaved both immorally and pusillanimously pervades official quarters as well and that, in fact, the agreement was more an accidental result of the play of immediate political pressures than of genuine political understanding. However, it is possible that I am doing an injustice to certain American policymakers, who may have understood what the nature of the controversy really was.

[12] The term "Papuan" is (apparently) a Malay term meaning "woolly-haired," originally applied by Moluccan peoples to coastal New Guinea peoples because of the latters' crinkly hair. Scientific analysis has hardly got much beyond this point; the linguistic, racial, and cultural substantiality of this group remains to be established and the word has tended to be used by Western scholars to mean "non-Malayo-Polynesian speaking inhabitant(s) of Melanesia." A good many of the ethnographic categories anthropologists use are pretty arbitrary, but for sheer vacuousness "Papuan" is probably unexceeded.

acterized.) And how about reversing the argument? Does "Malay" Indonesia have the legitimate claim to Brunei, North Borneo, and Sarawak that it lacks to New Guinea? Few (except perhaps, now that they have, for all intents and purposes, won Irian, some Indonesians) would care to carry logic to such extremes. The point is that the issues involved in the dispute could not be made even intelligible morally, legally, or politically, in these terms. The issues themselves were (and perhaps still are) real enough, and eminently disputable. But the quasi-anthropological, even to put it more bluntly, racist, vocabulary in which they were discussed by all parties was hardly conducive to understanding them.

As a political issue, and one whose resolution could hardly be much longer delayed, there were perhaps but four major possibilities for West New Guinea's disposition: (*a*) the territory could remain a Dutch preserve, under some form of trusteeship, with the idea that the indigenous peoples would be prepared by the trustee for eventual self-rule; (*b*) it could be granted independence; (*c*) it could be included, with the remainder of the island, in some larger independent Melanesian federation, or at least a pan-New Guinea state; or (*d*) it could be handed over to Indonesia.

The first two of these proposals were hardly feasible. Even if one were to grant, somewhat in the face of the Netherlands East Indies experience, that the Dutch would prove to be effective modernizers of perhaps the most untouched tribal peoples in the world, it is hard to imagine that the tutelage pattern would be regarded as a realistic possibility in the Southeast Asia of 1962 by any but the most steadfast member of Holland's evangelical Anti-Revolutionary Party (the revolution it is against is the French). As for granting West New Guinea's Papuans a separate independence, the only result one can even imagine is chaos followed by a rather rapid loss of the independence. The latter two possibilities contain, however, more substance and at least some promise of practicability. The Melanesian federation notion has the attraction of grouping people together in an ethnographically somewhat more reasonable way (for it is not part of my argument to deny that cultural, racial, or linguistic realities, or even imagined realities, have serious political implications). However, such a federation has not even a prospective existence at the moment, and one cannot very well integrate a colonial territory into a nonexistent, and perhaps never-to-be-existent, state. Had the various colonial powers of Melanesia, including the Netherlands, spent the last decade working out a concrete, workable, well-staged plan for an eventual Melanesian state, they would have had a far better argument against Indonesian claims to set before the world than the combination of white-man's-burden moralizing *cum* cold war gamesmanship upon which they in fact relied. As for the Indonesian solution, the one, whatever the letter of the agreement may seem to say, that has in effect been chosen, has the advantage of bringing the territory into a large, established, and at least potentially rich and powerful state, and the disadvantage of turning the Papuans over to a disorganized, hyperideologized, nearly bankrupt government whose future is highly uncertain. But the point is not whether one believes (as I do) that the decision to deliver West New Guinea to Indonesia represents—for the Papuans, for the Indonesians, for the Dutch, and for world peace— the best gamble among the sorry options actually available. Respectable arguments can be brought (though they rarely have been) from either side. The point is that the arguments for or against the concrete alternatives must be fundamentally civil and not anthropological ones, ones concerned with the establishment in Southeast Asia of a set of viable polities, strong enough to defend their independence, vigorous enough to advance the interests of their members, and sober enough to carry on peaceful international relations with one another and with the world in general. To such discussions, linguistic, cultural, and even skin-color or hair differences are far from irrelevant. But the nature of their relevance can emerge with any clarity only if ethno-cratic doctrines of political legitimacy are resolutely aban-doned.

The proposal to form a Malaysian Federation out of Malaya, Singapore, Sarawak, Brunei, and British North Borneo illustrates the reverse side of the coin from the New Guinea issue. Here the differential political histories and, hence, social-economic organization of the proposed com-ponent elements were the main obstacle to success; and the very existence of genuine, and radical, ethnic discontinuity was the prime mover of the whole enterprise. The seeming paradoxical quality of this situation—that it was cultural diversity which was making for political unity—derived, again, from the axiomatic, and for Southeast Asia completely errant, assumption that states are nations and nations states. The Malaysian Federation is perhaps the most interesting political experiment so far attempted in Southeast Asia, and its course and outcome will have implications far beyond its borders, perhaps especially for Africa, where colonial rule also left behind a debris of small and unworkable politi-cal units that must eventually find a place in some larger polity if they are to come into the modern world. The gamble of Prime Minister Tengku Abdul Rahman of Malaya is not a paradox but a portent; and like all portents it must be read with an informed eye.

The biethnic character of the Federation of Malaya (i.e., Malaya proper) was, as mentioned earlier, never more than minimally dissolved by the symbolic necessities of the in-dependence struggle into a single, colony-defined ideological "nationality." The contrast between the two communities (actually three, including the Indians) was too great to make any theory of a Malayan cultural identity over and above those of Malay and Chinese more than a transparent strategy. Instead, ethnogenesis here took the form of lump-ing what was originally a set of local or regional communities, crosscut with linguistic, racial, and cultural differences, into two state-wide ethnic blocs:

[In the colonial period] the social map was . . . made up of a kaleidoscope of small culturally defined units rearranging themselves in accordance with local conditions. "The Malays" did not interact with "The Chinese." . . . Some Malays interacted with some Chinese. . . . But as "Malays" [and] "Chinese" . . . come to be realized as structural entities on a nation-wide scale, they can begin to have total relations with one another. . . . Through most of its modern history Malaya has shown important cultural and "racial" divisions, but these divisions had not created cleavages running the length and breadth of the society. The social ideals of Malays [and] Chinese . . . were different and their interrelations governed by narrowly defined political and economic interests; but there was not framework for the massive alignment of ethnic forces. In the Federation of Malaya the attainment of Independence has furnished conditions for such an alignment. Malays [and] Chinese . . . are forced to confront one another and pushed into speaking for their own ethnic communities on a national scale.[13]

In itself, such a confrontation need not be politically disruptive. In fact, under the enfolding umbrella of the Alliance, Malaya's dominant political party, it has so far animated one of the most effective democracies in Asia. But, as in Indonesia, one item of unfinished political business remained to plague it and render it permanently unstable —the future of Singapore, 78 per cent Chinese in population and virtually 100 per cent in social outlook. Like New Guinea, Singapore was originally excluded from the transfer of sovereignty over the former colonial territory to the new indigenous elite at least in part on ethnic grounds.[14] And,

[13] Freedman, *op. cit.* I have removed all references to the Indian group for purposes of simplicity.
[14] For a résumé of the somewhat involved political history of the Malay peninsula, see Silcock, T. E., "Singapore in Malaya," *Far*

like New Guinea, its future had become increasingly problematical as the date approached when continued colonial rule became impossible. But whereas in the New Guinea case the problem was one of a government deprived, so it felt, of a legitimate part of its heritage, in the Singapore case it was one of a government most reluctant to absorb a territory which, though very difficult to separate from its domain economically, politically, or even psychologically, it regarded not so much as a lost jewel as an unextractable thorn.

The reason for this ambivalence toward Singapore on the part of the leaders of the Federation was again the divergent pull of cultural and political (or political-economic) factors. Adding Singapore to the Federation would change the country's Malay-Chinese population balance from about 50%:37% to about 41%:44%, something the Malay leaders of the Alliance, and probably even the bulk of its Chinese leaders as well, regarded as a far from pleasing prospect. The change of proportions in favor of the richer, more energetic, and (somewhat) more rapidly multiplying Chinese would destroy the precarious "communal" balance by which Malaya had lived, and indeed flourished in a modest way, since independence. Yet at the same time, though almost certainly not independently viable either politically or economically, Singapore represented Southeast Asia's greatest commercial and industrial center and thus perhaps the key to Malaya's future as a modern state and regional power. The exclusion of Singapore from the Federation, which was itself, of course, mainly a primary producer, hampered the long-run economic and social development of Malaya at the same time as it assisted its short-run stability; and it left Singapore

---

Eastern Survey, Vol. 29, No. 3, March 1960, pp. 33–39, who remarks . . . "The inclusion of Penang, first in the Malayan Union and then in the Federation, while Singapore remained separate, probably indicates that economic and geographic arguments carried little weight, while the racial balance of Malaya and the strategic significance of Singapore to the British may have been the determining factors."

in a political limbo which could not be endured much longer. Half-in, half-out of Malaya (the Federation and Singapore had a common currency and banking system, and a great many large businesses had branches in both territories), half-colony, half-independent city-state, Singapore could not, as T. E. Silcock has pointed out, "be floated away with all its problems into the middle of the China Sea, nor yet absorbed into the Federation without major changes in the balance of . . . power." [15]

The proposal by Tengku Abdul Rahman in May 1961 for a new Malaysian Federation that would include not only Malaya and Singapore but the three Bornean territories as well—a complete and sudden reversal of policy for him and for the until-then resolutely antiaccession Alliance government—was both a recognition of this home truth and an ingenious plan for muffling the communal issues it presented by placing them in a larger, more complex political context. The Tengku and his followers seemed not only to have realized that either a way must be found to bring Singapore and Malaya together or the moderate Singapore government would soon fall to pro-Peking, anti-Malaya elements, but also that this could only be accomplished if an ethnic counterbalance to the increased Chinese population could be found. The inclusion of the Bornean territories created such a counterbalance.[16] But it also created a socially, economically, and politically (not to say geographically) very much more diverse and loose-limbed state. To a very large extent, the future of Malaysia depends on which of these considerations—ethnic balance or social-economic hetero-

---

[15] *Ibid.*, p. 38.

[16] Over-all Malaysian "ethnic" distributions are about 42 per cent "Malay," 38 per cent "Chinese," 10 per cent "Indian," and 10 per cent "Other Indigenous." See Hanna, W. A., "Malaysia, A Federation in Prospect, Part I: The Proposal," American Universities Field Staff Report, Southeast Asia Series, Vol. 10, No. 1 (1962). If the "Other Indigenous"—mainly Malayo-Polynesian speaking tribal peoples of Borneo: Dyaks, Kedayans, etc.—eventually line up as "Malays," then the proportions of Chinese and Malays will be virtually unchanged in Malaysia from what they have been in Malaya.

geneity—proves to be the most consequential for national evolution.

As a matter of fact, it was not in Singapore, for whose delicate sensibilities the whole plan was designed in the first place, that the main threat to Malaysia developed. Singapore opted for federation by a whopping 70 per cent in the referendum of September 1962; but in Sarawak, Brunei, and British North Borneo a number of unforeseen complications developed. The most serious, or at least the most violent, of these was the reaction of Brunei oil workers under the leadership, at once Indonesian irredentist, Brunei imperialist, and pro-Communist, of A. M. Azahari's Partai Rakjat. Perhaps the most surprising, and most discouraging, was the irredentist claim suddenly advanced by the Philippines against the least developed of the territories, North Borneo. And in Sarawak, where the Chinese were both the most numerous and, probably, the strongest, they initially united in opposition to Malaysia, perhaps as much to maintain their local position as anything else. The details, uncertain in any case, are not, however, what is important here. What is important is that in undertaking to resolve one thorny political problem, the status of Singapore, the Tengku saddled himself with at least three more that were equally difficult. The original notion that the three Bornean territories could be absorbed into Malaya proper, with only Singapore having a special status in the larger union, evaporated in the face of political realities. It became clear that if and when the new Federation finally came into being, it would consist of a motley collection of special cases.

Thus, what started out as a device to maintain a delicate interethnic relationship within Malaya by projecting the pattern of balance upon which it rested over a much wider domain, ended by becoming a problem of adjusting the diverse social-economic requirements of a primary producer, a commercial-industrial city-state, and a set of largely undeveloped hinterlands so as to integrate them into a workable, overarching political framework. What began as a "nationality" problem in the ethnic sense ended as a "national" problem in the civil sense. The solution of the problem of preventing the accession of Singapore to Malaya from disrupting the latter's ethnic balance created, in turn, a set of wicked problems in political negotiation. This was undoubted progress: progress away from thinking about states as ethnic (or, in this case, biethnic) entities to thinking about them as autonomous civil communities within which ethnic realities are an important, but not a defining, element. Malay communalists, clinging to Malayan isolationalism and Malay special privilege on the peninsula and looking to Indonesia or the Philippines in Borneo, or Chinese communalists looking toward Peking in Singapore and their own local communities in Borneo, might well have disrupted the federation proposal. But such an outcome (again, independently of whether one favored, as I did, the proposal or not) would have represented not a triumph of "national" self-determination and cultural self-expression but a failure of political genius.

The partition of Indochina is, of course, the outstanding example in Southeast Asia of what happens when such genius does fail and a viable political unit is dismembered into less ethnically heterogeneous parts.[17] Whether partition was unavoidable—or, more precisely, when it became unavoidable—is hardly worth additional discussion at this date; by the time the American government became directly involved, the choice had narrowed down to large-scale military intervention in favor of the demoralized colonial power or partition, and few even now, after the Laotian fiasco and the South Vietnam emergency, would question the wisdom of our selection between those two alternatives. What is worth looking at, however, are the political results of such

[17] The parts are still, however, not entirely homogeneous: ethnic Laotians (i.e., lowland, Buddhist, Thai-speaking) comprise only about half the total population of Laos, and there are important tribal minorities in Vietnam as well. Also, of course, partition split the Vietnamese into two states, and there is the Buddhist-Catholic contrast in the south.

balkanization; for if the Malaysian Federation represents one sort of pattern of relations between governmental and ethnic units in Southeast Asia, the existing Indochinese fragmentation represents another.

The most immediate result of balkanization is that the hand of the dominant ethnic group is immeasurably strengthened vis-à-vis whatever minorities may still be present within the parceled polity. Relieved of the necessity of striking domestic political bargains with other large and important ethnic groups, it can more easily attempt to press the temper of its own personality upon the whole country. Instead of a civil state straining to contain a variety of powerful peoples within a single governmental framework, there results instead a strong movement toward ethnocracy. The hill peoples of South Vietnam, North Vietnam, Laos, and, to a lesser extent, Cambodia, are unable to play the Lao, Vietnamese, and Khmer off against one another in order to protect their own integrity against the cultural imperialism of these powerful lowlanders.[18] The system of ethnic checks and balances is disrupted, or, more exactly, not allowed to develop, and each minority is left to the mercy of the single dominant ethnic group of its reduced state. That is unless, as of course has been the case, it can gain its ethnic allies from outside the state's boundaries through the useful device of a common, supposedly supranational social ideology, and in so doing reduce those boundaries, as has also been the case, to an open sieve through which pour the political solvents that threaten to dissipate the entire structure of the state.

In turn, this accession to dominance of a single ethnic group within a small state tends to lead to a much more traditional pattern of government. Relieved of the necessity of developing the sorts of modern political skills which are necessary to keep a large, multiethnic state going, the elite

[18] Members of majority groups living "on the wrong side" of state lines—e.g., the Khmers in South Vietnam—are, of course, victims of the same situation.

is almost bound to try to rule by methods derived from their own classical culture, only slightly updated to look as though they were parliamentary, bureaucratic, or popular. In each of the partition-formed states (except, perhaps, North Vietnam, which has been reabsorbed into a larger political entity which, whatever else one may say about it, belongs to this century), the movement away from the political forms of traditionalism is sharply retarded: in Laos, an ideologized version of segmentary politics; in Cambodia, a republican renovation of divine kingship; in South Vietnam, a Romanized mandarin familism. Thus to the simple facts of their small size, economic weakness, and exposed position must be added antiquated government and an enfeeblement of the civil sense.

Again, though the comparison will stand only so much inspection, one is reminded of the Southeast European situation. There too, the fragmentation, after World War I, into small, ethnically more or less homogeneous units isolated the region from the processes of political change, both "good" and "bad," that were taking place in the rest of the continent. There too, weak, archaic, wholly defensive governments, anxious mainly to hang on, drifted out of touch with their masses, despite the (assumed) commonalities of "blood" and "culture" uniting them, while the political capacities of the masses themselves remained stunted. There too, the tendency for ethnic animosities and political divisions to coalesce, compassing each petty state with a nest of familiar enemies, made stable international relations extraordinarily difficult to achieve. (Perhaps nothing in Southeast Asia is so reminiscent of Ruritanian politics and the sort of thing which used to start world wars than the Cambodia–Thailand temple dispute—unless it be that Eastern version of an opening to the sea problem, the Cambodia–Vietnam controversy over Phu Quoc.) There too, the political-economic unworkability of a collection of mutually hostile lilliputian states made them an easy prey to the unifying power of an externally rooted totalitarian ideology and a leviathan empire—first Nazi, now Communist. Whether this will be the outcome on the Indochinese peninsula is, of course, far from certain. But the virtual collapse of Laos after a major, if ill-devised, American effort to render it viable; the increasing inability of Cambodia to escape a total absorption in the immediate ethnic threats with which its separate "national" existence has surrounded it and to pursue a more realistic foreign policy in the interests of its own growth and security; and the extreme tenuousness of the American attempt to breathe life into a tottering South Vietnam would, I should think, lead one to consider whether one-state, one-nation doctrines were not rather more to the advantage of our political opponents in Southeast Asia than to ourselves.

III

Political stability in Southeast Asia depends most importantly on the formation of a small set of reasonably large, vigorous polities shaped into some sort of regional balance of power in which no one state is simply dominant and no one state simply impotent. The political autonomy of the region, in the sense of freedom from domination by external powers, depends upon the same condition. Even that elusive summum bonum, the creation of effective supranational checks upon national sovereignty, depends upon it. Aside from the inevitable outbreaks of political megalomania on the part of arriviste statesmen, perhaps the most formidable obstacle to the formation of such a system is the extreme variegation of the cultural landscape with its constant invitation to separatism, isolationism, racialism, and xenophobia. The wide and chronic divergence in this cluttered corner of Asia between the ethnic or primordial meaning of "nation" and its political meaning gives to the problem of "nation building" an immanent ambiguity that folkist concepts of the sources of legitimacy only deepen.

Both the maintenance of cultural integrity and the

achievement of political viability are crucial to the peoples of Southeast Asia as to any other people. But there—perhaps more than elsewhere, perhaps not—the realization of each of these goals depends upon its being disentangled from the other and pursued separately. The search for a social identity and the demand for social progress are, as always, intimately related, and react back and forth upon one another. But they are not the same thing, and when, at least in a culturally heterogeneous state, they are confounded one gets an ersatz identity on the one hand and political enervation on the other, a combination whose outcome is either national disintegration or totalitarian integration, or perhaps the one giving way, in time, to the other. If the notion that an effective political community can only grow out of a pre-existing cultural consensus is true, then Southeast Asia's future looks dim indeed, for, except in part for Thailand, no such consensus exists, nor is likely to exist in the foreseeable future, over any area wide enough to be meaningful in a world of powerhouse states. If the notion that cultural freedom can only exist in an ethnically homogeneous state is true, then there is even less hope—for such, in this area necessarily minuscule, states can in the mid-twentieth century be but transient realities. The conditions for an Eire do not exist any more than those for a Germany. But neither of these assumptions is true unless Southeast Asians and we ourselves regard them as so, and so regarding them cloud the fundamental nature of the immediate political task in the region: the construction of workable multi-ethnic states.

The interests of the United States in Southeast Asia lie on the side of the rapid growth of political competence and civil sense on the part of both the leaders and the peoples of the various states that are now taking shape there. No more than any other social change can such a development be forced—certainly not from outside. But we can avoid hindering it and perhaps can even encourage it, first, by recognizing the somewhat peculiar context in which it must take place, and second, by communicating this recognition to the governments and peoples of the region themselves through our actions toward them. By reacting to them as states rather than tribes we may induce them to act like states rather than tribes. By insisting on the distinction (but not the irrelation) between cultural and political concerns we may help them perceive the distinction, particularly if we should suddenly develop the ability to judge their policies in terms of their own purposes and abstain from attempting to pressure them into political arrangements which serve our interests but not theirs. By understanding the nature of their own uncertainties we may help convince them that they can be understood and, understood, resolved. Though they will be much more difficult to deal with and will tax far more strenuously our own political capacities, we need powers in Southeast Asia, not satellites.

Our actions and policies are not, and are not likely to become, the only, or even the main, factor in bringing these various results about. The United Nations is doubtless even more important; and I sometimes imagine that when we look back, if we are still here to look back, in future years on the first decades of the United Nations, its greatest significance will be seen to have been not so much its broker role among the great powers, which is perhaps more apparent than real, but its function as a sort of school for aspirant states, a mechanism for socializing a set of rather amateur governments, and through them their peoples, into a workable international order, and teaching them, thereby, what it means to be a modern political entity and what it takes to survive as one. The growth of relations among the several states themselves will also have more effect than American policy (unless that policy be unusually inept). So, too, will the simple experience of dealing with domestic problems— not the least of them ethnic diversity, which, with luck, could prove the salvation of libertarian government in Southeast Asia rather than its undoing—in a systematic and self-conscious way. But American policy will matter. In the wavering balance between regional fragmentation and regional integration, it may even turn out to be decisive.

4

THE PATTERN OF SOUTHEAST ASIAN RESPONSE TO INTERNATIONAL POLITICS

ᏋᎧᏌᏋᎧᏌᏋᎧᏌ

DAVID WURFEL

CHARLES BEARD HAS RIGHTLY said that "foreign policy rests upon an image of the world." [1] But assessments by political leaders concerning the main forces in internal politics are also crucial. It is the purpose of this essay to attempt to discern the world images held by the political elites of Southeast Asian states, to describe the relevant internal factors, to trace the impact of both on the developing patterns of national foreign policies, and finally to note the implications of these patterns for United States policy toward the area.

The "image of the world," or definition of international reality, of Southeast Asian political elites has been determined primarily by history and by geopolitical realities. The most significant experience for most of these leaders has been participation in anticolonial nationalist movements.

[1] Beard, Charles, A Foreign Policy for America (New York: Knopf, 1940), p. 5.

Out of this experience they have acquired the ideologies and attitudes that inform their interpretation of the geopolitical configuration of the world scene. Thus history and geography determine the over-all goals of foreign policy. In Southeast Asia these goals, subsumed by some under the general heading of a "quest for power," have been variously expressed as security, territorial expansion, greater national prestige, greater national unity, and always independence from external restraints, the protection of sovereignty.

Within the broad framework of long-term definitions of reality, national leaders must interact with a variety of immediate situations in making policy decisions. These decisions are influenced by the leaders' operational values, such as a preference for adjusting to, rather than attempting to remold, a new situation, by current assessments of their own national power, by domestic political relationships such as the strength and policy position of the real or imagined opposition, and by the demands of other nations. In Southeast Asia, as among other new states, domestic political considerations are usually more important than in the case of older, more stable governments.[2]

I

Southeast Asia is not a homogeneous region. It is very difficult to generalize about its foreign policies. Thus, keeping in mind the factors influencing both the broad definition of international reality and the making of particular policy decisions, let us examine some of the countries of Southeast Asia separately.[3] We shall treat them according to their position in the foreign policy spectrum.

[2] See Good, Robert, "State-Building as a Determinant of Foreign Policy in the New States," Martin, Laurence, ed., *Neutralism and Nonalignment* (New York: Praeger, 1962).

[3] For descriptive material on national foreign policies see Fifield, Russell, H., *The Diplomacy of Southeast Asia, 1945–1958* (New York: Harper, 1958); and appropriate sections in Kahin, George McT., ed., *Governments and Politics of Southeast Asia,* rev. ed. (Ithaca: Cornell University Press, 1963). Also Dudman, Richard, "Asia's Frontiers of Freedom," *St. Louis Post-Dispatch,* February 3–8, 10–13, 1963.

THE PHILIPPINES

Despite recent manifestations, it is still possible to say that in domestic politics as in foreign policy orientation, the Philippines stands closest to the West of any country in Southeast Asia. The Philippines was given the longest training in democratic self-government of any colony in Southeast Asia. As an independent nation it has in the best sense "nationalized" democratic procedure, enabling Filipinos to change national leadership via the ballot box on several occasions, an unmatched record in the area. The same historical experience which has made of the Philippines a democracy has also produced an "image of the world" quite compatible with our own. The Catholic religion has fostered vehement opposition to communism among the elite, and widespread fear of it among the masses (although not enough to prevent peasant support for a Communist-led agrarian movement which was felt to be working for their interests). Exclusion of a Yugoslav basketball team, which caused cancellation of an international tournament, is a recent manifestation of an attitude which shuns all knowing contact with Communists of any variety. The association of communism with China in recent years, reinforcing the traditionally anti-Chinese element in Philippine nationalism, strengthens this bias. Conversely, the ease with which independence was gained has inhibited the growth of virulent or widespread anti-Americanism. Such anti-American outbursts as have occurred voice particular grievances, not a fundamental antipathy. The clear displeasure in 1961 at the initial failure of the United States Congress to pass a war damage bill, for example, was largely justified.

The Philippines' insularity has tended to isolate the country, until recently, from the political currents of Southeast Asia. Furthermore, it has made the presence of American air and naval power a plausible policy for the national defense. At the same time, the proximity of Formosa has made the preservation of a non-Communist regime there a matter of essential national interest. On more than one occasion,

Philippine spokesmen have declared their determined refusal to recognize Communist China even if the United States should do so.[4] The strongest geographical link which the Philippines has with Southeast Asia is through Borneo, a political terra incognita until a very few years ago. Now the Borneo problem has involved the Philippines directly in one of the most serious intraregional disputes since World War II.

Let us delve into the Borneo dispute in more detail, treating it as an example of the forces determining Philippine foreign policy today.[5] There is no space here to detail the complicated history of the legal status of British North Borneo, which has ramifications enough to fill an international law textbook. It is sufficient to say that the present Philippine claim, based on the historical rights of the Sultan of Sulu, is not frivolous. But why should it receive public attention only after announcement of plans for the formation of Malaysia? The chain of events now seems clear. Ever since Britain annexed North Borneo in 1946, the heirs of the Sultan of Sulu, from whom the territory had originally been leased (or purchased, that is the question), have been asking to negotiate with the British Crown. In 1957 Nicasio Osmeña, acting as attorney-in-fact of the heirs, asked the British for $15 million to settle the claim, which entails claims both to sovereignty and to proprietary rights; the British were unresponsive and unperturbed. When it became apparent that the British were planning to transfer the territory to the proposed Federation of Malaysia,[6]

[4] For an extended public debate on Formosa, see Collas, Juan, ed., *Senator Claro M. Recto on the Formosa Question* (Manila: Carmelo and Bauermann, no date).

[5] The fullest scholarly account is by Ortiz, Pacifico, "Legal Aspects of the North Borneo Question," *Philippine Studies*, Vol. 11, No. 1, January 1963, pp. 18–64. See also Rama, Napoleon G., *Philippines Free Press*, December 30, 1961; January 20, 1962; March 10, 1962; April 7, 1962; April 21, 1962; and Meadows, Martin, "The Philippine Claim to North Borneo," *Political Science Quarterly*, Vol. 77, No. 3, September 1962, pp. 321–335.

[6] See below, pp. 78–80.

Osmeña acted quickly. He felt it would be even more difficult, both legally and politically, to deal with the successors to the British interest. In February 1962, the heirs of the Sultan transferred their "sovereign rights" over British North Borneo to the Philippines, and requested the Philippine government to pursue their proprietary claims through diplomatic channels. Osmeña was astute enough to recognize that the claim would attain importance only if it could be clothed in nationalist garb. The necessary press coverage and the appropriate speeches in Congress followed. President Diosdado Macapagal, having been acquainted with the claim since his days in the Philippine Foreign Service, pushed it on patriotic grounds. The Philippine government acted quickly, and was as quickly rebuffed by the British. Not until Vice President Emmanuel Pelaez brought the Philippine claim to the attention of the United Nations and, more significantly, not until a revolt broke out in Brunei while its leader, A. M. Azahari, was in Manila, did the British agree to negotiate. The first round of talks was held in January 1963 when Vice President Pelaez went to London. Although these talks produced no agreement, direct conversations in April between Macapagal and Prime Minister Tengku Abdul Rahman of Malaya finally brought greater understanding. In June, the Philippines agreed to drop its opposition to Malaysia when the Malayans offered to entertain the Philippine claim subsequent to formation of the new Federation. Philippine protests were renewed, however, on the eve of Malaysia's September birth on the grounds of alleged irregularities in the procedures of the United Nations mission sent to determine the wishes of the Bornean people.

It is clear, first of all, that the most important operational value in the Philippine policy process is initiative and action, *if* national interest and/or influential individual interests are involved. In comparison with other Asians, Filipinos are not by nature passive. This is revealed in their foreign policy style. Furthermore, it is obvious that the Philippines does not differ from its neighbors in the power of nationalism, once mobilized, to determine the direction of foreign policy. Nationalist flames had been vigorously fanned by the apparently disdainful British attitude. The momentum was so strong that at one point it appeared the Philippines was willing to wreck the recently formed Association of Southeast Asia rather than modify or delay the Borneo claim; cooler heads eventually prevailed. For the fullest understanding of Philippine action, we must also take account of domestic political alignments. Both President Macapagal and Vice President Pelaez had been accused, during the 1961 election campaign, of being "America's candidates," of being insufficiently nationalistic. Though they wisely did not attempt to disprove this with wild oratory before election day, they have not overlooked any opportunity to create a more nationalistic image since inauguration.

In sum, Philippine foreign policy may be characterized as active and aligned (pro-Western), a policy which is sometimes determined by internal politics and nationalist psychology, and at the same time by a world view that might be considered rational from the Western point of view. The domestic pressures toward external aggression which might be observed in Indonesia, for example, are not present in the Philippines. Nor do internal politics have any significant effect on policy regarding major cold war issues.

MALAYA

Regardless of the 1962–1963 controversy between them, Malaya has been next only to the Philippines as a firm democratic ally of the West. Malayan democracy, however, has a much shorter history than the Philippine variety, and today suffers from restrictions. Freedom of speech, for example, is not as uninhibited as in the Philippines. Nor is the social-cultural base for democracy in Malaya as strong as in the Philippines. Malaya is still to a large extent a plural society. Although a workable compromise between racial communities has been achieved for the moment, the penetration of ideologies and the impact of economic development will undoubtedly upset it. Whether or not a new compromise adjusted to changed conditions can be worked out at the proper time within the democratic process is the brooding question mark in Malaya's future.

The Malayan political elite, like the Philippine, has a very westernized image of world politics, which is, however, supported by a somewhat less broad national consensus than in the latter country. Since independence, in fact, this image has been largely the reality defined by Tengku Abdul Rahman, both foreign minister and prime minister. British-educated himself, he heads a civil service also very much British-oriented. The friendly negotiations which led to independence were not conducive to an upsurge of anti-British nationalism; furthermore, the Malays, who are in political control of the Federation, are rightly grateful for British policy which made this pre-eminence possible. By the same token, however, the politically conscious Chinese, an ever growing segment of the population, have reason to be dissatisfied with the government's strong British orientation. While Abdul Rahman maintains a military alliance with Britain, and until recently has tended to rely almost entirely on the British presence for defense, he has stayed out of SEATO. Perhaps this is simply based on the judgment that SEATO's political liabilities are more important than its military assets, a judgment easily justified, but Malaya's nearly insular position also allows it. Recent cooperation between Malaya and Thailand in policing their common border reinforces this insularity.

Malaya's insularity, however, does not imply isolation, for Malaya is an "island" at the crossroads of Southeast Asia. This circumstance, together with the personality of Malayan leadership, has insured an operational value that puts a premium on initiative and action. The case of Malaysia shows this most clearly. Since the formation of Malaysia has been clearly the major foreign policy goal of Malayan political leadership in recent years, and since it reveals graphically the impact of both domestic and foreign influences on the Malayan policy process, let us examine this problem in some detail.[7]

Although its creation would allow the present political elite of Malaya to play the major role in governing a larger territory, the drive for Malaysia should not be thought of as simply a policy of territorial expansion, Sukarno's epithets notwithstanding. Formation of the Federation of Malaysia was primarily a technique for preserving after merger with Singapore the compromise among ethnic communities within Malaya, on which the power of the ruling Alliance is based. Malaysia was designed to balance the increased Chinese population with an increase in Malays, even though the net result would be a reduction of the Malay majority in Malaya to a mere 42 per cent plurality in the new Federation. The merger with Singapore itself was conceived as the most effective means of dealing with the danger of that city becoming a Communist-dominated island right on Malaya's front doorstep. The crises believed to be inevitable in the British territories of North Borneo if they achieved separate independence were also thought to be more manageable and less dangerous to Malaya within a federation than without.

Agreement on conditions of merger with Singapore became possible only because of the particular character of the balance of forces in that intensely political community in 1961. Lee Kuan Yew was the third prime minister to come to power in Singapore on a radical platform, only to turn right and be challenged by the more radical left after he assumed office. He had won electoral victory under the People's Action Party banner, supported by its Communist allies. When the PAP split in early 1961, his major opposition became a Communist Chinese labor leader. Both Lee and

[7] For the most detailed and up-to-date information on Malaysia, see Hanna, W. A., *Malaysia, A Federation in Prospect,* American Universities Field Staff Reports Service, Southeast Asia Series, Vol. 10, Nos. 1–12, Vol. 11, Nos. 1–3, 5–7, 10–13, 1962–1963.

Abdul Rahman recognized that the cycle could not be repeated. Merger with the Federation had been a major plank in Lee's platform; for the first time, it was unquestionably in Malaya's interest to agree to that merger on terms which the prime minister of Singapore could sell to the island's voters. Lee was able to gain a 71 per cent majority in the September 1962 referendum on Malaysia, but only by using a brilliant combination of Machiavellian tactics, "a virtuoso performance in counter-Communist one-upmanship." [8]

The decision to launch the Malaysian scheme, therefore, was a result of the coincidence of the partisan political interests of the two prime ministers, and of their assessments of the national interests of their respective countries. It was at first assumed that the Borneo territories, not yet politically articulate, and as members of the Commonwealth still subject to considerable British influence, would quickly acquiesce in the plan. But politics is never so simple. What had been a political backwash spawned nearly a dozen new political parties in little more than six months after announcement of the Malaysia proposal. The first reaction of the major leaders in the three territories was to reject the scheme as it stood. They talked more favorably of independence for a Federation of Northern Borneo. Ethnic realities cooled this ardor, however. Reactions to concrete proposals inevitably differed in Brunei, where Malays dominate, from Sarawak and British North Borneo, which are dominated by dynamic and sizable Chinese minorities.

Eventually the main weight of Bornean opinion was moved to support the Malaysia project by the brash acts of its leading opponent, Indonesian army veteran and Brunei's Partai Rakjat leader, A. M. Azahari. The Brunei revolt launched on December 8, 1962, which was undertaken with Indonesian approval and support, revealed Azahari's intentions, his connections, and his weaknesses. He proclaimed himself prime minister of the "Revolutionary Government

[8] See Hanna, *op. cit.*, "Singapore—The Strategy and Tactics of Merger," Vol. 10, No. 7, September 1962.

of Northern Borneo," including Sarawak and North Borneo as well as Brunei, but his followers were able to capture only one town, from which they were soon dislodged by British forces. Even as the rebels were being captured or scattered, Indonesian officials in Djakarta, both civilian and military, were increasingly vehement in their expressions of support, and in their attacks on Abdul Rahman. The revolt proved that the Borneo territories would not be politically quiescent partners in Malaysia, but it did not prove that they would stay out.

Two weeks after the revolt an election in British North Borneo, the territory's first, resulted in a landslide victory for the pro-Malaysian Alliance Party. Indonesian leaders talked in January 1963 of sending "volunteers" into the North Borneo territories. The dangerousness of the situation attracted United Nations Secretary General U Thant's attention. A dramatic meeting between Sukarno and Abdul Rahman in Tokyo in June, followed by a July summit meeting with Macapagal in Manila, brought a temporary end to the warlike Indonesian stance; and resumption of Djakarta's outspoken opposition a month later did not suffice to delay formation of the new Federation in September 1963. Significantly, however, the Sultan of Brunei declined, for a variety of reasons, to join in the enterprise.

Abdul Rahman's Malaysian policy was motivated primarily by a desire to consolidate internal unity, and to forestall the development of an external threat to security. He will probably be more successful in the latter than in the former. Abdul Rahman's international prestige has undoubtedly been enhanced by establishment of the broader Federation of Malaysia; but it should also be pointed out that he has not used an adventure in foreign policy as a substitute for serious grappling with internal problems. The Malayan economic growth rate has been the most rapid in Southeast Asia. The determination to expand the minuscule Malayan armed forces, in response to Indonesian saber-rattling, was undoubtedly a reluctant one, in view of the budgetary competition it will pose to development projects. In sum, we can say that the foreign policy of Malaya, which will be the policy of Malaysia too, as long as it is led by Abdul Rahman, has been active but not aggressive, pro-Western but not slavishly so, and determined by definitions of external threat as well as by internal political exigencies.

THAILAND

Although now a military ally of the United States, Thailand can in no sense be termed a democracy. Furthermore, there are grounds for believing that its pro-Western orientation is less firmly based than in the case of the Philippines or Malaya. In the first place, the Thai political elite is not nearly so westernized as their Philippine or Malayan counterparts. Western influences in Thailand have been both briefer and less intense than in the two former colonies. Furthermore, westernization was selective, with the Thai elite doing the selecting. Western values that have appeared inconsistent with Thai values have been particularly unacceptable.[9]

Thai values have led the Thai elite to a pragmatic assessment of world politics that has given particular attention to the strengths and goals of the great powers. Thailand's geographic position has often brought it in contact with these powers. Until World War I, Thailand was caught precariously between the colonial ambitions of France and Britain. Today the country finds itself on the border between Chinese Communist and American spheres of influence. Throughout, the guiding principle of Thai foreign policy has

[9] See Wilson, David A., "Thailand and Marxism," Trager, Frank N., ed., *Marxism in Southeast Asia* (Stanford: Stanford University Press, 1959), especially pp. 65–70, 74–79. See also Wilson, David A., *Thailand 1962* (Santa Monica: The RAND Corporation, December 1962); and Insor, D., *Thailand: A Political, Social and Economic Analysis* (New York: Praeger, 1963), Chapter 6.

been willing adjustment "to the world as defined by the Great Powers." [10]

Thus, even though the West could hardly ask for greater realism from Thai policymakers, the basis of their present alignment is largely an assessment of the existing world power structure, not a common ideological commitment. (The Thai military assistance agreement with the United States was made in October 1950, before the first successes of Chinese intervention in Korea.) Thai values stress the virtues of reserve and emotional noninvolvement, and therefore adjustment to any given circumstances. The style of Thai foreign policy is clearly distinct from the activism of the Filipinos or the Malayans. Throughout the cataclysmic events of the last three decades, Thailand has always managed to be an ally of the dominant power in the area.

Recent events reveal a continued loyalty to these principles of Thai policy. In Laos, Thailand gave strong support to the Boun Oum–Phoumi Nosavan faction when it was supported by the United States. When American policy in 1961 shifted to support for neutralism, the Thai were understandably dismayed. They regarded it as a sign of weakness. They were further shaken by the inability or unwillingness of SEATO, in which the Thai had put great faith, to take action against Communist advances in Laos. Washington wisely gave both diplomatic assurances and direct military evidence that Thailand was in no sense being abandoned. In March 1962 Secretary of State Dean Rusk declared that the United States would come to the defense of Thailand whether the SEATO Council agreed to or not. In May, American marines flew into northeast Thailand when there were reports that Pathet Lao troops had reached the Thai border. The Thai were reassured. Hints that Thailand might "go neutral" in order to protect itself were not repeated.

[10] Wilson, David A., "Thailand," Kahin, George McT., ed., *Governments and Politics of Southeast Asia* (Ithaca: Cornell University Press, 1959), p. 9.

The stability of the Thai political system despite successive coups d'état, and the insignificance of political parties in the policy process (except for the brief period from 1955 to 1957) have meant that internal political considerations have been less important in influencing foreign policy than elsewhere in Southeast Asia. Nor does Thailand lack national cultural unity, a lack which often tempts leaders to foreign adventure. There are two ways, however, in which domestic conditions have been influential. For most of the postwar period Thailand has been a military dictatorship, albeit with constitutional trappings. Thus the reigning political elite has been delighted to find in the American military assistance program a means for strengthening its own position. Not until recently has the size of the Thai military establishment been justified by any comparable external threat, but the United States has been supplying it with equipment since 1950.

The nearly 2.5 million Chinese in Thailand, larger by percentage than in any Southeast Asian country except Malaya, have strongly influenced the character of Thai nationalism, as well as affected its foreign policy. To a considerable extent, foreign relations have been seen as a means of balancing the domestic influence of the Chinese community. One could perhaps predict, therefore, that if Red China were willing to abandon its nationals in Thailand, and if there were a shift in power relations, Peking might be able to woo Thailand to neutralism. Should China attempt to use its minority in Thailand as a weapon of Communist infiltration, however, the government would be pushed into even closer alliance with the West, unless Peking proved skillful enough to bargain a voluntary restraint on Communist activity for some Thai concession. Intensified Chinese Communist subversion in Thailand would probably not be viewed as merely a shift in the power balance but as a direct threat to the ruling elite.

In sum, Thailand has within its culture the psychological basis for nonalignment, if the conditions upon which it has

pragmatically based a pro-Western alliance should shift.
The Thai political elite believes on the basis of past experience that transferring external allegiances need not threaten
its own power. Thai foreign policy, although capable of
territorial aggression, as against Cambodia during World
War II, is just as capable of surrendering its fruits
when objective conditions change, as after the end of the
war.

SOUTH VIETNAM

While it is a more repressive dictatorship, South Vietnam
is much less stable than Thailand. Although much more
dependent on the United States than the Thai, the Vietnamese regime is also a much more precarious ally. It is a
regime that today effectively controls only a small part of
the territory to which it lays claim. Despite official claims
to the contrary, Vietcong forces on the countryside grow
steadily stronger, and the elite is unable to offer a political
program that might compete with the Communists. Nevertheless, the American commitment to such a regime is frequently reaffirmed.

It would seem that both geographical relationships and
recent historical experience should teach the South Vietnamese elite that the Communists are the enemy and the
Americans its friends. In addition, many of them have had
a Western education, and quite a few share with the West
its religious beliefs. In some respects, the policymakers of
Saigon are more westernized than those in Manila or Kuala
Lumpur. But their orientation is more French than American, and their definition of reality is not always what Americans assume it to be. Ngo Dinh Nhu, the President's brother,
and his wife, whom most observers believe to be the most
powerful pair in South Vietnam, are capable of viewing the
United States as an enemy, as anti-American diatribes in the

controlled Saigon press have frequently revealed.[11] One cannot assume that they have completely identified their own careers with a free, anti-Communist Vietnam, as has President Ngo Dinh Diem. An American challenge to their power is as much feared as a Communist one, and perhaps more so, since they apparently believe that it is more immediate. Does this mean that the Ngo Dinh Nhus would be willing to negotiate with the Communists in order to resist American pressures for their removal? This is the position which many observers believe Chiang Ching-kuo is in today. Unlike the Nhus, however, Generalissimo Chiang Kai-shek's son has enough influence with the army to attempt such a policy if he desires. But the point here is that an influential, perhaps dominant, segment of the Vietnamese political elite does not regard the national struggle against communism, which is properly both foreign and domestic policy today, as a personal matter of life and death. American helicopter pilots are being asked to make a greater commitment.

Vietnamese foreign policy, the exclusive domain of the President and his family, has ceased to have much relationship to objective definitions of national interest. It has been reduced to the primary task of preserving the Ngo family's power. The journalist, the lobbyist, the diplomat are all used, some knowingly, others not. The Ngos have realistically assessed the situation, and concluded that they can maintain their position only if American aid is continued, and thus they have concentrated their efforts on keeping it flowing. Since the United States relaxed its pressures for reforms in late 1961 in the face of stormy resistance, the Ngos estimate, perhaps correctly, that Washington would not dare to halt aid in order to force political changes. Yet the more successful the Ngos are in this tactic, the less responsive they become to the needs of the Vietnamese situation and the

[11] See Thai, Nguyen, "A Vietnamese Speaks Out," *New Republic,* Vol. 148, No. 23, June 8, 1963, pp. 14–17; and *Is South Vietnam Viable?* (Manila: Carmelo and Bauermann, 1963).

less likely American aid is to achieve its true objective: the defeat of the Vietcong. Nowhere in Southeast Asia today is the United States so deeply involved in the support of a non-Communist government against both an external and internal threat, yet in no place is American policy, unless revised, more certain of ultimate failure.

CAMBODIA

Cambodia, Vietnam's unfriendly neighbor, has a neutralist foreign policy, but is perhaps more capable of serving American interests, that is, the preservation of an independent non-Communist government, than is Vietnam.[12] Cambodia's historical experience parallels that of Vietnam in a number of respects, but the differences are perhaps more important. Cambodia is a Theravada Buddhist country which received its major cultural influences from India; Vietnam is culturally a Sinitic land. The veneer of French civilization laid down by colonialism in both countries—much thinner in Cambodia, however—was not able to bridge the ancient rift. The underlying values of Cambodian society are thus more similar to Thailand and Laos, its western and northern neighbors. But modernizing and westernizing influences in Cambodia have been even less widespread than in Thailand. The colonial regime did not, for example, create a Cambodian civil service, but relied largely on Vietnamese and Frenchmen. A dearth of trained leaders for a modern government was, in fact, one of the main factors (aside from his own personality) which led King Norodom Sihanouk to step down from the throne to become his country's chief of government. In Cambodia, to a greater extent than in

[12] See Leifer, Michael, *Cambodia and Neutrality* (Canberra: Australian National University, 1962); Smith, Roger M., "Cambodia's Neutrality and the Laotian Crisis," *Asian Survey*, Vol. 1, No. 2, July 1961, pp. 17–24; and Fall, Bernard B., "Cambodia's International Position," *Current History*, Vol. 40, No. 235, March 1961, pp. 164–170.

any other country in Southeast Asia, foreign policy is the decision, and the whim, of one man.

It is Sihanouk, a dynamic, French-educated prince, unchallenged leader of a traditional Buddhist society, who has determined the goals of Cambodian foreign policy within the inevitable geopolitical limits. Geographically, Cambodia lies between two long-time enemies, Vietnam and Thailand, on the east and west; is unprotected by natural boundaries; and is separated on the north from an expansionist China only by Laos, which is largely a political vacuum. When the independent Cambodian government was launched into the international arena in 1954, both Vietnam and Thailand had American-supported regimes. History gave Sihanouk ample reason to believe that these two neighbors posed a threat. (For example, in 1941 Siam had, with Japanese approval, seized three Cambodian provinces.) It seemed plausible that Cambodia would be best protected by balancing American and Soviet influences.[13] This interpretation, called "active neutrality," was confirmed by the Bandung Conference and by Chinese emphasis on the so-called Five Principles of Peaceful Coexistence.

Neutralism quickly contributed to a self-fulfilling prophesy about South Vietnam's position. Sihanouk's announcement that he would recognize neither half of that divided nation caused Saigon to blockade the Mekong River, Cambodia's only water route to the sea. Although this potent economic pressure forced de facto Cambodian recognition, diplomatic exchanges between the two countries have since suffered from an overdose of vitriol. Vietnam has charged Cambodia with harboring Vietcong forces, while Cambodia has alleged violation of its territory by the South Vietnamese army and persecution of the Cambodian minority in Vietnam. Relations with Thailand have been no less stormy. Even though

---

[13] According to Leifer, however, such an interpretation was not actually made by Sihanouk until after Nehru's visit to Phnompenh in November 1954. See Leifer, *op. cit.*, p. 10.

the major bone of contention, jurisdiction over the Prah Vihar temple, has now been settled by the International Court of Justice, diplomatic contacts are not yet on a friendly basis.

In the course of these disputes with its neighbors, Cambodia sometimes has been able to use its neutralist position as a club with which to threaten the United States into restraining our allies. But the major premise behind Cambodian neutralism is a principle also held by the Thai, that is, that the nation's foreign policy should adjust to the existing international power structure. This is essentially a passive principle. On it, however, the Cambodian leader draws a conclusion opposite from the Thai's. He believes that Communist China is the most powerful nation in Asia, and that it will ultimately dominate the whole Indochinese peninsula. Sihanouk expects to enjoy the same success as Thailand had during World War II in adjusting to changing overlords. In 1962 he told his people, "We will become Communists together and our union will still be preserved." [14] In fact, however, he has suppressed domestic Communist opposition. Should Communist subversion ever pose a major threat to his own leadership position, his foreign policy stance might change. It has not yet become clear how Sihanouk applies the lessons of Laos to Cambodia; but he is certainly deeply concerned.

Another justification Sihanouk has presented for Cambodian neutralism is that it allows Cambodia the opportunity to receive large amounts of foreign aid from both sides in the cold war. In this respect, success has been obvious. Although a country one-quarter the size of Thailand, Cambodia has received only slightly less American economic aid than its western neighbor. The Communist bloc since 1956 has added more than one-half the amount of total United States aid. While Sihanouk has accepted military assistance from the United States but not from the Communist bloc, he has maintained his neutralist posture by repaying

[14] *Réalités Cambodgiennes*, January 26, 1962, p. 6.

the United States with a larger quota of verbal abuse. Although he recently offered to cut off American military aid as a token of his neutralism, he has on several occasions in the past requested additional military equipment from Washington, and has been refused.

Cambodian neutralism is not all rational calculation. Shifts may sometimes as readily be explained by Sihanouk's moods as by an attempt to balance the two blocs. Furthermore, the "active" element in Cambodian foreign policy is largely Sihanouk's attempt to project his personality onto the world scene, as in the Geneva Conference on Laos. In sum, we can say that the style of Cambodian foreign policy is active, at least as compared with other Buddhist countries, nonaligned, in a neutral sort of way, verbally aggressive but physically defensive, and largely determined by the intellectual perspectives and psychological complexes of one man. Nevertheless, its goals of preserving Cambodian independence, protecting its territory, and promoting its development have, so far, been achieved.

BURMA

Until 1962 Burma could be classified as a democratic neutral. However, under the military regime of Ne Win—a not-always benevolent dictatorship—Burmese neutralism has shifted somewhat to the left.[15] During the British colonial era in Burma, the educational and political sys-

[15] See Rose, Jerry, "Burma and the Balance of Neutralisms," *The Reporter*, Vol. 28, No. 1, January 3, 1963; Tinker, Hugh, *The Union of Burma* (London: Oxford University Press, 1959), Chapter 12; Badgley, John H., "Burma: The Nexus of Socialism and Two Political Traditions," *Asian Survey*, Vol. 3, No. 2, February 1963, pp. 89–95; Hanna, W. A., "Re-Reviving a Revolution: Political Stress in Burma, 1963," American Universities Field Staff Reports Service, Southeast Asia Series, Vol. 11, No. 4, January 24, 1963; Trager, Frank N., "Burma's Foreign Policy, 1948–56: Neutralism, Third Force, and Rice," *Journal of Asian Studies*, Vol. 16, No. 1, November 1956, pp. 89–102; and Moorthy, K. Krishna, "The Shake-up in Rangoon," *Far East Economic Review*, Vol. 39, No. 9, February 28, 1963, pp. 433–439.

tems trained a generation of leaders who, to a considerable extent, understood and were sympathetic to the Western democratic tradition. It was this generation which achieved power in independent Burma and which occupied prominent positions in U Nu's successive governments. Under such leadership, Burmese neutralism became known as the most pro-Western in Asia. From the Third to the Fourteenth sessions of the United Nation's General Assembly, Burmese votes on issues regarding world peace, atomic energy, and disarmament agreed with the United States 65 per cent of the time and with the Soviet Union only 37 per cent. During the simultaneous Hungarian and Suez crises of 1956, Burma took the lead within the Afro-Asian bloc in condemning Soviet aggression. There was a very conscious effort to levy consistent moral judgments on both sides of the cold war. The style of Burmese neutralism was different from that of Cambodia in other ways as well. When American aid came to be considered an undue influence, it was stopped, not repaid with diatribe. Nor was Burmese foreign policy a reflection of the Prime Minister's personal ambition, except partly in the case of the two-year celebration of the Buddha's 2500th anniversary. Aside from initiating the Asian Socialist Conference, Burma made no attempt to assert leadership among other neutralist countries.

Today, the military leadership no longer has a common ideological commitment with the West. Though perhaps it was done to provide a precedent for excluding Chinese Communist banks, private American agencies working in Burma have been forced to withdraw, the most prominent being the Ford and Asia Foundations. Most of the officers now in power have had little personal contact with Westerners. The number of Chinese technicians working in the country, on the other hand, has increased, as have Communist aid programs generally. And yet, while the elite's definition of Burma's international situation has changed, the fundamental determinants of Burmese policy have not.

Geographically, Burma has common borders with both of the two largest Asian nations, India and China. While the Indian border is no problem, the Chinese border has long been disputed.[16] When the Communists seized power on the Chinese mainland, they continued to publish maps, as had previous regimes, that showed areas which the Burmese believed to be theirs as Chinese territory. In November 1955 several hundred Chinese Communist troops occupied nearly 1,000 square miles of Burmese territory. When this became public knowledge in Rangoon, the Burmese government utilized public indignation to press for negotiations with Peking. Despite several visits by U Nu, U Ba Swe, and Chou En-lai back and forth between Peking and Rangoon, no agreement was reached for more than three years. The Chinese demanded territory which the Burmese, or more particularly the Kachins, were not willing to surrender, and they failed to offer concomitant concessions. Finally, in 1960, the greater decisiveness of Ne Win and the sudden sweet reasonableness of Peking made possible a treaty which stipulated only minor territorial losses for the Burmese. This can now be recognized as part of the Chinese plan to humiliate India and isolate that nation from its neighbors in Southeast Asia. Burma's attitude throughout was to avoid provoking the Chinese but also to avoid any substantial loss of territory. These objectives were achieved. Friendship for China has seemed to the Burmese to bear fruit.

Ever since independence, Burma has also been plagued with unrest, and sometimes rebellion, among its political and ethnic minorities. The political minorities, which were Communist or Communist-oriented, ceased to be a serious threat by the mid-1950's, and were reduced to insignificance during Ne Win's first regime, 1958–1960. The Burmese have long considered the ethnic rebellions more serious and have

[16] See Woodman, Dorothy, *The Making of Burma* (London: Cresset Press, 1962), Chapter 19; also Maung, Maung, "The Burma-China Border Settlement," *Asian Survey*, Vol. 1, No. 1, March 1961, pp. 38–43.

often charged that they were Western-supported. Although the Western role has certainly been exaggerated in the Burmese mind, it is true that certain Protestant missionaries have acted as advisers to the Karens, and that rebel Shan chieftains have been able to obtain supplies smuggled from Thailand.[17] Chinese Nationalist troops fleeing from the victorious Communists operated on Burmese soil for some time and were also viewed as a potential stimulus to rebellious tribes. Indirect American support for these forces, which lasted until 1961, was easily established. Ethnic disunity is a serious and continuing problem for Burma. The fall of U Nu's government in 1962 was caused in large part by the army's dissatisfaction with Nu's indecisive handling of the Shan question.

Thus the drive for national unity and the attempt to maintain territorial integrity have both led Burma to neutralism. The two goals are, in fact, closely related. Should the time ever come when the Chinese Communists make a serious effort toward infiltration and subversion of hill tribe leadership, Burma might concede that neutralism had failed and change its policies. Perhaps recognizing this possibility, the Chinese are now concentrating on infiltration and subversion of the national elite in Rangoon. The fact that the Burmese, who once condemned Soviet aggression in Hungary, have not been willing publicly to criticize Chinese incursions into India may indicate partial success. It also indicates, incidentally, the importance which the personal friendship between the two prime ministers, Jawaharlal Nehru and U Nu, had for Indo-Burmese relations.

In sum, Burmese foreign policy, once directed by a relatively westernized elite, is now controlled by a young, rather anti-Western nationalist officer corps. Both adjusted, in somewhat different ways, to a similar concept of reality, in which fear of the Chinese colossus on the north, and re-

[17] For a perceptive account of the subtle and unintentional way missionaries contributed to separatism, see Brant, Charles, and Khaing, Mi Mi, "Missionaries Among the Hill Tribes of Burma," *Asian Survey*, Vol. 1, No. 1, March 1961, pp. 44–51.

bellion among ethnic minorities enjoying some Western sympathy and support, were prominent features. Burmese policy can now be characterized as passive, defensive, and nonaligned, with a somewhat greater tendency to yield to Eastern gales.

INDONESIA

Indonesian foreign policy, once classified as pro-Western neutralist, was until very recently more pro-Communist than the Burmese.[18] This phenomena finds explanation in Indonesia's history, geography, and internal politics, and also in that enigmatic but all-important personality, President Sukarno.

Indonesia, Southeast Asia's largest and most populous country, passed through a profoundly traumatic experience in throwing off the mantle of colonial rule. If one marks Dutch relinquishment of West New Guinea as the culmination of the anticolonialist struggle, then that struggle went on longer in Indonesia than in any other former European colony in Asia. The clean sweep of Dutch influence has been no less thorough than removal of the French legacy in North Vietnam. In the course of this struggle, the most westernized, and pro-Western, elements in the political elite have been gradually, and now almost entirely, eliminated; they are in voluntary exile or in well-silenced opposition.

Geographically Indonesia enjoys the security of insularity. With the last vestiges of Dutch colonialism eliminated, and with the great distances that separate Indonesia from China, it is difficult to imagine a direct external threat to Indonesia's

[18] See Hanna, W. A., "A Note on the Republic of Indonesia," American University Field Staff Reports Service, Southeast Asia Series, Vol. 8, No. 16, August 1960; "The Irian Barat Settlement," *ibid.*, Vol. 10, No. 18, October 1962; and "The Politics of Sport," *ibid.*, Vol. 10, No. 19, October 1962; Feith, Herbert, *The Decline of Constitutional Democracy in Indonesia* (Ithaca: Cornell University Press, 1962); Pauker, Guy, "Indonesia: Internal Development or External Expansion?," *Asian Survey*, Vol. 3, No. 2, February 1963, pp. 69–75; and Pauker, Guy, "The Soviet Challenge in Indonesia," *Foreign Affairs*, Vol. 40, No. 4, July 1962, pp. 612–626.

security (although Sukarno, in some recent statements about Malaysia, exhibited an almost unbounded imagination). In any case, since the external threat of Communist China is more remote than in the case of Burma, a somewhat different rationale for neutralism must be found.

Geography has not only set Indonesia apart from mainland Asia but has also set Indonesians apart from each other. In addition, Indonesia suffers from a greater problem of ethnic and cultural diversity than Burma. Furthermore, the rebellions that have taken place in Indonesia have not been merely the sniping of disgruntled tribal chieftains, as was often the case in Burma. They have usually been led by highly competent civil and military officers with an openly pro-Western political orientation who, with better coordination and greater decisiveness, some feel might have succeeded. In 1958 the United States gave covert aid to rebellion in Indonesia,[19] and Nationalist Chinese aid was also forthcoming. Dutch army veterans were implicated in earlier uprisings. Thus Sukarno and his advisers were given frequent justification for continuing to identify "Western imperialism" with the threat of national disintegration. A foreign policy that developed counters to this threat was appropriate and at the same time served a variety of domestic objectives.

The events of 1958 in particular helped to lead Sukarno toward such a policy. The Java-based Communist Party (PKI) became the most powerful political grouping in the country; the previously influential anti-Communist Masjumi was discredited for its implication in the Sumatra rebellion. The Communists thereafter developed a symbiotic relationship with Sukarno, by which they provided mass support for him in exchange for their protection from army repression internally, and Sukarno's support of the Soviet position internationally. The military leadership, which Sukarno could not control, and which feared the growing power of the

[19] See Mossman, James, *Rebels in Paradise, Indonesia's Civil War* (London: Jonathan Cape, 1961).

PKI, nevertheless could not object to the President's foreign policy since it was only from the Soviet Union, after American refusal, that it was able to obtain substantial amounts of military assistance. Pro-Soviet neutralism was implemented by expanded economic, as well as military, aid and by a multiplication of official visits between Djakarta and Moscow.

Sukarno's relations with Peking have not been as cordial as with Moscow. The Chinese embassy in Djakarta has on several occasions attempted to frustrate Indonesian government policies restricting the economic activities of the local Chinese community and has reportedly given substantial financial aid to the PKI. Nevertheless, Indonesia did exchange ratifications of a dual nationality treaty with China in 1960; Chinese economic aid was expanded in 1961; and Liu Shao-chi visited Indonesia in April 1963.[20]

It should be clear that in Indonesia, internal political considerations, ethnic and cultural disunity, plus the precarious political balance which maintains Sukarno's leadership, are more important in determining foreign policy than are international realities. Some observers believe that Sukarno needs to maintain the popular focus on an external enemy in order to preserve a modicum of national unity and to divert popular attention from the ever-worsening economic situation. With Indonesian administration established in West New Guinea, the Dutch can no longer provide this focus. There seems to have been a brief attempt to develop Malaysia as a substitute, though opposition to a continuation of British bases in Borneo is an understandable neutralist position. But Abdul Rahman's firm determination, with British support, to prevent any Indonesian intrusion in the northern Borneo territories, and the quick suppression of the Azahari rebellion, may have caused Sukarno to regard that as too

[20] See Mozingo, David, "The Sino-Indonesian Dual Nationality Treaty," *Asian Survey*, Vol. 1, No. 10, December 1961, pp. 25–31; and Williams, Lea, "Sino-Indonesian Diplomacy: A Study of Revolutionary International Politics," *The China Quarterly*, No. 11, July–September 1962, pp. 184–199.

costly an adventure. Portuguese Timor, however, could be an easier alternative.

Since domestic political factors are decisive in determining Indonesian foreign policy, only a change in those conditions will bring a major policy shift. If Sukarno should attempt to implement fully his plan to end martial law and to remove restrictions on political party activity in preparation for elections, 1963 could prove to be a year of decision. Elections in present circumstances could mean a PKI victory. A more likely alternative would be an anti-Communist military coup to forestall elections or formation of a PKI cabinet, unless the military leadership has been more heavily infiltrated by the Communists than is now known. Success of another assassination attempt against Sukarno is also possible.

In August it appeared that, even without violence, Indonesian policy had shifted somewhat. Deepening economic crisis seemed, at least temporarily, to have impressed on Sukarno the desirability of caution abroad. Or perhaps Sukarno was simply adjusting to a strengthening of the army's position. In any case, it was a surprise to most observers that he would sign a pact with the Philippines and Malaya in Manila. The outbreaks on the occasion of the proclamation of Malaysia raise the question, however, whether the pact will be implemented.

LAOS

The situation in Laos is perhaps even more complicated to analyze. The country today should perhaps be thought of as three distinct political units rather than as a single entity. One of these units, controlled by the Pathet Lao, is already Communist-dominated. The second, held by the Phoumi Nosavan–Boun Oum faction and based in southern Laos, is staunchly anti-Communist. In between are the so-called neutralists, headed by the nominal prime minister, Prince Souvanna Phouma. Laos is the only place in Southeast Asia where the United States and the Soviet Union have openly supplied opposing military forces engaged in open conflict. Communist North Vietnamese advice to, and at times direction of, the Pathet Lao has been continuous. But the United States has also intervened directly and actively in Laotian politics, more so perhaps than in any other place in Asia since the end of the Japanese Occupation. On four different occasions, American intervention determined the composition of the cabinet, three times in favor of Phoumi Nosavan and the last time against him.[21] Indeed, at certain times the Laotians have had less to say about the direction of events in their own country than have foreign governments.

Laos is a small country with an extremely small elite. Very few of these have had the opportunity for higher education.[22] Most of the present elite participated in the Lao Issara movement during and just after World War II. The development since then of sharp divisions within the elite, even to the extent of rival groups establishing themselves in distinct territories, has been in large part the result of foreign influence, primarily Vietnamese and American, although traditional ethnic and geographical cleavages have also been partly responsible. It is perhaps understandable that those who were primarily concerned about national unity should also want to follow a neutral policy between the contending world power blocs. Rigid American anti-neutralist policy up to early 1961 had the effect of pushing the neutralists into a temporary and reluctant alliance with the Communists. In view of the pro-Communist image of Souvanna Phouma which had been projected in the United States, it took some courage on the part of the United States government to reverse its course, withdraw its previously exclusive backing for Phoumi Nosavan, and transfer its sup-

[21] See Smith, Roger M., "Laos in Perspective," *Asian Survey*, Vol. 3, No. 1, January 1963, pp. 63 ff.
[22] See Halpern, Joel M., "Observations on the Social Structure of the Lao Elite," *Asian Survey*, Vol. 1, No. 5, July 1961, pp. 25–32.

port to him. As a result, the major pressures on the neutralists since 1962 have been Communist. In Spring 1963, fighting broke out between the Communists and neutralists. General Kong Le, the outstanding neutralist military figure, is now clearly aware of the threat he faces. He may soon be receiving American military assistance again, as he did before 1960.[23]

This experience is clear proof that a "hard line" is no way to make friendly neutralists. Ironically, the recent aggressiveness of the Pathet Lao may well turn Souvanna Phouma and Kong Le to nonalignment. If this should occur, and if they are able to develop dynamic domestic programs for the still free portions of Laos, complete Communist take-over of the country may yet be frustrated. The experience would also have a sobering influence on other neutralists.

II

Having attempted to describe and analyze briefly the foreign policies of each Southeast Asian country, let us now try to discern the pattern which emerges. It would appear that in Southeast Asia today the three major internal factors determining foreign policy are the presence or lack of national cultural unity, the stability or instability of the regime, and the training and ideological orientation of the leadership. The importance of external factors varies according to the character of internal factors. Nations having both unity and political stability can afford to determine foreign policy to

[23] See Modelski, George, *International Conference on the Settlement of the Laotian Question, 1961–62* (Canberra: Department of International Relations, Australian National University, 1962); Halpern, A. M., and Friedman, H. B., *Communist Strategy in Laos* (Santa Monica: The RAND Corporation, 1960); Fall, Bernard, "The Laos Tangle," *Current History*, Vol. 42, No. 245, January 1962, pp. 8–14, 27; Smith, Roger M., "Laos in Perspective," *op. cit.*, pp. 61–68; and Crozier, Brian, "Peking and the Laotian Crisis: A Further Appraisal," *The China Quarterly*, No. 11, July–September 1962, pp. 116–123.

a greater extent on their assessment of external conditions. Here the power positions of the great powers, and the kinds of policies they follow, are crucial. Variations in the content of policy among Southeast Asian nations in this category are caused by the variety of experience and the ideology of the leadership. North Vietnam, the Philippines, Thailand, and Cambodia would fall in this category, although all have Chinese minorities large enough to have some impact on policymaking.

In a second category are nations which have national cultural unity, but unstable regimes. While some would point to the problem of the montagnards, in relative terms within Southeast Asia, South Vietnam falls in this grouping. Such a nation's foreign policy is designed simply to preserve the regime. Third, nations having stability but not unity develop policies which attempt to secure the missing quality. Although the desire to forestall a potential external threat has also entered his thinking, Abdul Rahman's Malaysia should be placed essentially in this category. The only unity which he can hope to secure in the foreseeable future will arise from a peaceful balance of ethnic communities.

Finally, nations having neither stability nor unity must attempt to develop both through foreign policy. Burma, Laos, and Indonesia should today be classified in this group, although Ne Win's regime is probably more stable than the others. The differences in the content of foreign policy among these three countries, which are faced with the most serious problems of national integration, can best be explained by noting the source of the threat to national unity in each case. For Burma and Indonesia, the threat in the past to cultural and ethnic unity has appeared to be inspired in large part by the West or its agents. For Laos, the threat has appeared to be alternatively Western and Communist. (For Malaya, on the other hand, the threat has been clearly Communist.) Each nation has attempted to find in foreign policy a counter to the particular threat it faces. We must remember that Southeast Asian political elites have generally tended to fear challenges to their hegemony from political groups having a particular ethnic or cultural base more than threats from those that do not.

A general conclusion which can be drawn from this type of analysis is that domestic political considerations in Southeast Asian foreign policies must be given greater attention in the process of United States foreign policy formulation.

III

The kind of foreign policy which the United States has had most difficulty in dealing with in Southeast Asia is neutralism. Perhaps it deserves, therefore, special analytical attention.[24] Neutralism in Southeast Asia, as can be seen from the foregoing survey of national foreign policies, is the result, among others, of a bitter colonial experience and struggle for independence, of a desire to avoid antagonizing a potential aggressor, and of an attempt to balance potentially aggressive forces by relations with their competitors. The neutralist wants neither to be abandoned nor overwhelmed, whether by charity or by military force. These desires stem both from a need for ego satisfaction, whether on the part of the leaders or of their people, and from a duty to protect national interests. The neutralist leader also wants assistance in support of his domestic political position. Neutralism is thus both a psychological phenomenon and the product of a rational calculation of interests.

United States policy toward neutralism has become much more sophisticated in recent years. American diplomats now recognize that a neutralist may be just as capable of defend-

[24] See Martin, Laurence, *op. cit.*, especially articles by Liska, George, "The 'Third Party': The Rationale of Non-alignment," and "Tripartism: Dilemmas and Strategies"; Kissinger, Henry A., "The New Cult of Neutralism," *Reporter*, Vol. 25, No. 9, November 24, 1961, pp. 26–29; and Scalapino, Robert A., "Neutralism in Asia," *American Political Science Review*, Vol. 48, No. 1, March 1954, pp. 49–62.

ing himself against Communist pressures as an ally. We have shown much greater understanding of divergent points of view in our recent relations with the neutralists. What principles should determine those relations? Greater recognition needs to be given to the strong psychological need for prestige and international status among the leaders of the new nations. Only recently, Ne Win's self-effacing request for non-VIP status during an American tour was taken too much at face value, with unfortunate consequences for the Burmese general's attitude toward the United States. Nor have we been willing to try to match the pomp and circumstance afforded a Sukarno or a Sihanouk in Peking. In foreign aid programs as well, we have often shown incomprehensibly puritanical attitudes to Asian requests for prestige projects which happened to lack adequate economic justification.

In dealing with neutralist regimes, policy must maintain a necessary balance between support, pressure, and aloofness. Certainly neither extreme of withdrawal [25] or of maximum pressure[26] is appropriate. Total withdrawal of American assistance or guarantees from a neutralist country would not bring it crawling on its knees, begging for us to return. Now that Chinese and Soviet missions are present in most neutralist nations, our withdrawal would simply allow their influence to become predominant. Furthermore, even if they should be required to withdraw formally, they have avenues of continued access and influence which the United States does not, such as Chinese minorities, Communist parties, and poorly guarded borders. On the other hand, vigorous pressure on neutralists usually brings negative results. The most obvious example of this is Laos. Here the United States government not only put pressure on a neutralist regime both overtly and secretly but actively intervened to over-

[25] See Brzezinski, Zbigniew, "The Politics of Underdevelopment," *World Politics*, Vol. 9, No. 1, October 1956, pp. 55–75.
[26] Kissinger, *op. cit.*, advocates this course on the assumption that the neutral will always take a position equidistant between the two blocs.

throw a neutralist regime. The move did not establish a stable ally, but instead stimulated Communist reaction and drove the neutralists into the Communist embrace. Withholding aid as a technique of pressure against neutralist governments has also produced unintended results, as in the case of Indonesian reliance on Soviet military equipment since 1958. To refuse to provide a neutralist state with assistance or guarantees which it feels are essential for national security, or to press upon it a policy which is felt inimical to its national interests, is to leave the field open for Communist penetration. In short, the doctrine of the mean should guide policy toward neutrals.

Not all pressure by one bloc on a neutralist government in a bipolarized world political system causes it to approach the other bloc. If the neutralist believes that rejection of pressures from one side is a greater risk to its security than compliance, pressure can be effective. But this will be true only when the side exerting pressure is perceived by the neutralist to be at the same time potentially more powerful when protection is needed, and also to be immediately less threatening to the ruling elite. In this respect the United States is sometimes at a disadvantage in Southeast Asia. Communist China's size and geographical propinquity, when coupled with a believable peaceful coexistence line, makes a persuasive combination. Furthermore, Marxist influences on Asian neutralist thinking prejudices their perception of American intentions, while the airy consistency of the SEATO "paper tiger" results in a low evaluation of the American ability to protect a neutralist country seriously threatened from the other side. American performance in India will be closely watched in this regard. On the other hand, if aggressive Communist party tactics in Indonesia, for example, should be convincingly linked to Chinese foreign policy at a time of internal Chinese economic crisis, the West would have the advantage.

The situation becomes more complicated when rigid bipolarity is lost, of course. The neutralist is given greater freedom of choice, and the effectiveness of pressure from any single power diminishes. Thus in Indonesia, Chinese pressures on behalf of the Chinese minority were less effective because of Soviet competition for influence in the country; and the Dutch withdrawal of interisland shipping did not have the desired impact because of the eagerness of Japanese shipping lines to provide an alternative.

In assessing the effects of American influence on a neutralist country, the United States should never make the mistake of treating such a nation as a unit, but rather should always recognize the interaction of competing elements within the political elite. This point is particularly pertinent to the Indonesian situation today. While it is hard to justify additional aid to Indonesia on the ground that it will be well used, or that Indonesia has been our friend, it can be classified as urgent in terms of intraelite competition. An approach of not too much pressure, but not too much withdrawal, needs to be applied toward prominent members of the elite as well as toward nations. If anti-Communist elements in Djakarta today should come to feel abandoned by the West, the result could well prove disastrous. Fortunately the Executive seems to have recognized the dangers, but many in the Congress have not.

How can United States military commitments be reconciled with an effective policy toward neutralism? As we have noted, SEATO looks increasingly like a paper tiger to the neutralists, and to its members as well.[27] SEATO was conceived in an earlier era when official American policy toward neutrals was strongly moralistic in tone. In the haste to construct a treaty organization in 1954, more Western than Asian members were brought into the pact. Today it is a weak and ineffective symbol of the Western military presence in Asia, and for the neutrals often appears as a reminder of the lingering power of Western imperialism. It

[27] For an excellent discussion of SEATO, see Clubb, Oliver E., Jr., *The United States and the Sino-Soviet Bloc in Southeast Asia* (Washington: Brookings, 1962).

is hard to see what advantages SEATO now has for United States policy.

Among its numerous disadvantages, let us mention here only its impact on the neutralist countries and on genuine regionalism in Southeast Asia. We have said that the neutralist nations want assurances from the West for their security and at the same time the appearance of independence from outside pressure. Yet SEATO gives maximum publicity to the possibility of intervention and a minimum of actual security. It has the power to repel without the power to attract. Because of the sharp distinctions it draws between aligned and nonaligned, it renders very difficult, if not impossible, the development of a genuine and effective regionalism.

IV

The trend toward intraregional solidarity is one of the major patterns of postwar international relations in Southeast Asia.[28] Southeast Asia is not, of course, a single culture area. The first common experience to be shared by the entire region was the Japanese Occupation during World War II. Since the war there have been various initiatives for joint regional action. Almost every nation in Southeast Asia has sponsored some kind of regional conference or proposed some regional organization. It is an important part of the policies of prestige pursued by these newly sovereign states.

The relevant "region" is still poorly defined, however. Some of the meetings which have brought Southeast Asian states together were initiated by powers outside the region, as for example, the Asian Relations Conference at New

[28] See Fifield, *op. cit.;* Bone, Robert C., *Contemporary Southeast Asia* (New York: Random House, 1962), pp. 119–128; Henderson, William, "The Development of Regionalism in Southeast Asia," *International Organization*, Vol. 9, No. 4, November 1955, pp. 463–474; and Ingraham, Edward C., "Regionalism in Southeast Asia," unpublished seminar paper, Cornell University, April 1958.

Delhi in 1947, the Manila Conference for the creation of SEATO in 1954, and the Bandung Conference in 1955. Nonpolitical regional meetings have been stimulated or actually organized by UNESCO, ECAFE, and private American foundations. But no regional meeting of an intergovernmental nature has ever met which was composed exclusively of Southeast Asian states and at which all of them were represented.

There are, indeed, still important obstacles to Southeast Asian unity. Aside from the general lack of intraregional trade and cultural contact, the competitive character of national economies,[29] and the nearly complete absence of a sense of regional identity even among the intellectuals, there are specific differences between states which, until resolved, will seriously inhibit greater regional cooperation. We have mentioned the most prominent of these conflicts: Thai-Cambodian, Vietnamese-Cambodian, Philippine-Malayan, Indonesian-Malayan; there is also the more serious confrontation between Communist and non-Communist Vietnam.

Yet there are also forces on the move which increase prospects for the growth of effective regional organization in the future.[30] An especially significant step was formation of the Association of Southeast Asia (ASA) established by Malaya, Thailand, and the Philippines in July 1961, the first permanent (or so it was intended) intergovernmental organization made up exclusively of Southeast Asian states.[31] Its purposes include the creation of an "effective machinery for friendly consultations and mutual assistance in the economic, social, cultural, scientific and administra-

[29] See Gordon, Bernard K., "Economic Impediments to Regionalism in Southeast Asia," *Asian Survey,* Vol. 3, No. 5, May 1963, pp. 235–244.

[30] See Gordon, Bernard K., "Problems of Regionalism in Southeast Asia," a paper read at the meetings of the Southern Political Science Association, Gatlinburg, Tennessee, November 10, 1962, unpublished.

[31] For the text of the Bangkok Declaration, the nearest thing to an ASA charter, see Pacis, Vicente Albano, *Philippine Government and Politics* (Quezon City: Bustanente Press, 1962), Appendix 9.

tive fields" and provision for "machinery for fruitful collaboration in the utilization of . . . natural resources, the development of . . . agriculture and industry, the expansion of . . . trade." The ASA was specifically defined by its founders as "in no way connected with any outside power or power bloc and . . . directed against no other country." It was so designed in order to attract neutralist countries, but so far none of them has been attracted. The fact that two of the three members are also members of SEATO makes the ASA declaration of independence somewhat unconvincing to the suspicious neutralist.

Yet the best long-term hope for collective concern for the security of Southeast Asia, and for a realistic appraisal of threats to the region, is a closer association among pro-Western and neutralist leaders of the area. Such an association could be effective today only if it were outside the framework of a military alliance. Since it is in the best interests of the West to promote such an association, it would appear desirable now either to dissolve SEATO or to relegate it to an inactive status. Its nonmilitary functions could easily be transferred to ASA. The Philippines already has a bilateral defense pact with the United States and would lose little or nothing in terms of a formal guarantee of its security. Thailand has a less formal understanding with the United States and would probably prefer a formal bilateral arrangement to the existing SEATO commitments. There is considerable evidence, moreover, that this type of relationship would be less offensive to the neutralists than SEATO has been.

The surprising agreement reached at Manila in June 1963 between Indonesia, Malaya, and the Philippines to establish machinery for regular consultation on internal security, as well as on economic and cultural matters,[32] which followed so closely on some rather bitter quarreling among the three countries, indicates that the trend toward regional cooperation in Southeast Asia is perhaps stronger

[32] *The New York Times,* June 12, 1963.

than has often been thought. If this organization for a "Maphilindo" does, in fact, become operative, it would seem only logical that it be coordinated in some way with the already existing ASA. The United States should give every encouragement to such developments as these.

United States policy in Southeast Asia should be designed to promote the development of political freedom, and of social and economic progress, in the countries of the region. To the extent necessary, the United States must also guarantee the security of these Southeast Asian countries from external military threat. But our military policy must avoid interference in the internal affairs of these countries and must never preclude the political, social, and economic measures essential to achieve national progress in freedom.

5

SOME SOUTHEAST ASIAN VIEWS

OF AMERICAN FOREIGN POLICY

ROGER M. SMITH with the assistance of LIONEL LANDRY

I

Since World War II Southeast Asia has come to command
high priority in the foreign policy of the United States.
Eager to establish amicable and mutually beneficial relations with the countries of the region, whether allied to the
United States or nonaligned, we have lent assistance to all
of them (with the exception of North Vietnam) to further
their political, economic, and social development.

Our efforts, unfortunately, have not always yielded the
intended results. Nor have they yielded the important by-
product which, it has seemed to many, should come as an
inevitable consequence of our acts, namely, the emergence
of a picture of the United States and its policy as reliable,
generous, and altruistically motivated. On the contrary, our
actions have frequently been misconstrued by Southeast
Asians and have at times alienated them instead of drawing
them closer to us as we had hoped. And even where our
actions were not to blame, negative beliefs about the United
States have arisen in Southeast Asia from a number of

sources, domestic and foreign. These beliefs, painful and unjust though they may often appear to us, do exist and are important political factors with which we must deal. Any American embassy has a certain number of objective problems to cope with in executing United States foreign policy in a given Southeast Asian country. But it must also take account of those attitudes that happen to be prevalent among government leaders and the molders of national public opinion. Such attitudes, if they are favorable, provide a helpful climate for negotiation or, if they are not, can render difficult or impossible even those diplomatic approaches that we would consider logical, necessary, and ultimately beneficial to the given nation as well as to ourselves.

The purpose of this essay will be to identify some of these attitudes toward the United States and our foreign policy. The problem is complicated by two important contemporary factors: (1) the recentness of the emergence of these new nation-states, which are still torn by the pangs of political and social revolution, and (2) an international environment not of their making, in which they are buffeted by the contradictory interests of two large power blocs ideologically at war with each other. Domestically, the stresses within these nations in a period of acute revolutionary change have divided their peoples into congeries of more or less hostile groups ranging the political spectrum from right to left, all agitating in the name of domestic progress, but whose concepts of which may approach or depart from ideals held among Americans. In addition, strong echoes resound from abroad, where a pitched struggle is going on between nations professing a more or less orthodox communism and those committed to concepts of freedom as the West understands it.

Thus the United States emerges with an identity often twice distorted and with policies whose motives appear twice deformed: through the slogans of domestic nationalists and revolutionaries, on the one hand, and through the political defamation of professional Communist propagandists on the other. There is evidence, also, that foreign pressures as well as domestic considerations, and often the two acting simultaneously, can lead to extreme anti-American statements on the part of leaders who, as their private statements and personal orientation reveal, are not basically inimical to the United States. In terms of the general opinion of many people in Southeast Asia, however, this cannot afford much comfort to the United States in view of the tendency of the masses to be more loyal to dominant personalities than to abstract principles. Thus it is only of secondary importance for us to know, in this context, whether or not a violent political speech at an important mass meeting, attacking United States "capitalism," for example, is motivated more by a desire to placate Communist China than to "take the wind out of the sails of the Communists" for purely domestic purposes. The important thing is that a mythical American "capitalism," decked in the bogeyman's clothes fashionable among cartoonists of half a century ago, is being attacked and with it the so-called basis of United States foreign policy.

The too often negative image of the United States and its policies among Southeast Asians is, therefore, as much the product of irrelevant domestic and international issues as it is the consequence of objectively real foreign policy irritants in the conduct of American relations with a given Southeast Asian country. Whatever the cause of distortion of the image of United States foreign policy, it exists and poses in itself a fairly serious political problem.

This essay cannot report on the almost infinite range of attitudes toward us in Southeast Asia today, in view of the lack of proper documentation. It does propose, however, to point out some of these attitudes as specimens of what exists and what must be faced in various instances and at various times. The opinions and evaluations of the United States studied below should not, of course, be universalized or given more than their just weight. Yet their very existence and the extent to which they do prevail, especially in the nonaligned nations, can give none of us any conspicuous gratification, with the few exceptions that will be examined.

What are some of the ways in which United States foreign policy is viewed and judged in Southeast Asia? What are some of the prevalent attitudes in the region with which an American diplomat must cope?

II

Before we describe specific attitudes, it may be well to pause to examine what many Southeast Asians had imagined the future role of the United States among them would be after World War II.

Chiefly, many hoped that certain signs could be read as portending future American assistance in their struggle against European colonial powers for eventual self-rule and national independence. The most important of these signs were: (1) expressions of American sympathy during World War II for the political and social aspirations of those guerilla nationalist leaders most useful in the harassment of the Japanese invaders; (2) the well-known eagerness of President Roosevelt to see colonies become self-governing; and (3) the hopeful words of the Atlantic Charter of 1941.

The post-World War II preoccupations of the United States, however, centered on the new struggle with world communism, and our first and overwhelming concern lay in shoring up against a common enemy the very European powers against which people like Ho Chi Minh had begun to struggle for independence. Partly because of the sheer momentum of our European programs, partly because of distrust of some of the nationalist leaders (some of whom, like Ho, were themselves Communists), the United States re-entered the Southeast Asian scene in a role considerably different from that anticipated. By the end of the 1940's, the first preoccupation of the United States was no longer primarily with political and social inequities in the region but rather with the need to confront what we regarded as massive Communist penetration in Southeast Asia.

To those Asian leaders to whom colonialism, not communism, was the first peril, the new American posture meant disappointment and, later, rancor; and these feelings were not restricted to leaders on the Communist or Communist-sympathizing left of the political spectrum. Attitudes struck at that time have contributed to a persistent feeling of disillusionment about America, and Communist propaganda has been only too happy to intensify this disillusionment over the years.

The fall of the Kuomintang government, the Korean war, and the Vietminh victory in Vietnam eventually completed and confirmed the change in official American thinking about Southeast Asia. The region was no longer regarded as merely an underdeveloped area in need of economic and technical assistance and of political emancipation. The United States came to interpret the Indochinese war, for instance, less as an anticolonial struggle, which many Southeast Asians still believed it was, than as a confrontation between the Communist and free worlds, which is how United States policymakers primarily assessed the situation.[1]

The disparity between the region-wide preoccupation of the United States and the domestic or national preoccupations of the Southeast Asian nationalist leaders often made communication and negotiation difficult to carry out and mutual trust difficult to establish and maintain. If we add to this the difficulties inherent in crossing the cultural frontiers between Asia and America and the gratuitous claims of a never-idle Communist agitation and propaganda, it

[1] Following the Geneva negotiations in 1954, which partitioned Vietnam into Communist northern and anti-Communist southern states, the United States began to concentrate on strengthening the defense of South Vietnam and converting Laos into a pro-Western stronghold that would shield Thailand from North Vietnam and render inaccessible to the Vietminh a major thoroughfare into South Vietnam.

should not be surprising that there have arisen assessments of United States policy among Southeast Asians which Americans often find it difficult to face without exasperation, especially in the neutral countries, as we shall see, but in the allied countries as well.

III

Views in the Nonaligned Southeast Asian Nations. There is an important qualitative difference, for the most part, between the assessments made of United States policy in the nonaligned countries and those made in countries with a formal pro-Western orientation.

In the former, although condemnation of everything the United States stands for and does is far from universal, there are attitudes which at times provoke acrimonious charge and defense on both sides; an atmosphere is fostered in which Americans fail to see the intelligibility of Southeast Asian aspirations and Southeast Asians fail to appreciate the legitimate security preoccupations of the West—in particular, the United States. If Southeast Asians seem at times not to understand that their safety has been assured only because of American vigilance, Southeast Asians in the neutral countries feel that they have good reasons for making a number of charges against the United States.

Among the more commonly heard, and sometimes the most important, complaints are the following:

1. *The United States is so intent on winning the cold war in Southeast Asia that it often overlooks the basic political, economic, and social needs and desires of the Southeast Asian countries.* Economic assistance, according to these critics, appears to take second place to military aid, while the amount of economic assistance seems to vary not with the needs of the recipient nations but with their willingness to commit themselves to the Western, anti-Communist alliance. Thus, for instance, it has been said that the United

States has overlooked the desire of many Vietnamese for the reunification of their country in accord with the provisions of the Geneva agreements of 1954. Instead, the charge goes, Washington has made the split between North and South Vietnam permanent by providing military and economic backing for the Ngo Dinh Diem regime, which is accused of becoming increasingly repressive.[2] The fact that Diem is wedded to the anti-Communist cause and is not afraid to suppress rival political elements, proponents of this view continue, is the sufficient and only criterion by which the United States chooses him as the beneficiary of its assistance on a massive scale, no matter what Vietnamese aspirations are overlooked. Hence the United States is content to ignore the political aspirations of the Vietnamese, both north and south. It seeks only to serve its own cold war purposes.

To the American observer, this may seem a rather simple-minded statement of the situation and coincidentally one very much like the Communist claims with respect to Germany and Korea as well as Vietnam. The fact that this attitude prevails, not its rightness or wrongness, nor its sources for that matter, is what concerns us here. The implication of American indifference to social and political aspirations cannot be overlooked in the total context of this belief. Thus, while United States strategists view the present war in South Vietnam as a battle of government forces against Communist infiltrators from North Vietnam, the opinion

[2] On several occasions in 1955 and 1956, American policymakers publicly expressed United States support for President Diem's determination not to participate with North Vietnam in the elections which were to be a prelude to reunification. See, for example, Secretary of State Dulles' statements as reported by *The New York Times*, August 11 and 31, 1955, and the remarks of Walter S. Robertson, Assistant Secretary of State for Far Eastern Affairs, in his "United States Policy Towards Vietnam," in *A Symposium on America's Stake in Vietnam* (New York: American Friends of Vietnam, 1956), pp. 17–19. It was this stated policy, plus massive American military and economic aid to the Diem government, that led some Southeast Asians to conclude that the United States was opposed to a reunified Vietnam in which Vietnamese Communists would have a role to play.

of many Southeast Asians appears to be that it is essentially a struggle of a politically oppressed populace against a foreign-supported, dictatorial government.[3]

Another example of this approach is the opinion of the Cambodian leadership with special reference to Laos. United State policy is regarded here as having, during 1958-1960, directly scuttled the Geneva accords by preventing Pathet Lao representation in the government. Many Cambodians have regarded the Pathet Lao as primarily a nationalist group, which, according to this opinion, had fought for the independence of Laos against the French and was now justifiably seeking representation in the government of a free Laos.[4] The United States, however, is considered to have regarded Pathet Lao participation in the government as tantamount to a Communist take-over. Thus when Prince Souvanna Phouma agreed in 1957 and in 1960 to include the Pathet Lao in a coalition government in an attempt to bring to an end the civil war that had been raging since the conclusion of the Geneva agreements, the United States is regarded as having worked actively to subvert his government by threatening suspension of economic assistance and by engineering a coup d'état. Ironically, according to this point of view, the very efforts of the United States to prevent the spread of Communist influence in Laos had the opposite effect. Souvanna Phouma was

[3] See Prince Norodom Sihanouk's remarks on this subject in *Neak Cheat Niyum* (The Nationalist) (Phnompenh), January 9, 1960. See also, President Sukarno's views on Vietnam as expressed in his address to the Conference of Non-Aligned Countries in Belgrade, September 1-9, 1961, in *The Conference of Heads of State or Government of Non-Aligned Countries* (Belgrade: Publicističko-Izdavački Zavod "Jugoslavija," 1961), p. 32; his address on the anniversary of Indonesia's independence, August 17, 1962, "A Year of Triumph," in *Antara* (New York: Indonesian National News Agency), August 23, 1962, p. 21, and his interview with Nguyen Van Hieu, head of a South Vietnam People's Movement delegation, as quoted in *Antara*, September 24, 1962, p. 1.

[4] For details of Cambodia's views of the Laos crisis, see Roger M. Smith, "Cambodia's Neutrality and the Laotian Crisis," *Asian Survey*, Vol. 1, No. 5, July 1961, pp. 17-24.

driven to request, for the first time, economic assistance and later military materiel from the Soviet Union.[5] (Until then Laos had not entered into diplomatic relations with Russia.)

Prince Norodom Sihanouk, in commenting on American actions in Laos, expressed the fear that his own country, which borders on Laos, might soon become a battleground between Communist and pro-Western forces. It was this belief, he said, which led him to propose in early 1961 a second Geneva conference to negotiate a peaceful settlement in Laos. While the Communist bloc immediately responded favorably to Prince Sihanouk's suggestion, the United States at first refused to participate in a conference which was bound merely to reaffirm the Geneva accords of 1954; we later agreed to take part, but only with visible reluctance. As a result of this position on Laos, the United States suffered a setback in the cold war, as far as Cambodia was concerned, since Washington appeared to have compromised its avowed belief in self-determination in order to protect its own immediate security interests in Laos.

2. The belief is held that *United States economic assistance in Southeast Asia is an instrument for recruiting new human and physical resources for the United States in the cold war and, a means of denying these to our Communist rivals.* Indonesia and Burma as well as Cambodia have given expression to this charge,[6] which, at its worst, would have

---

[5] *Ibid.* See also the views of Thai political leaders as quoted in Modelski, George, "Asian States' Participation in SEATO," in Modelski, George, ed., *SEATO: Six Studies* (Melbourne: Cheshire, 1962), p. 122; and in Wilson, David A., "Thailand: Old Leaders and New Directions," *Asian Survey*, Vol. 3, No. 2, February 1963, pp. 85–87.

[6] See, for example, *The Nation* (Rangoon), April 9, 1952, and *Réalités Cambodgiennes* (Phnompenh), June 24, 1960. See also, the discussion of the Mutual Security Agreement controversy in Indonesia, 1952, in Feith, Herbert, *The Wilopo Cabinet, 1952–1953; A Turning Point in Post-Revolutionary Indonesia*, Monograph Series, Modern Indonesia Project, Southeast Asia Program, Cornell University, 1958, pp. 57–65, and in Kahin, George McT., "Indonesian Politics and Nationalism," in Holland, William L., ed., *Asian Nationalism and the West* (New York: Macmillan, 1953), pp. 193–194.

the United States "bribing" Southeast Asian countries into adopting American viewpoints across the whole range of contemporary affairs.

According to such critics, this motivation in United States policy is sufficient to negate the good will which the aid itself might generate. Thus Mohammed Hatta, the former Vice President of Indonesia and hardly a sympathizer with Communist slogans, wrote in 1958:

> When it wants to help some country, the United States puts forward too many of its own views and ideas and pays too little attention to the desires and ideals of the nation involved. Everything is measured by American axioms, the American view of life. Consequently the help given by the United States does not produce effective results.[7]

American policy in Southeast Asia during the Eisenhower administration seemed to reflect Secretary of State John Foster Dulles' conviction that nonalignment in the cold war was not only "short-sighted" but "immoral." During this period the United States was widely thought to regard neutral countries as constituting a dangerous power vacuum susceptible to an inflow of communism, and some of its actions were construed by leaders of the nonaligned Southeast Asian countries as implying that continued or increased aid to these countries was conditional upon their assumption of an anti-Communist posture.[8] As Mohammed Hatta further wrote:

[7] Mohammed Hatta, "Indonesia between the Power Blocs," Foreign Affairs, Vol. 36, No. 3, April 1958, pp. 485–486. See also the editorial comments in The New Times of Burma (Rangoon) concerning American foreign economic policy, July 2, 1953, and October 16, 1954, and Prime Minister U Nu's comments as reported in The New York Times, October 14, 1954.

[8] See, for example, Prince Sihanouk's allegations concerning American pressures on Cambodia in early 1956 in La Libérté (Phnompenh), April 26, 1956. See also, Les Idées du Discours-Programme Présenté par le Prince-President devant l'Assemblée Nationale lors de l'Investiture du 3ᵉᵐᵉ Gouvernement Sangkum, le 29–2–56 (Phnompenh: 1956).

. . . not infrequently the help given to Indonesia is measured by her attitude towards . . . Communist states. It has happened that orders for goods vital to the daily life of the Indonesian people have not been attended to for months. Perhaps Westerners consider this merely a businesslike attitude. But such an occurrence hurts the feelings of Indonesians, and is put down to pride. They feel that an effort is being made to make them realize that they cannot exist without foreign aid, especially from the Western world. They feel they are being asked to go down on their knees in order to obtain it.[9]

And in his address to the United States Senate in June 1955, Prime Minister U Nu of Burma declared that,

The implication [of American policy] seems to be that a nation which does not choose sides and join irrevocably with one or the other camps in the armed truce that exists in the world today lacks courage and conviction. And very often the inference which seems to be drawn is 'if you are not with us, then you are against us.' And if you are not with us, you must be either openly or secretly in tow with communism.[10]

Such statements as the few cited here reveal that there was considerable suspicion in the minds of leading political figures in Southeast Asia that United States aid was not merely the product of a philanthropic American tradition but an instrument for bending Southeast Asian wills to American policy. What those political figures expressed was certainly not a private or an unrepresentative view of the problem as conceived in the cabinets and much of the press in their countries. It should be remembered that critics of the United States and of American policy in such countries are apt to keep on expressing such opinions long after the circumstances have passed which gave rise to them.

[9] Hatta, *op. cit.*, pp. 484–485.
[10] U Nu, *An Asian Speaks* (Washington: Embassy of the Union of Burma, 1955)

3. *The United States is not beyond engaging in subversion to overthrow neutralist regimes in Southeast Asia or at the very least to threaten them ominously,* according to the publicly expressed fears of leading political figures such as Burma's U Kyaw Nyein, Indonesia's President Sukarno, and, once again, Prince Norodom Sihanouk. If an implied threat of withdrawal of aid is considered an economic lever of United States security policy, the overthrow of a government is considered the ultimate political weapon.

In Burma during 1950–1953, the United States was believed to be supporting remnant Kuomintang forces based in northern Burma for an eventual attack on China, which was to be coordinated with the "unleashing" of Nationalist armed forces from Formosa.[11] Some Burmese were even persuaded that the United States backed plans to engulf Burma in this manner in a new Korean conflict which, if it did not topple the U Nu regime, would have the far more disastrous effect of plunging a still war-crippled Burma into further conflict.[12] Burmese suspicions of American intentions led them to demand the immediate termination of American economic aid.[13] In a press interview, Deputy Prime Minister U Kyaw Nyein justified his country's action in the following words:

[11] For a discussion of Burmese views on this subject, see Cady, John F., *A History of Modern Burma* (Ithaca: Cornell University Press, 1958), p. 622; Clubb, Oliver E., Jr., *The United States and the Sino-Soviet Bloc in Southeast Asia* (Washington: The Brookings Institution, 1962), pp. 85–87; and Johnstone, William C., *Burma's Foreign Policy, A Study in Neutralism* (Cambridge: Harvard University Press, 1963), pp. 65–66.

[12] See, for example, *The New Times of Burma* (Rangoon), February 3 and 5, March 3, 6, and 26, 1953, and *The Nation*, March 30 and April 5, 1953. See also, Tinker, Hugh, *The Nation of Burma* (London: Oxford University Press, 1957), pp. 345 ff; Johnstone, *op. cit.*, p. 73, and Cady, *op. cit.*, p. 623.

[13] For a discussion of other factors in the termination of the United States aid program in 1953, see Walinsky, Louis J., *Economic Development in Burma: 1951–1960* (New York: Twentieth Century Fund, 1962), pp. 126 n., 515–516.

With one hand we were accepting American aid while with the other we had to fight bandits armed by the same people who gave us the money. . . . If this KMT business continues, we may even be driven to accept aid from the Chinese. We shall always try to keep our independence, but no self-respecting people can put up with this insidious business. If the Americans press us too hard they may succeed in pushing us in the opposite direction.[14]

In Indonesia, in 1957, dissident army officers, especially in Sumatra, who had long conducted irregular trade in a variety of primary goods such as rubber and tin, found a cause for alarm at the new Djuanda cabinet's desire for the regularization of this foreign trade; they found another in the conspicuous efforts of President Sukarno to balance the constant strength of the Masjumi party with the fast-increasing power of Indonesia's Communist party, the popular appeal of which had become manifest in the 1956 national elections. These officers, natives of the outer islands for the most part, had also become irritated at the centralizing tendencies they observed in the Djakarta government, which they resented as corrupt and inefficient and as the source of a powerful Javanization of the economy (among other things), that they considered to be unfair in every respect to the peoples of the outer islands.[15]

The open rebellion which flared up in the Padang area of Sumatra at the close of the year was believed by many Indonesians to have been supported with American arms and even the services of American pilots.[16] The suspicion

[14] Quoted in Mende, Tibor, *Southeast Asia Between Two Worlds* (London: Turnstile Press, 1955), pp. 178–179.

[15] For a discussion of this situation, see Brackman, Arnold C., *Indonesian Communism: A History* (New York: Praeger, 1963), Chapters 20–22, *passim*.

[16] That many Indonesians believed the United States to be culpable was revealed in statements made by Prime Minister Djuanda, as quoted in the *Asian Recorder* (New Delhi), May 17–23, 1958, p. 2056; by Foreign Minister Subandrio, as quoted by Woodman, Dorothy, in the *New Statesman*, August 2, 1958; and by President Sukarno in an address, "A Year of Challenge," printed by the Ministry of Information in 1958. See also, *Antara*, January 7, 1958; *Review of*

of Indonesia's leaders was soon transformed by the press into widespread belief that Washington was involved in an effort to topple President Sukarno's government by playing on the grievances of the army and utilizing disgruntled Masjumi leaders.[17]

In Cambodia, too, the United States is regarded by Cambodian leaders as implicated in at least one major plot (1959) to subvert Prince Sihanouk's neutralist regime.[18] In that year royal army action broke up an anti-government conspiracy based in Siemreap province, where subsequent investigations uncovered American radio equipment and arms. Cambodians widely believed that the United States directed the intrigue, working through agents of the South Vietnamese government. While Washington denied participation in this affair, Prince Sihanouk declared before the United Nations General Assembly in September 1960:

> We are sincerely grateful for the aid granted to us by the great and rich powers, but we can only accept that aid which contributes to improving the lot of our people, and allows us to emerge from our under-developed state. For what many of you are perhaps unaware of, but what many small aided nations are perhaps not unaware of, is that too often a friendly aid, provided for in official agreements, is accompanied by a secret and far less friendly kind of aid. This latter kind of aid, which is never mentioned, and which arouses indignation if one mentions it, can take several forms: either direct subversion,

---

Indonesia (Washington: Embassy of Indonesia), Vol. 5, No. 2, February 1958, p. 1; and *The New York Times,* March 13, 1958.

[17] For a description of the Communist journalistic techniques used in this instance for the creation and spread of political and psychological warfare "news" items, see Kaznacheev, Aleksandr, *Inside a Soviet Embassy: Experiences of a Russian Diplomat in Burma* (Philadelphia: J. B. Lippincott, 1962), pp. 172–174.

[18] See *Principaux Discours et Allocutions de S.A.R. Le Prince Norodom Sihanouk en 1959* (Phnompenh: Imp. du Ministère de l'Information, n.d.), pp. 22–25; *La Dépêche du Cambodge* (Phnompenh), October 1, 1959, and *Agence Khmère de Presse* (Presse) (official government daily news bulletin) (Phnompenh), October 2, 1959.

the totally artificial support or the creation of opposition groups, or the purchase of the consciences of men considered strong enough to achieve secession of certain provinces, and torpedo neutrality and the national regime. . . .[19]

Cambodian wariness of American motives has been heightened by the frequent border incursions and economic blockades to which the country has been subjected from time to time by its neighbors and traditional enemies, Thailand and South Vietnam. The Cambodian government feels that since these two countries are so greatly dependent upon the United States for military and economic aid, Washington could easily dissuade them from such harassment if it chose to do so.

Thus we see a fairly widespread belief among those Southeast Asian neutralist leaders with wide and important constituencies that the United States, while giving assistance generously, is not beyond making more or less sinister efforts at the same time to gain by subversion what overt diplomatic policies for the "control" of neutral Southeast Asian governments fail to bring about. Whatever the facts of the matter, the important thing is the deep suspicion of the integrity of United States foreign policy. It goes without saying that even normal negotiations become difficult in this sort of psychological climate.

4. *The United States, in projecting its concern with communism into Southeast Asia, fails to make a correct assessment of the national foreign policy interests of the neutral Southeast Asian countries.* These countries can best assess their own national interests, according to this attitude, and Washington's impatience with nonalignment as a foreign

[19] Address by Prince Sihanouk to the fifteenth session of the United Nations General Assembly, September 26, 1960. Text in *Principaux Discours et Allocutions de S.A.R. Le Prince Norodom Sihanouk en 1960* (Phnompenh: Imp. du Ministère de l'Information, n.d.), pp. 189–209. See p. 207.

policy is clearly an indication of our inability to comprehend the realities of living in the Southeast Asian vortex.

To be sure, there is a threat to national sovereignty, whether by subversion or invasion, from neighboring Communist China. But this is a fear rooted at least as much in history and memory as in the current Marxist-Leninist-Stalinist ideology of the Peking regime, according to this attitude. Particularly during a period when the Soviet Union and the Chinese People's Republic appeared as a single vast and monolithic international force, an offense against one meant possible retaliation from the other. Nor have Southeast Asians forgotten such Communist bloc maneuvers as support of the Madiun rebellion in Indonesia in 1948, the Hukbalahap movement in the Philippines, or the anti-nationalist position vis-à-vis Cambodia and Laos adopted by China and Russia during the Geneva Conference on Indochina in 1954; they are not unaware of Chinese efforts to gain control over alien Chinese residents in Southeast Asia, nor are they unmindful of support given the Communist party in Burma, the Pracheachon in Cambodia, and the Pathet Lao in Laos.[20]

In the hope that such circumstances as these might make some impression on United States lawmakers, diplomats, and, indeed, the general public, the Burmese and the Cambodians have explained neutralism as a defensive posture which alone could guarantee continuity of sovereignty. Thus, U Nu declared in 1950:

. . . once Burma has taken sides with either the Anglo-American bloc or the Soviet bloc she must support the side taken in any and every thing right or wrong. We will have no choice. Our conviction is that in this world there is nobody who is always wrong or always right.

[20] See, for example, Prince Sihanouk's views on this subject in his *Le Cambodge et ses Relations avec ses Voisins* (Phnompenh: Imp. du Ministère de l'Information, n.d.), pp. 44–75; and Prime Minister U Nu's views, as reported in *The Nation*, June 24 and August 18, 1956, and *The New Times of Burma*, August 18, 1956.

. . . Therefore we cannot allow ourselves to fall into a position in which we must blindly support any country or countries right or wrong.[21]

and again in 1955, speaking in Washington:

> . . . Burma at the present time has no choice but to pursue her policy of neutrality if she wishes to preserve her independence, and that to us is more important than anything else. It is part of her defense, an important part, against subversion. . . . But in another way, she cannot abandon her neutrality without increasing the risk of losing her independence through subversion.[22]

In Cambodia, the position was explained with candor as follows:

> Our neutrality has been imposed on us by necessity. A glance at a map of our part of the world will show that we are wedged in between two medium-sized nations of the Western bloc and only thinly screened by Laos from the scrutiny of two countries of the Eastern bloc, North Viet Nam and the vast People's Republic of China. What choice have we but to try to maintain an equal balance between the blocs? . . . It would be absurd to suppose that a tiny country like mine, geographically situated as it is, would risk provoking the Chinese and Soviet colossi now that planes fly so fast and rockets so far.[23]

Still another reason that nonaligned nations in Southeast Asia have preferred to retain their neutral status is that they feel that involvement in the cold war will divert attention and energy from the internal development of their countries. As Prince Sihanouk declared at the fifteenth session of the United Nations General Assembly:

[21] Speech delivered in Parliament, September 5, 1950. Text in *From Peace to Stability*, Speeches of U Nu during August 15, 1949, to April 20, 1951 (Rangoon: 1951), pp. 95–101. See p. 101.

[22] U Nu, *An Asian Speaks, op. cit.*

[23] Norodom Sihanouk, "Cambodia Neutral: The Dictate of Necessity," *Foreign Affairs*, Vol. 36, No. 4, July 1958, pp. 583, 585.

For our part we believe we have the right, considering the vital problems which beset us, to stay away from the blocs and so-called "defensive" military organizations which in practice often show themselves to be of a nature which tends to draw peoples into adventures which do not concern them, and where they stand to gain little.[24]

As an obverse to this urge to explain and have understood the reasons for their neutrality, some Southeast Asian leaders of the nonaligned states believe that Thailand and South Vietnam have compromised their freedom by allying themselves too closely with the United States. It is widely known, for example, that the Thais were strongly opposed to the decision of the United States in 1961 to replace the pro-Western Boun Oum government in Laos with a neutralist regime and had even promised the pro-Western faction that Bangkok would provide the means to maintain it in power. However, when the United States finally committed itself to support the neutrals and began to put pressure on Boun Oum and Phoumi Nosavan to step down in the interest of a coalition government, the Thais, albeit reluctantly, fell into line with the American position.

Subsidiary virtues for nonalignment are equally unappreciated in the United States, according to exponents of this attitude. For example, nonalignment is regarded by some Southeast Asians as the wisest course to take from the point of view of domestic politics, as they feel certain a thoroughgoing pro-Western or pro-Communist orientation would encounter opposition from important and vocal segments of the population. Neutrality in international affairs is considered to be one of the most expedient means to maintain internal political stability. By remaining unaligned, neutral leaders also feel that their countries may be able to develop their own ideology, one particularly suited to their own history, needs, and evolving institutions. Only such an ideology, they believe, can be the basis for national unity; this point was emphasized by President Sukarno of In-

[24] *Principaux Discours . . . en 1960, op. cit.,* pp. 201–202.

donesia in his speech before the Belgrade Conference in 1961.[25]

Cambodia believes nonalignment is practical, also, from the point of view of its traditional suspicions of its neighbors Thailand and South Vietnam. Americans who are critical of Cambodia's friendly relations with China, according to this point of view, fail to realize that (1) to date the Chinese have not posed a direct threat to Cambodia's territorial integrity; whereas (2) the Thais and South Vietnamese, in addition to engaging in numerous border incidents with the Cambodians, have laid claims to territory over which Cambodia has historically exercised jurisdiction; and (3) in the light of the threat to Cambodia's security which is posed by its stronger neighbors, a friendly China is regarded as an important potential counterweight in helping Cambodia to maintain a balanced relationship with them.[26] The point which neutral Cambodia, for instance, would like to impress upon the United States is that the latter's division of the world into Communist and anti-Communist camps is not a realistic one for many countries which, for reasons peculiar to their own history, find it more practical to categorize nations in other ways.

It is interesting to note that, while leaders of the neutral nations have often been sharply critical of American foreign policy in not understanding their neutralism, at least one is ready to acknowledge publicly that the American presence in Southeast Asia is essential. Aware that any withdrawal of American interest or influence from Southeast Asia might upset the international political equilibrium there, Prince Sihanouk had this to say to an Asia Society audience in New York in 1961:

[25] *The Conference of Heads of State or Government of Non-Aligned Countries, op. cit.,* pp. 28 ff.

[26] On the latter point Sihanouk has asserted that ". . . it is only our relation with one of our powerful friends in the area which actually prevents our neighbors from succumbing to the temptation to wipe us out." See his address to the students of Kent State University (Ohio), October 3, 1960, as quoted in *Cambodian Commentary* (Phnompenh: Ministry of Information), No. 10, August 1961, pp. 21–33. See p. 25.

As far as our country is concerned, we are well aware that its survival as a free and sovereign nation depends entirely on preserving equilibrium and friendship with these two blocs. The day we find ourselves facing only one all-powerful bloc, the days of our independence—perhaps even our very existence—will be counted. This is why we are absolutely sincere when we say that we want the United States and our other Western friends to preserve and maintain their influence, their position and their prestige in our area.[27]

IV

The Views of the Western-Aligned Nations. The three nations closest to the United States in Southeast Asia—the Philippines, Thailand, and South Vietnam—have generally regarded with favor American foreign policy in the region. In general, this favorable attitude has been brought about by a number of factors: substantial consonance of foreign policy goals; satisfaction with the purposes and administration of various American aid programs; the transfer of their deep-seated fear of foreign intrusion away from Japan, which is now viewed more sympathetically than formerly, to Communist China and thus a continued acceptance of the United States' presence in Southeast Asia as a matter of national safety; and a good many more. Attitudes have emerged from time to time, however, which have threatened to impose strains upon relationships between these countries and the United States. Most of these attitudes have revolved about the occasional doubts of Thai, Filipino, and Vietnamese leaders as to the degree to which the United States actually feels committed to assist in their defense in the actual event of attack. In other words, *the steadfastness of the United States in the execution of its foreign policy,*

[27] *Address of H.R.H. Prince Norodom Sihanouk, Chief of State of Cambodia to The Asia Society, September 26, 1961* (New York: Permanent Mission of Cambodia to the United Nations, 1961), p. 18.

and especially its defense commitments, is sometimes considered questionable.

Two major events in recent years have led the Thais to examine closely their dependence upon the United States, especially for defense support. The sudden backdown of the United States from support of the pro-Western government in Laos, which it had helped bring to power, caused Thai leaders to question the reliability of their own alliance with the United States. The American decision to transfer support to a neutral government in Laos was interpreted by the Thais as an expression of a loss of interest in the fate of Laos and an abandonment of American responsibility. The issue loomed large in the minds of the Thais because of a reported increase in 1961–1962 in Communist activities in their own northeastern provinces, which were once part of Laos and which are still predominantly peopled by Lao. Thais fear that there activities reflect an attempt by the Pathet Lao to regain these provinces for Laos.[28] They began now to talk about a need for greater self-reliance in the spheres of foreign, defense, and economic policy. The United States, eager to maintain its alliance with Thailand, has tried to assuage these anxieties by formally assuring Thailand that our obligation under the Manila pact to assist it in case of armed attack by Communist forces does "not depend upon the prior agreement of all other parties to the Treaty, since this treaty obligation is individual as well as collective." [29] With the renewed outbreak of hostilities in Laos, the United States demonstrated its readiness to come

[28] Present-day Laos and the northeast provinces of Thailand once comprised the Kingdom of Lan Xang. Through wars and political intrigue, parts of Lan Xang were subjugated by the Thai. With the arrival of the French in Indochina, France signed an accord with Thailand by which the Mekong River was recognized as the boundary between Thailand and French Laos. The result of this demarcation of borders is that today more Lao live in Thailand than reside in Laos itself.

[29] This interpretation of SEATO obligations is found in the joint declaration of March 6, 1962, by Secretary of State Dean Rusk and Foreign Minister Thanat Khoman. See *Department of State Bulletin*, Vol. 46, No. 1187, March 26, 1962, p. 498.

to the defense of the Thais in the eventuality of an expansion of the war onto Thai territory by alerting the Seventh Fleet and dispatching several thousand American troops to northeastern Thailand.

Also contributing to Thailand's uneasiness over its relations with the United States was the increase in American military aid which was given to Cambodia in mid-1962, at a time when Cambodia's clamor about Thailand's provocative activities along their common border was at its peak. The American action appeared to Thais to lend credibility to Cambodian accusations. On this matter, Prime Minister Sarit Thanarat asserted at the Thai "Army Forward Headquarters Exercise" in 1962 that "I do not believe that Cambodian strength alone can match up against us. But the reason why Cambodia is so arrogant today is because it believes that it has allied protectors." [30] The American action also prompted some Thais to urge a reconsideration of their government's Western-aligned position in foreign affairs. The Minister of Interior, Praphat Charusathien, for example, hinted that United States willingness to please neutrals might force Thailand to change its policy.[31]

In addition, the American announcement in 1961 that aid to Thailand would be increasingly in the form of loans rather than outright grants did not sit well with Thai leaders, for example, Prime Minister Sarit, who, speaking on the occasion of the eleventh anniversary of the Thai-American aid agreement in September 1961, expressed dismay that ". . . we in Thailand who are true friends of the United States have received less than some countries who are not and who sometimes showed open hostility to the United States." [32]

[30] Quoted in *SEATO Record* (Bangkok: SEATO Public Relations Office), Vol. 1, No. 11, October 1962, p. 16.

[31] *Bangkok Post*, September 6, 1962. See also the address of Foreign Minister Thanat Khoman at the Seventeenth Session of the United Nations General Assembly, September 27, 1962, as quoted in *SEATO Record*, Vol. 1, No. 12, December 1962, p. 16.

[32] Quoted in *Foreign Affairs Bulletin* (Bangkok: Ministry of Foreign Affairs) Vol. 1, No. 1, August-September 1961, p. 66.

Filipinos, as well as Thais, by and large have reacted favorably to American foreign policy in Southeast Asia. In 1961–1963, two major sources of friction between the two countries were eliminated when the United States acceded to Filipino demands on the issues of war damage payments and military bases.

In the Philippines, however, and perhaps less visibly elsewhere, there is the concern that *certain aspects of common United States–Philippines security arrangements in Asia are irrelevant to the security of the Philippines itself; and that the common plane on which our mutual relations should be conducted—one of ideological and spiritual preoccupation —is largely overlooked by the United States.*

With respect to the first outlook, the Philippines has been fearful than its commitments to SEATO may embroil it in issues in which it has no stake (for example, an attack on Pakistan), perhaps at the risk of jeopardizing its own defensive security. At the same time Filipinos have worried over the fact that the Manila pact does not contain a clause which would require the automatic commitment of troops by other SEATO nations, in particular by the United States, in case of an attack on their own islands.[33]

With respect to the second point, Filipino leaders would like to see the United States conduct a more intensive ideological campaign in the whole conduct of its foreign policy in Southeast Asia. Speaking at the Manila Overseas Press Club in September, 1962, President Diosdado Macapagal declared:

American leadership of the free world has not been as effective as it could be because it has relied more on material power and less on spiritual and ideological weapons. The ironic fact that although America spends billions of dollars in foreign aid, she appears not to be popular in the recipient countries may find explanation in

[33] See Smith, Roger M., "The Philippines and the Southeast Asia Treaty Organization," in Smith, Roger M., and Somers, Mary F., *Two Papers on Philippine Foreign Policy*, Data Paper No. 38, Southeast Asia Program, Cornell University, 1960, *passim.*

the lack of proper attention to spiritual and ideological values. For instance, the United States has often given the impression that it lacks a proper regard for the pride and sensibilities of other peoples, a proper recognition of the need to put a premium on the loyalty of steadfast friends as against fickle fencesitters, and a proper degree of consistency in upholding principles in her dealings with nations big and small, instead of sacrificing such principles to maintain the support of the big powers.[34]

Of all the Southeast Asian nations, South Vietnam has received the largest amount of military and economic aid from the United States. No nation in Southeast Asia, including the Federation of Malaysia, which has just come into existence, is presently in such a state of flux, and perhaps equally unstable are attitudes there which could have been described objectively only a short time ago. While consonance of foreign policy aims between South Vietnam and the United States might have been great until relatively recently and may continue into the future, it is undeniable that the chief negative attitude toward the United States and its foreign policy centers at this moment about the belief that *the United States can and does interfere in the internal affairs of a nation, contrary to diplomatic tradition, if the national security interests of the United States, rightly or wrongly assessed, are conceived to be threatened.* Whatever the American rationalization, no nationalistically inclined Southeast Asian leader can brook such intrusion without feelings of outrage, and President Ngo Dinh Diem, whatever the shortcomings of his regime, is no exception.

Thus, American advocacy in 1961 of certain political, economic, and social reforms designed to win a popular base for the government and to assure the success of joint military efforts against the Vietcong were not favorably received by the Ngo regime. Jealously guarding its right to administer South Vietnam in the manner it deems best, the Ngo government has also been bitterly critical not only of more recent

[34] Quoted in *SEATO Record*, Vol. 1, No. 11, October 1962, p. 15.

American efforts to induce it to halt repressive measures taken against the Buddhist clergy and their supporters but also of strong suggestions to remove certain of President Diem's advisors from office.

Another important South Vietnamese grievance, which, however, has been overshadowed by recent events, involves the American decision to support a neutral coalition government in Laos. The approach of the United States to the Laos situation was not acceptable to many of South Vietnam's political leaders for two reasons: First, it was believed that establishment of a coalition government in Laos, in which the Pathet Lao would undoubtedly exercise great influence, would permit unchecked Vietcong use of that country as a thoroughfare from North to South Vietnam. In connection with this, there was also apprehension that the unwieldy coalition government would give way in the near future to a Vietminh-controlled Pathet Lao regime, in which case South Vietnam would be confronted by two hostile countries along its borders. In the second place, the Ngo government was concerned lest the neutralization of Laos serve as a precedent for American support of a similar international solution to the civil conflict in Vietnam.

In varying degrees, therefore, ranging from casual doubt to near outrage, even Western-oriented nations in Southeast Asia show attitudes of greater or lesser apprehension on aspects of United States foreign policy. This does not reverse the Western orientation of the leaders of these countries, however, any more than occasional words of praise for American policies in the neutral nations are a sign of their abandonment of nonalignment policies.

V

The specimen attitudes reported in this essay are far from reflecting a consensus of Southeast Asian opinion, whether among the masses or the elite. They are important, nevertheless, despite the ceremonial context in which some of them were expressed, both in view of their authorship and in view of the often crucially important elite constituencies of their authors and the mass loyalties which these authors more often than not command.

Nor are these the only noteworthy attitudes to be met with among Southeast Asian leaders of any echelon of importance. Such attitudes vary with the times, the place, the occasion, and the issue. They have been adduced, rather, as evidence that attitudes, whether based on fact or not, are important political factors which add yet another hazard to the difficulties that must be met in the execution of United States foreign policy overseas and in Southeast Asia no less than elsewhere.

6

THE COMMUNIST CHALLENGE

IN SOUTHEAST ASIA

ಐ೦ಜಿ೦ಜಿ೦ಜಿ

FRANK N. TRAGER

THIS ESSAY DEALS WITH THE present and prospective Communist challenge in Southeast Asia, with special reference to its changing strategy and tactics, the strength of indigenous Communist movements, and the implications of the Sino-Soviet debate upon the area. The background for this discussion will be supplied only to the extent necessary to understand the present situation.[1]

THE PRIZE TO BE WON

The Communist challenge in Southeast Asia seeks a valuable prize. Mainland and island Southeast Asia are strategically

[1] The reader interested in the recent past may easily fill in the gaps by referring to such studies and their accompanying bibliographies as: Brimmell, J. H., *Communism in Southeast Asia, A Political Analysis* (London: Oxford University Press, 1959); Rose, Saul, *Socialism in Southern Asia* (London: Oxford University Press, 1959); and Trager, Frank N., ed., *Marxism in Southeast Asia, A Study of Four Countries* (Stanford: Stanford University Press, 1959).

located on the sea lanes and under the airways which divide South Asia from the western and southern Pacific Ocean. Control here would add an eastern to the already existing northern Communist flank athwart South Asia, while depriving both India and Japan of important economic and strategic interests in Southeast Asia. It would also endanger Oceania and the still-free countries on the western rim of the Indian Ocean. If Southeast Asia were to fall, exit from the Persian and Aden gulfs, as well as from the ports of East Africa, could be seriously interfered with in a shooting crisis.

Southeast Asia, belonging to the "third" or underdeveloped world, is important on another score. It is a rich resource base of primary products: food, industrial raw materials, and fuel. Its tropical, monsoonal climate makes possible its present production of food and fibers, and could with moderate investment in skills, machinery, fertilizer, irrigation, and water storage provide vastly higher productivity in a twelve-month-long agricultural year. Prewar mainland Southeast Asia, that is, Burma, Thailand, and French Indochina, was capable of feeding its population and annually exporting 7 million tons of rice. Though international and domestic upheavals have inhibited production and export in the area, Burma and Thailand today rank first and second, respectively (the United States is third), among the world's exporters of that commodity. Southeast Asia accounts for almost 90 per cent of the world's supply of natural rubber. Indonesia, Malaya, and Thailand together contribute to world trade about 60 per cent of its tin. Other primary products in less commanding positions, such as petroleum and other mineral products, tea, copra, palm kernels and oil, hemp, and hardwoods, are nonetheless plentiful.

The countries of Southeast Asia with approximately 200 million people are, relative to the land base, in general not overpopulated, although there are some particular areas, for example Java, where the population problem has become

acute. Population statistics for Southeast Asia found in
standard reference books[2] are based largely upon projections
of prewar estimates or small postwar samples. Only in the
case of Thailand do we have a complete postwar census
(1960), and it revealed the inadequacy of earlier estimates
and growth rates. Hence population figures and projections
based upon them must be carefully weighed against other
evidence. Table 1 is offered within these liabilities.

TABLE 1

AREA AND POPULATION OF SOUTHEAST ASIAN COUNTRIES

	Area (square miles)	Estimated population, 1960–1961 (millions)
Burma	262,000	21.5
Cambodia	67,000	5.0
Indonesia*	756,000	95.7
Laos	90,000	2.0
Malaysia	130,000	9.9
Philippines	115,000	27.5
Thailand	200,000	25.5
North Vietnam	65,000	15.0
South Vietnam	66,000	14.0

* Including West Irian, which has an area of approximately 180,000
square miles and a population estimated at 0.7 million.

*The strategic location, with good inland waterways and
harbors, the exploitable land, the exportable primary prod-
ducts, the lebensraum of Southeast Asia have made it historically a target for China and Japan and for Western imperialist powers. Today it is a prime target for Communist
China and, to a slightly lesser degree, for the Soviet Union
as well.*

Western imperialism has been almost completely elimi-

[2] *Economic Survey of Asia and the Far East 1961* (New York:
United Nations, 1962), and *Demographic Yearbook 1962* (New York:
United Nations, 1962), are most useful.

nated from the area. With the emergence of the Federation of Malaysia in 1963, all that remains territorially of Western empire in Southeast Asia, after four and a half centuries, is Portuguese Timor, which occupies the lesser part of the island of Timor, and Brunei, which will almost certainly become part of the Federation of Malaysia within a year or two. Marxist-nationalist amalgams succeeded after World War II in bringing about the independence of Burma, Laos, Cambodia, Vietnam, and Indonesia. The Philippines achieved independence in 1946 upon fulfilling the terms of a timetable enacted by the United States Congress in 1934. In analogous fashion Malaya became independent in 1957. And Thailand had never wholly lost its independence.

But it is not enough to know that Western-style imperialism has come to an end in Southeast Asia. For the fact of its long sway has strikingly conditioned the present Southeast Asian generations who have lived under its less-than-benign rule. Half a century hence, this experienced event will have more thoroughly passed into history. To be sure, it will continue to be cited, but it will no longer be as relevant to Southeast Asian politics as it has been until now. Today the countries of the area tend to glorify the history of the precolonial era, even though it is inadequately studied; while the colonial period is always denigrated, and the nationalist revolution and nationalist revolutionaries are raised to heroic proportions. These extravagances must first be understood, then lived with, and gradually trimmed to true historic proportions. For not everything in the dynastic past of the warring states of Burma, Siam, Cambodia, Vietnam, Malaya, Indonesia, and the Philippines deserves glorification; nor does everything in the colonial past merit vilification.

Western imperialism provided the various Southeast Asian nationalist movements, both before and after they achieved independence, with a "cause" for many of their difficulties. After independence, Soviet propaganda terms such as "neo-colonialism" and "economic imperialism" were also adopted to explain away various local shortcomings. But in today's context of domestic and international politics, such scapegoating is less and less persuasive and is less and less heard outside of Southeast Asian Communist and crypto-Communist circles. For the real challenge to survival in Southeast Asia—the need to create national unity out of ethnic and linguistic diversity; to establish and maintain internal stability, law, and order; to bring about the conditions for economic and social improvement; to engage fruitfully and, where possible, democratically in the many-sided and difficult task of nation building—comes in part from within these independent states and in part from the new imperialism launched by Moscow and Peking. A decade ago a Burmese Socialist leader, U Kyaw Nyein, identified this new imperialist venture as "the Soviet type . . . perhaps more dangerous, because it is more ruthless, more systematic and more blatantly justified in the name of world communist revoluion." [3]

U Kyaw Nyein's words were not idle. Since the end of World War II and the coming of independence, every state in Southeast Asia, with the possible exception of Cambodia, has been or is now the object of a Communist revolutionary uprising, guided or supported and endorsed in one way or another by Moscow or Peking, or both. The political character of the particular Southeast Asian government in power at the time of the Communist rebellion made no difference to the rebels. Socialist-nationalist Burma and Indonesia were included along with the capitalist-nationalist Philippines, French Indochina, and Malaya. And today armed conflict continues in Vietnam and in Laos, while Thailand is said

[3] U Kyaw Nyein, Speech to the Anti-Colonial Bureau, Asian Socialist Conference, *Socialist Asia*, (Rangoon), Vol. 3, No. 2, June 1954, p. 9. This is not an isolated theme in Burmese leadership thinking. The recently published *Burma Socialist Program Party Philosophy* (see *The Guardian* [Rangoon], January 18, 1963, for text), issued by General Ne Win's regime, criticizes the "vulgar materialism" of the "leftists" who are "heading towards the reverse of the socialist aim." The text leaves no doubt that the reference is to "countries" as well as to group deviationists.

to be at the preinsurgency stage in the sixteen northeastern provinces abutting on Laos. Remnants from earlier Communist uprisings are still active in Burma and the Philippines, while Malaya suffers from some remnants of the old rebellion along its border with Thailand, and also faces some danger from Communist and other rebel elements in the Borneo territories included in Malaysia.

COMMUNISM IN SOUTHEAST ASIA, ITS CHANGING STRATEGY AND TACTICS

"The strictest devotion to the ideas of Communism must be combined with the ability to effect all the necessary practical compromises, to manoeuvre, to make agreements, zigzags, retreats and so on." [4] These words of Lenin are peculiarly apposite in any attempt at understanding the changing strategy and tactics of communism in Southeast Asia. Lenin emphatically turned to the East at the 1920 Congress of the Third International, the Comintern. Communist interest in Asia was fostered during the early 1920's partly by Communist failures in Europe after World War I and partly by Lenin's views, supported by Stalin, of the importance of the Asian "colonial and semi-colonial" peoples as temporary allies of the professional revolutionaries who composed the proletarian or Communist parties.[5] The Comintern succeeded in presenting itself as the champion of the "oppressed peoples" of Asia. Its anti-imperialist ideology was congenial to whatever radical indigenous nationalist leadership was then and later on the scene.

However, prior to the end of World War II, the influence of the Comintern (which was dissolved in 1943) in Southeast Asia was relatively slight. Its agents had been successful in forming Communist parties only in Indonesia

[4] Lenin, V. I., " 'Left-Wing' Communism—an Infantile Disorder," *Selected Works,* Vol. 2 (Moscow: Foreign Languages Publishing House, 1951), p. 424.

[5] See Trager, *op. cit.,* pp. 244–248.

and French Indochina. In these two colonial areas the leaders of the Communist struggle emphasized its anti-imperialist orientation. In the former, an abortive Communist insurrection was crushed by the Dutch in 1927. The illegal Communist Party of Indonesia (PKI) operated through various fronts in the 1930's. It emerged partially "above ground" once again in 1945 under Jussuf, and fully in the spring of 1946 under Sardjono. In Indochina, the Communist leader Ho Chi Minh survived innumerable vicissitudes to triumph in North Vietnam after World War II. Lesser Communist or Communist-controlled fronts, more overtly based on "class" organization, had a brief existence in the Philippines (for example, the Congress of Filipino Workers, which became the Communist Party in 1930), and in Singapore-Malaya, where various efforts were made after 1924 to organize as the South Seas Communist Party and, later, as the more successful Malaya Communist Party (MCP).

The "united front from above" or "soft" strategy, again initiated after failure of the Nazi-Soviet Pact brought World War II to the Soviet Union, substantially advanced the fortunes of international communism both in Europe and in Asia. Stalin had been prepared for this. From 1925 onward, in accordance with his so-called law of the ebb and flow of revolutionary tides, he had talked, in reporting to various Communist party congresses, of the inevitability of war and its aftermath of revolutions. The expected "imperialist war," he said at the Seventeenth Soviet Communist Party (CPSU) Congress, in January 1934, "is sure to unleash revolution and jeopardise the very existence of capitalism." [6] Its crises would deepen, and the whole imperialist camp would deteriorate because of internal contradictions. Hence, it was necessary for the Soviet Union to aid and abet the revolutionary uprising. And this he and Moscow did.

[6] Stalin, Joseph, "Report to the Seventeenth Party Congress on the Work of the Central Committee of the CPSU," *Works*, Vol. 13 (Moscow: Foreign Languages Publishing House, 1955), p. 300.

The European satellites, North Korea, and China were added to the orbit of international communism between 1945 and the end of 1949.

In February 1946, Stalin began to shift Communist policy once again to the "hard" or revolutionary line. This was formalized in October 1947 by organization of the Information Bureau of the Communist and Workers Parties, the so-called Cominform. (The latter was dissolved after the de-Stalinizing Twentieth CPSU Congress in 1956. It was to be replaced by Conferences of Communist and Workers Parties, such as those held in Moscow in 1957 and 1960.) The shift to a hard revolutionary line, signalized by organization of the Cominform, had direct consequences in Southeast Asia. There, in rapid succession, every country except Thailand experienced a Communist-instigated and Communist-led rebellion directed against both newly independent nationalist and colonial regimes. The series of Communist and front conferences organized in Bombay and Calcutta between November 1947 and March 1948 was the main fuse setting off these 1948 rebellions in Burma, Malaya, and Indonesia; while the struggle in Indochina, after a period of fruitless negotiations during 1946, flared into open warfare in late December of that year. Vietminh representatives were in attendance at Calcutta. The Philippine Communists and the Hukbalahaps (The People's Anti-Japanese Army), like the Philippines generally in this period of its history, appear not to have been part of Southeast Asian political life. The Huks, with mass support in the Central Luzon provinces from an impoverished, landlord-ridden peasantry (although infiltrated and later controlled by avowed Communist leaders such as Luis Taruc, Castro Alejandrino, and Vicente Lava), originally came nearest to being genuine examples of "agrarian reformers" and traditional Filipino peasant rebels against wartime collaborationists and corrupt political leaders who managed to gain American support before 1950.[7]

[7] Scaff, Alvin H., *The Philippine Answer to Communism* (Stanford: Stanford University Press, 1955), is a valuable resource on this phase.

The subject of the Bombay and Calcutta conferences has been debated by Western scholars in terms of their presumed causal relationship to the (South and) Southeast Asian Communist rebellions.[8] Were the latter, so the question goes, "orders from Moscow" or "orders from Peking," or both, or neither? In fact, the question is somewhat beside the point. The meetings in India heard expositions of the "liberation struggle" line laid down in A. Zhdanov's thesis presented at the 1947 Cominform meeting. The latter, like earlier meetings of the Comintern, merely closed the debate on the new line which, as indicated above, had been in the making since early 1946. Various Communist leaders and parties throughout the world, including those in Southeast Asia, are always in some disarray while a new line is in process of adoption. Intense internal debate and factional rivalry virtually never cease despite monolithic public action, unless there is an open split in the party or, as in the case of Yugoslavia, between the parties. But sooner or later, up to the late 1950's and the period of the Sino-Soviet debate (see pp. 158–164), those who remain within the Communist movement conform to the major directions of the line, operating under the party principle of democratic centralism.

Thus to ask the question, did the meetings in India "cause" or instigate the rebellions, is relatively meaningless. The international Communist movement, then taking its unchallenged direction from Moscow, geared itself to the tasks called for by the new zigzag in the line. (As Harold R. Isaacs pointed out long ago,[9] the international Communist movement originally used both written and oral communications between its organs and their affiliates for transmission of policy, strategy, and tactics. After 1926, the system of publication of internal documents was largely scrapped, and semiconspiratorial and underground techniques were

---

[8] See Trager, *op. cit.*, pp. 263–273.
[9] Isaacs, Harold R., *The Tragedy of the Chinese Revolution*, rev. ed. (Stanford: Stanford University Press, 1951), pp. 58 ff, pp. 239 ff.

henceforth employed for these purposes.) Thereafter the application of the Communist hard-line strategy in Asia, including Southeast Asia, was everywhere in evidence, although its timing varied somewhat from country to country in terms of what Communists call "objective conditions," and in terms of domestic Communist readiness to apply the line. International Communist monolithicism has never required international simultaneity as a necessary characteristic in the execution of strategy and tactics. Where loyalty to any existing Moscow line and especially to the indisputable leadership of Stalin were unquestioned, minor and temporal variations in Communist action were tolerated. At worst, such variations would cause the rating of the non-Soviet party or front to move up or down on the scoreboard of parties in Moscow. In this context, the Bombay and Calcutta meetings simply instructed, readied, and made more certain that the 1947 line was understood in South and Southeast Asia.

A new change in Communist strategy and tactics began to take place in Southeast Asia tentatively in 1953 and certainly in 1954. Once again the line zigzagged to the "soft" or so-called "right" line. Its symptoms can be found in one of Stalin's last writings, *Economic Problems of Socialism*, published in October 1952. His death in March 1953 and the subsequent contest for power within the Soviet Union, which led to a loosening of restraints upon the lives of Soviet citizens, to the Korean armistice in July 1953, and to the Geneva Conference of 1954 which recognized the consolidation of Communist power in North Vietnam, are among the earlier manifestations of the new policy. The conciliatory posture of the Chinese Communists as represented by the Chou–Nehru–Nu Five Principles of Peaceful Coexistence of 1954, the Bandung Conference of 1955, and the Bulganin–Khrushchev visit to Southeast Asia in the same year, are major items in the development of this period of Sino-Soviet policy.

As always, such a shift did not and does not alter Lenin's

dictum concerning "the strictest devotion to the ideas of Communism." Both Moscow and Peking, and all other Communist parties, adhered to the two-camp analysis of the world, that is, the "capitalist–imperialist" camp versus the "socialist" camp. They retained the ideology of historical materialism. They merely found new "objective conditions" and reverted to other, already tried methods for forging ahead on the road to power. The "soft" or "right" strategy characteristic of the Comintern in its united front period before the Sixth Congress in 1928, and in its people's front period between 1935 and 1939 following the Seventh Congress, was again trotted out for the Asians (and others).

But there was a difference which must be carefully noted. This time, that is by the early 1950's, the Communist world had established itself beyond the confines of the Soviet Union and Outer Mongolia. It included the European satellites, mainland China, Tibet, North Korea, and North Vietnam; and it had also acquired, by international agreement at the Geneva Conference of 1954, a foothold in the two northeastern provinces of Laos, Phongsaly and Samneua. The new application of the old "soft" line could be more flexible, and it was. At Bandung, for example, the Communists did not distinguish between Southeast Asian (and other) neutralist countries and those which had joined with the United States in collective security agreements. It extended the olive branch of the Five Principles on a government-to-government basis. At the same time, the Communists initiated in Southeast Asia their trade-and-aid program with those governments whose neutralist policies they favored, that is, Burma, Cambodia, and Indonesia, and a trade program only with Malaya and Thailand. Parenthetically, it should also be noted that the bloc aid program has also been extended to such nonneutralist governments as Pakistan, Turkey, Argentina, Bolivia, and Brazil.

Thus the Communist strategy of government-to-government relations in this post-Stalin era exhibited a two-pronged attack. It was seemingly prepared to cultivate all newly independent and ex-colonial nations in the interest of "peaceful coexistence," but it was especially prepared to reward those governments which were or became neutralist. The scale of rewards tended to be directly proportional to the degree to which the neutralists moved closer to support of international Communist policies—as for example, India and Indonesia—or at least restrained Western influence or avoided formal Western alliance, such as Burma and Cambodia. The so-called third world was to be weaned from association with the West, wooed to some kind of dependence upon the Communist bloc, and thereby made more accessible to eventual Communist "peaceful" take-over.

This new policy received its official blessing at the Twentieth Congress of the CPSU, in February 1956, where it was coupled with the supposedly secret but actually well-publicized anti-Stalin line of Khrushchev. As many have since pointed out, the Sino-Soviet leaders were now cultivating the third world as a "zone of peace." Moscow, Peking, and the satellite capitals courted non-Communist governments by stepped-up programs of political, economic, and cultural exchanges, as Tables 2 and 3 suggest.

TABLE 2

BLOC NONMILITARY CREDITS AND GRANTS TO NON-COMMUNIST
ASIA, JANUARY 1954—JUNE 1962 *
(*Millions of United States dollars*)

Afghanistan	$ 515
Burma	93
Cambodia	65
Ceylon	58
India	950
Indonesia	641
Nepal	55
Pakistan	33
TOTAL	$2,410

* The Sino-Soviet Economic Offensive through June 30, 1962 (mimeographed research memorandum RSB-145, unclassified) (Washington: Department of State, September 1962), p. 9.

TABLE 3

BLOC EXPORTS AND IMPORTS TO SELECTED COUNTRIES
OF NON-COMMUNIST ASIA, 1959–1961 *
(*Millions of United States dollars*)

	Exports	Imports
Afghanistan	$ 96.2	$ 53.7
Burma	86.4	70.5
Cambodia	32.9	13.6
Ceylon	87.	95.1
India	277.9	334.
Indonesia	210.8	211.4
Malaya	187.	460.9
Pakistan	33.4	68.6
Taiwan	5.1	. . . .
Thailand	14.9	13.3
TOTAL	$1,031.6	$1,321.1

* Adapted from *ibid.*, pp. 39, 42. "Recent Soviet statistics on trade
with nonbloc Asian countries indicate that in 1961 it was eight times
that of 1955 when the aid-trade program got underway." *Current
Notes on International Affairs,* Vol. 33, No. 12, December 1962, p. 50.

However, throughout this period of the soft line on a
government-to-government basis, which extended roughly
from 1954 onwards, the Communist bloc did not apply this
strategy to the divided Southeast Asian countries, South
Vietnam and Laos. With varying intensity, especially increased since 1958–1959, the bloc and its parties supported
armed insurrectionary campaigns against the existing government in South Vietnam and, except for a brief coalition
interlude in the summer and fall of 1957, against Laos. The
Geneva Conference of 1954 on Indochina hardly inter-
rupted the attack; nor did the 1962 Geneva Conference on
Laos succeed in stopping it. Further, and what is generally
overlooked by many who eye the current Sino-Soviet debate, at no time before or since 1954 have the Moscow or
Peking regimes, or the Soviet or Chinese parties, disavowed
or used influence to end the Communist rebellions in Burma,
Malaya, and the Philippines. In these three countries, the

Communists have maintained insurrectionary activity since 1948, despite especially friendly Soviet and Chinese Communist governmental relations with Burma, and extensive Soviet trade relations with Malaya (second in Asia to Japan). Only in Indonesia where the PKI, the largest party outside the bloc, has been figuratively embraced in the tenuous political consortium of Sukarno's guided democracy, and in Cambodia where Prince Sihanouk's unique influence surmounts the scene, have the Communists pursued their objectives by "peaceful" means. And now Thailand, brought dangerously close to direct contact with the Chinese Communists and Pathet Lao in northwestern Laos, has begun to experience Communist infiltration and preinsurgency efforts in its northeastern region.

The Communist combination of a soft-line strategy applied on a government-to-government basis in Southeast Asia (and elsewhere) and of the maintenance of a party organization engaged in overt and covert revolutionary activity and "wars of national liberation" is not a new phenomenon invented or devised by Khrushchev and/or Mao in the post-Stalin period. It is merely a more adroit (because there are more Communist national centers to draw upon), more widespread application of the strategy and tactics clearly set forth by Dimitrov and Wang Ming at the Seventh Comintern Congress in 1935. Then, while emphasizing the people's front line which entailed government-to-government relations, these spokesmen for the Comintern did not fail to voice the classical Leninist position on the importance of the revolutionary party and the ever-continuing actions of its cadres. Their language called for a "united front from below," although this aspect of the Communist strategy was then frequently overlooked, as well as "from above." A "united front from below" in Communist terms means the continuing effort of the Communist party first to unite with, and thereby to gain hegemony over, its temporary non-Communist allies in "imperialist," ex-colonial, or "national democratic" states. An essential ingredient in the dominating leadership of Lenin, Stalin, Khrushchev, and Mao has been their ability to advocate and apply, singly or simultaneously, the hard and soft strategies whenever and wherever their analysis of "objective conditions" has warranted the application. In a sense, only Trotsky appears to have been devoid of this capability. For most of his mature life, certainly after 1917, he was an undeviating, inflexible advocate of the hard or revolutionary line. Among Southeast Asian Communist leaders, only Thakin Soe of Burma exhibits such inflexibility, and this in turn has erroneously given rise to the allegation that he is a Trotskyite. Soe is really a splinter leader, no more, no less. He has had virtually no external connections.

It is in the sense of the preceding paragraph that the more serious danger emanating from the soft, as compared to the hard, Communist line should be emphasized. Southeast Asian countries today and, indeed, ever since their nationalists achieved independence, have been the object of alternating and simultaneous application of both strategies. On a government-to-government basis, they suffered first from the hard, and more recently—excepting for the divided countries—the soft strategy. But since the end of World War II, their governments and peoples have also been the relentless object of the revolutionary or hard line, the united front from below, conducted under the covert or overt insurrectionary policy of the respective indigenous Communist parties.

THE CURRENT STRENGTH OF INDIGENOUS COMMUNIST MOVEMENTS

The provable strength[10] of Communist parties is difficult to establish. The extent of their influence in front groups,

[10] Some of the statistics in this section have been drawn from *World Strength of the Communist Party Organizations* (Washington, D.C.: Department of State, January 1963).

trade unions, and related organizations requires even greater effort to validate. Reliable membership figures are virtually unobtainable and usually unverifiable. At the end of 1962, *Pravda* listed a total of 90 Communist parties having a claimed membership of 42.5 million. All but 7 million of this figure came from bloc countries. Outside the bloc, Indonesia (approximately 2 million), Italy (between 1.2 and 1.5 million), France (between 240,000 and 430,000), India (150,000), and Cuba (60,000) are supposed to have the largest party memberships.

In Southeast Asia, Burma (October 1953), Malaya (July 1948), the Philippines (June 1957), Thailand (November 1952), and South Vietnam (October 1956) have proscribed the Communist party. However, Communist movements or crypto-Communist parties, whether legal or illegal, operate in all Southeast Asian states.

Burma's Communist movement is divided into three main sections. The official party, known as the Burma Communist Party (BCP), is estimated to have a membership of 1,500. A splinter group, separated from the BCP in 1946 and outlawed since then, is known as the Communist Party (Burma), or CP (B); its membership is held to be about 500. Aboveground, a crypto-Communist movement led by the Burma United Workers Party and the Burma Trade Union Congress received about 5 per cent of almost 8 million votes in the 1960 general election, but failed to elect a single representative to either house of parliament. (Burma's parliament was dissolved on March 9, 1962, by General Ne Win and his Revolutionary Council.) Communist insurgency, although still continuing, is certainly no present threat to the incumbent military regime. From time to time, Communist leaders have sought to "cooperate" with ethnic insurgent groups, such as the Kachins, Shans, and Karens, but they have never succeeded in forging a durable united insurgent front. In the future, however, dissident Kachins and Shans might align themselves with the so-called Free Kachin and Free Thai autonomous movements sponsored by the Chinese Communists and based in Yunnan. The continuing depredations of former Kuomintang troops, numbering up to 4,000, on the Burma-Laos border, is a constant invitation to Chinese Communist intervention in Burma.

Martial law in Thailand, together with the legal ban on any Communist party, has severely curtailed any aboveground Communist activity. There are no known Communists among the membership of the constituent assembly appointed in February 1959. The Thai Communist Party and its companion, the Chinese Communist Party (Thailand), have had little effect on the population. However, the CCP (Thailand) can exploit grievances among the considerable Chinese minority (about 3 million); and both parties together, with assistance from abroad, are now obviously active in the depressed northeastern region. Some 50,000 Vietnamese, refugees from war in French Indochina, live in this section. Many are said to be loyal to Ho Chi Minh. They and the indigenous population, who are ethnically akin to the Laotians, make the area vulnerable to a combination of Chinese, Vietminh, and Pathet Lao subversion. Some guerilla activity has already been encountered. In the interim, the Soviet Union has been alternating threats and cajolements to lure Thailand out of the Southeast Asia Treaty Organization (SEATO).

As of Summer 1963, the disastrous troika coalition which we unwisely accepted as the basis for Laotian peace and neutrality at the Geneva Conference in 1962, continues in jeopardy because of armed Communist attack. Advent of the 1963 rainy season did not halt hostilities. The Vietminh-supported Pathet Lao acquired still more territory during 1962–1963, and have largely invalidated the position of Souvanna Phouma as the neutralist leader of that coalition.

The nature of a coalition government inclusive of a Communist party or movement may have received attention from United States officials before they entered into the 1962 Geneva negotiations, but, if so, the record is not available. Coalition government as usually understood in the West is a temporary combination between or among political parties which retain their distinctive principles, but agree for a period on support for special or well-defined programs. During such a coalition there exists a political truce. In principle, no party of the coalition seeks domination, for that would most probably end the agreement on which the coalition is based. Where such coalitions in Western countries have included the Communists, as for example in France, they have rested upon fairly firm institutional bases and upon rather well-informed national electorates. Even in such instances, coalitions are dangerous in that a Communist party gains access to democratic respectability, and also acquires a degree of power with respect to essential elements of national security, which in the short or long run it seeks to overthrow.

In Southeast Asia, the national and institutional basis for any government—its electorate, party structure other than Communist, and public opinion—has been and still is relatively weak. A determined, well-oriented minority such as a Communist cadre can, therefore, readily exploit a coalition to gain dominance. For what is most important to recognize is the fact that in Communist theory and practice a coalition, where permissible, is not a political truce; it is a united front which remains always to be exploited by the party. "Who dominates whom" and "who destroys whom" are questions which all Communist parties professing loyalty to Leninism must necessarily endeavor to settle in their own favor.[11]

[11] The variations on this theme are endless and hardly need further documentation. Lenin, and after him Stalin, altered the formula slightly as they constantly repeated it: "Who will chase whom away or who will dissolve whom"; who will "smash" whom, "who will defeat whom," etc. See Leites, Nathan, *A Study of Bolshevism* (Glencoe: The Free Press, 1953), pp. 429–449. And Mao Tse-tung, whatever else he may be, regards himself as a Leninist. In his most extended treatment of this theme, at the height of his party's advocacy of the two-stage road to power, he puts forth the need for a "new-democratic state system . . . a united front . . . based on the over-

It is in the light of the foregoing that one may seriously question the wisdom of the 1962 Geneva settlement on Laos. It is probable that any coalition involving a Communist party in an emerging, underdeveloped country severely endangers the non-Communist partners. In Laos, weakest of all Southeast Asian states, and least developed in terms of nationhood, the danger was compounded. The demise of this coalition is highly probable and will likely lead to a still greater loss of Laotian territory.[12] Early armed intervention may yet be able to save the vital Mekong River valley, the royal and administrative capitals of Luang Prabang and Vientiane, and the Laotian panhandle bordering on Thailand, Cambodia, and Vietnam. If this does not occur, if the United States and some of its Asian and other allies do not intervene, the Communist challenge on mainland Southeast Asia will be further advanced into these three latter countries. Effective military resistance to, and interdiction of, Vietminh advances in Laos constitute the present price we must pay for earlier reliance on the folly of coalition with Communists.

Cambodia has a national assembly all of whose members belong to Sihanouk's People's Socialist Community Party. The Communists operate covertly through the Pracheachon Party, which has about 1,000 members and perhaps as many as 30,000 sympathizers. It did not contest the elections. Cambodia is for the time being safe with Sihanouk and his

whelming majority of the people under the leadership of the working class." But he makes clear that "We Communists never conceal our political stand . . . our future or maximum program is to head for socialism and communism." See Mao Tse-tung, *On Coalition Government* (Peking: Foreign Language Press, 1955), pp. 46, 51.

[12] See Trager, Frank N., *The Struggle for Mainland Southeast Asia: Laos, A Pivot* (forthcoming). It should be pointed out, in fairness, that even those government officials who engineered the Souvanna Phouma-led troika were not optimistic about its future. But such Washington official sentiment generally beguiled itself with the view that although the Communists would continue to try to get power, they would do so by political and subversive means. Obviously, they are again wrong. The Communists are using military means.

neutralist policy, which openly balances support from both East and West. Sihanouk has gained added protection because his neighbors, Thailand and Vietnam, which he alleges are his principal "enemies," are defending his flanks. The fall of Laos could change this fairly comfortable picture.

No one knows how many Communists there are in South Vietnam. Estimates of hard-core Communist guerillas circle about the figure of 20,000. Many thousands more are subject to their control, or willingly support them logistically and otherwise. South Vietnam is at present the major focus of active United States counterinsurgency efforts. On the Malayan analogy, each Communist guerilla requires about fifteen (or more) dedicated counterinsurgents. The most optimistic estimates hold that it will take three years to win the war in Vietnam. Undoubtedly military progress has been made since President Kennedy authorized implementation of General Maxwell D. Taylor's 1961 recommendations. More than 12,000 United States military personnel are now serving as advisers and trainers of the Vietnamese armed and paramilitary forces. Reports of political conflict—especially the current mishandling of the Buddhist majority—with the Ngo Dinh Diem regime fall outside the scope of this chapter but merit careful United States action and substantial criticism. The primary objective of Ho Chi Minh, which he has never concealed, is to unify North and South Vietnam under Communist control. A probable interim objective is international Communist recognition of the National Front for the Liberation of South Vietnam, which operates clandestinely although it has been publicly announced in South Vietnam as the only "legitimate" government in the south.

The Malayan Communist Party, predominantly Chinese in character, with an estimated hard-core guerilla membership of about 500, is now confined to the jungle border area between Malaya and Thailand. Whether it has lost its appeal for the almost 40 per cent of Malaya's population which is Chinese, is difficult to ascertain. The twelve-year state of emergency was ended on July 31, 1960. Malaya retains stringent security laws, however, enforced by an able police force which in turn is backed by British-Malayan armed forces.

More dangerous are Communist threats to the proposed Federation of Malaysia, which took shape in 1963. Malaya thus acquired the difficulties inherent in Singapore's illegal MCP, and in the legal but Communist-infiltrated, if not dominated, Barisan Socialis Party (BSP). The latter tactically supports the federation idea, but is working for the downfall of the incumbent People's Action Party government in Singapore, which led Singapore into merger. Compounding this problem is Sino-Indonesian support for the "liberation" of the North Borneo territories. Liu Shao-chi's endorsement of the Indonesian position[13] followed earlier Soviet expression of opposition to the Federation. The Philippines has separately engaged in this fight against Malaya. Whether Indonesia will train and use "volunteers" to support this "war of liberation" or has already used such forces in alliance with indigenous Communists is very much on today's agenda. It is probable that some permanent solution can be found between Manila and Kuala Lumpur. But over the long term, the opposition of Sukarno and Indonesia may not be so easily eliminated.

These complications feed on political uncertainties in the North Borneo territories. Some tribal suspicion of the Malays of Malaya is evident, although the latter are seemingly preferred to the Indonesians. The Chinese-dominated and Communist-infiltrated Sarawak United People's Party (SUPP) fears the loss of the preferred economic and political position hitherto enjoyed by the local Chinese population if Malays from Malaya come into Sarawak. The Partai Rakjat of Brunei (PRB), supported both by Indonesia and the Philippines, launched an abortive revolt in December 1962 against the Sultan of Brunei, while the Sultan himself

[13] See *The New York Times*, April 20, 1963.

objected to the financial conditions attendant upon entering the Federation. Finally, there are supposed to be some 30,000 Indonesian migrants in North Borneo.

The Federation of Malaysia was probably designed to accomplish the following objectives. It would dilute the growing Communist threat in Singapore, chiefly Chinese in composition, in the larger Malay population—anti-Communist and opposed to Chinese domination—of the Federation. It would solve most of Great Britain's remaining colonial problems in Asia, and it would cement the British-Malayan defense arrangement which both the Conservatives and Labour parties have always supported. In a not unusual fashion these days, Malaysia's birth was also dependent upon the continued health, political and biological, of Tengku Abdul Rahman, prime minister of Malaya and leader of its carefully balanced Alliance Party.

The Communist Party of the Philippines (CPP) was declared illegal by a Supreme Court ruling in 1932. This did not prevent its rise and spread illegally and otherwise in the intervening years, until it was specifically outlawed by the Anti-Subversion Act of 1957. Today's estimate gives the CPP some 1,500 to 2,000 members, of whom 300 to 500 are Huks and 300 to 400 are Chinese. There is still a Communist-led insurrectionary movement of some 300 to 500 guerillas located in the mountains of central and southern Luzon. The deterioration of public and economic morale prior to the present Macapagal administration made for a rise in Communist strength and attacks. The CPP had some success at infiltrating non-Communist organizations and winning over various dissidents. However, the Macapagal regime's "New Era" social and economic program, its war on graft and corruption, and its obvious independence in foreign policy have combined to widen the base of the regime's support in the countryside. This, in turn, and the long experience of the armed forces in containing the area of guerilla mobility have again brought about a decline in Communist strength and activity.

Finally, Indonesia is the troubled paradise. Of the 283 members in its appointed parliament, at least 30 are identified as PKI members, and 34 others as Communist representatives from functional groups. Several leading Communists hold office in various top advisory councils. The respectability of the PKI, gained in no small measure as a consequence of Sukarno's public support of the party as a constituent element, with the Nationalist party (PNI) and the Moslem Scholars (NU), in the so-called Nasakom coalition, has added significantly to its membership, now claimed at 2 million. In addition, its influence and controls extend to the largest labor federation in Indonesia, SOBSI, with a claimed membership of 2.7 million strategically organized in transportation, estate agriculture, government employees, and the oil fields. Other Communist-dominated organizations include the Peasants' Front with 3.7 million claimed members, the People's Youth with 1 million, and the Women's Movement with 800,000.[14]

Most probably these totals overlap and do not represent cumulative numbers. But the strength of the Communist movement in Indonesia is, by any count, formidable. In December 1962, Sukarno announced that the state of emergency, imposed on Indonesia during the crisis precipitated by the rebellion of the so-called Revolutionary Government of the Indonesian Republic (PRRI) in 1958, would be lifted in May 1963. If this relaxation is really implemented, political parties may again be permitted to campaign; and if this were to come to pass, the PKI, unless thwarted by the army, might achieve a crucial minority position without whose support no other party could rule. Indeed, an electoral victory for the PKI cannot be wholly discounted. In this event, a severe contest among the Communists, the non-Communist sectors of the armed forces, and those Indonesians led by the charisma of Sukarno would most probably follow.

[14] See also Pauker, Guy J., "Indonesia: Internal Development or External Expansion?" *Asian Survey*, Vol. 3, No. 2, February 1963, pp. 69–75. Pauker's figures vary upwards from those made available by the Department of State.

This overview of indigenous Communist movements in the several Southeast Asian countries leads to the following summary conclusions, presented in no rank order.

1. In Burma and Cambodia, indigenous Communist strength lacks the internal power and sufficient external bloc support needed seriously to affect the ruling governments. The BCP and CP (B) appear to be at their lowest ebb since Burmese Communists formally organized their party in the early 1940's. Burma's danger stems from other domestic and external factors. The Pracheachon Party of Cambodia, through which the Communists work, alone of all Southeast Asian Communist parties, has not yet tried the path of insurrection.

2. The Philippines and Malaya (apart from the Federation of Malaysia) have quite thoroughly but not absolutely liquidated indigenous Communist insurrectionary activity. These governments, the Philippines even more than Malaya, need not suffer from a local Communist revival if they continue to register significant political, economic, and social gains at home. Malaya's Communist problem inheres in the delicate ethnic balance of Malaya's plural society.

3. The Federation of Malaysia, chiefly Singapore and the North Borneo territories, face a potential Indonesian "confrontation" [15] in conjunction with an indigenous Communist revolutionary threat. Chinese Communists, active in Singapore and in the Borneo territories, have links with Peking. British-Malayan forces have already been used to quell one rebellion in Borneo and may well be called on to maintain security within the new Federation.

4. South Vietnam and Laos are in varying stages of active or "second stage" Communist insurgency supported primarily by North Vietnam. Hanoi, in turn, enjoys Sino-Soviet support.

5. Thailand, without any indigenous Communist move-

[15] See van der Kroef, Justus M., "Indonesia, Malaya and The North Borneo Crisis," *Asian Survey*, Vol. 3, No. 4, April 1963, pp. 173–181, for a useful review of recent events.

ment of consequence, is experiencing the first thrusts from Hanoi-dominated Communist cadres.

6. Indonesian Communist strength presents four possibilities: (a) a Kerala-type electoral victory promoted to national proportions; (b) a Czechoslovakian type of take-over, in reality a not too violent form of coup d'état; (c) a new and far-reaching civil war, the scope of which will vastly dwarf the recent PRRI affair or the 1948 Madiun revolt; and (d) a new alliance among Sukarno, Mohammed Hatta, the PNI, the NU, and the non-Communist sectors of the armed forces, with Sukarno's charisma helping to withdraw popular support from the PKI, while Hatta or someone like him attends to the economic reconstruction of the country. In the distortion usually exemplified by personalizing historical forces, four men may determine the outcome of this difficult period in Indonesia's fretful postindependence course: President Sukarno; General A. H. Nasution; D. N. Aidit, chairman of the PKI, who for guidance and support ostensibly looks to Moscow; and his supposed competitor, M. H. Lukman, vice-chairman of the PKI, who ostensibly turns to Peking.[16]

THE IMPLICATIONS OF THE SINO-SOVIET DEBATE FOR SOUTHEAST ASIA

Millions of words have already appeared on the Sino-Soviet "dispute," "rift," "conflict," "schism," or "break," which in my view should more properly be called a "debate." Serious students of communism have presented various interpretations of this phenomenon across a spectrum which ranges from those who view it as a bloc strategy carried out

[16] This view of the respective positions of Aidit and Lukman is held by Pauker, Guy J., op. cit., p. 73. For the opposite view, holding that Aidit has gone farther than most in declaring for Peking as against Moscow, see Lowenthal, Richard, "Schism Among the Faithful," Problems of Communism, Vol. 11, No. 1, January–February 1962, p. 12.

in different ways by Moscow and Peking or a form of planned public antagonism coordinated on a global basis; to those who see it as the forerunner of a conciliar model of world Communist states and autonomous parties held together by a common ideology and by successive compromises among various national and group interests; to those who hold that the centralized world party, created by Lenin and subjected to the ideological authority and organizational discipline of a single center, has gone forever.

Still others see the debate as a passing and familiar item in the internal life of Communist parties that will disappear when Khrushchev, Mao Tse-tung, and their contemporary epigones yield to inevitable death. Who will run the show has always been a basis for party conflict. But in this view, the ideological and organizational ties that bind and advance the movement are more lasting than the terms of the debate because the Communist states and parties need the reinforcement and protection of solidarity if they are to weather continuing crises. The writer holds this view.[17]

Whatever be the terminal interpretation of this phenomenon, there is a wide consensus as to the major points supposedly at issue in the dispute. Presumably, (a) Moscow supports, and Peking rejects, the concept of peaceful coexistence with the "imperialist camp," that is, the free world; (b) Moscow supports, and Peking rejects, the concept that imperialist wars or general wars are no longer inevitable; (c) Moscow in the main supports, and Peking in the main rejects, the possibility of a peaceful road to power, that is, of a peaceful transition of capitalist states and "national democracies" (mainly the ex-colonial and neutralist states)

[17] See Trager, Frank N., "Communist China: The New Imperialism," *Current History*, Vol. 41, No. 241, September 1961, pp. 136–140. In this connection it is instructive to reread Liu Shao-chi, *On Inner Party Struggle* (Peking: Foreign Language Press, no date). This July 1941 lecture makes clear that such struggle "is absolutely necessary and cannot be avoided . . . [it protects] the purity and independence of the Party." The problem is "how to conduct" such struggle. These views are also applicable to interparty struggle, which has characterized the Communist movement since its beginnings.

to socialism; and (*d*) Moscow supports the principle of continuous interpretation of Marxism-Leninism in the light of new "objective conditions," while Peking rejects this as hated "revisionism" and calls for true or orthodox Leninism.

These are the allegedly high or "principled" bases for the dispute which the Chinese have aired so thoroughly. But perhaps even more serious have been a number of strategic and tactical issues. These relate to bloc allocation of scarce resources to member states and others; to the sharing of nuclear power; to the contest for ideological primacy between Mao and Khrushchev; to the occurrence of a severe famine in China following Khrushchev's scornful and accurate prediction of failure for China's "Great Leap Forward"; to Soviet "caution" about, and Chinese "recklessness" toward, nuclear brinkmanship and local wars; to Chinese "caution" about, and Soviet "recklessness" toward, the de-Stalinization campaign, the treatment of Albania, and so forth.

The dispute is current. But how has it affected, and how does it continue to affect Southeast Asia? Recently, Robert A. Scalapino prepared a scoreboard of Asian Communist responses to the debate. He concludes that in the struggle for ideological and political leadership, "Khrushchev is not at this point doing well. At present, he has the upper hand in Outer Mongolia and Ceylon. . . . Perhaps he can gain a lasting advantage in India. . . . But everywhere else . . . in Indonesia, North Korea, North Viet Nam, Japan, Burma, Thailand and Malaya—he has not been able to get acceptance of his position on Albania, de-Stalinization or other various issues, large and small. In general, the stance of these parties is one of non-alignment, but often a non-alignment that favors Peking." [18] Scalapino believes that the Asian Communist parties have more in common with Communist China and its problems of development than they

[18] Scalapino, Robert A., "Moscow, Peking and the Communist Parties of Asia," *Foreign Affairs*, Vol. 41, No. 2, January 1963, p. 337.

have with Moscow. He is aware, however, that Asian Communists are also unwilling to lose their "independence" to Peking. "Thus Sino-Soviet differences offer [them] . . . [the] opportunity . . . to secure greater independence through non-alignment; [and] the threat [of] internal schism." [19]

I believe that Scalapino has accurately gauged the prevailing public temper of the Southeast Asian Communist parties. That is, they prefer to remain nonaligned in the debate. But if they had to choose, I do not think that the choice would uniformly fall to Peking. With the exception of the Malayan Communist Party and its associated groups in Singapore and the North Borneo territories, whose membership is overwhelmingly Chinese, no party aspiring to mass leadership in Southeast Asia can risk an embrace with Peking. The feared and distrusted economic role of the overseas Chinese, the memories of an historically aggressive China under any regime from the Han dynasties to Mao, their "march to the tropics," are too prominent for close political association. This is as true for Indonesians as it is for Burmese, and indeed for all the other ethnic groups of mainland Southeast Asia. On the other hand the Southeast Asian fear or caution with respect to Peking does not necessarily promote, as for other reasons it has promoted in India, a favorable posture toward Moscow. The Communist parties of Southeast Asia will continue to seek whatever support they can get from both Moscow and Peking. It is worth noting that since the Communist rebellions of 1948, there have been no splits in the Communist parties of Southeast Asia as there were in the era of the Stalin-Trotsky struggle.

More important than the momentary stance of the Southeast Asian parties on the debate is the relationship of Moscow and Peking to the governments of Southeast Asia. That relationship has been peculiarly synchronized since the end of World War II. Moscow pursued its hard line toward these newly independent countries until approximately the end of Stalin's life. During all this period, both before and

[19] *Ibid.*, p. 342.

after the Chinese Communists came to power, their policy toward Southeast Asia publicly and operationally supported Moscow's. When Moscow changed in 1953–1954, so did Peking. And the Sino-Soviet bloc has not altered its similar if not concerted policy toward Southeast Asian countries since then.

Concern with the divisive terms of the Sino-Soviet debate should not obscure the similarities of Chinese and Soviet activity in the several Southeast Asian states. If Peking now charges Moscow with improper, excessive regard for national "bourgeois" or nonbloc states, Peking has also demonstrated, with Moscow since 1954, extraordinary consideration for neutralist Burma and Cambodia. If Peking charges Moscow with less than proper zeal for wars of national liberation, Moscow as well as Peking can point to its direct aid to the Pathet Lao and its material support for Hanoi as the major and appropriate instruments for promoting such wars in Laos and Vietnam. If Moscow has supplied the Indonesian government with $1.1 billion in military and related goods and services, Peking concluded with that government, perhaps for the first time in Chinese history, a treaty which recognized the possibility of Chinese becoming citizens of another country; and Peking followed Moscow in supporting Indonesia's adventurist policy in the Malaysian issue. Neither Peking nor Moscow appears to have found ways tangibly to support the Communist rebels in the Philippines and Malaya. And finally, both Peking and Moscow, while advancing considerable government-to-government aid and maintaining trade relations with Burma, found ways to carry on espionage and subversive actions[20] in the electoral campaigns of that country and provided training facilities for Burmese Communists in Yunnan.

In sum there is little, if any, evidence that the Sino-Soviet debate has in any material way inhibited the international

[20] See, for example, Kaznacheev, Aleksandr, *Inside a Soviet Embassy, Experiences of a Russian Diplomat in Burma* (Philadelphia: Lippincott, 1962).

advance of Communist policy in that strategic area, Southeast Asia. The debate may be real, but its reality is about the tactics of how to "bury" us, to use Khrushchev's vivid word. The "us" in this context not only applies to the Western democracies, it also applies to the eight still-free states of Southeast Asia—seven soon if we fail Laos—and six potentially if the danger in Indonesia is not thwarted by Indonesians who have once fought to gain their freedom and may have to fight again to preserve it.

To support this view of the Communist challenge in Southeast Asia, one does not have to argue for a supposed total identity of Sino-Soviet objectives, strategies, and tactics in the area, that is, for world Communist monolithicism. It may be readily admitted, as indicated above, that China, as China, has had historical interests in gaining sway in Southeast Asia which historically Russia never had, and that these historical interests to some extent color Chinese Communist policy perspectives. Also, Chinese regimes, past and present, have been concerned about the 12 to 14 million overseas Chinese in Southeast Asia, while in this sense there are no "overseas" Russians. China, furthermore, is an Asian power both geographically and racially, and gains thereby, it is thought, some advantage from such slogans as "Asia for the Asians"; while the Soviet Union, although in part Asian and inhabited in part by a Mongoloid population, is not regarded as a fellow Asian power by the Southeast Asians. But these differences between the Soviet Union and Communist China do not automatically favor the latter. Again it can be argued that such advantages as Peking presumably enjoys in pressing its Communist policies over those of Moscow create equal and opposite disadvantages among Southeast Asians who have historically feared a rampant China, distrusted the overseas Chinese, and been burned for some time to come by the Japanese variant of China's Nanyang or South Seas drive and racial slogans.

In brief, the presence of some variable interests between Moscow and Peking in Southeast Asia confers no significant advantage to either in terms of their ideological interparty debate. On the other hand, the variations help make it possible for Moscow and Peking to advance their overriding Communist objectives. Separately or together, they acquire more strings to their respective bows for the greater success of the Communist symphony. And, no matter what temporary cacophony may be forthcoming from the Communist orchestra(s) because of uncertainty about the conductor(s), there should be no doubt that the basic purpose of the exercise in both Moscow and Peking is to overwhelm, that is, to communize Southeast Asia. Southeast Asian nationalism, which was capable of bringing about independence, is not yet sufficiently strong in itself and by itself to withstand the continuing pressures of the Communist threat. Southeast Asian neutralism in Burma, Cambodia, and Indonesia has bought a little time. On the other hand, neutralism and coalition government have advanced the Communist timetable in Laos, and endangered all of mainland Southeast Asia. Island Southeast Asia, that is, Malaya and the Philippines, presumably benefits respectively from defense agreements with the United Kingdom and the United States.

There may, indeed, be ideological, military, and economic restraints on Sino-Soviet strategy, but the debate has not produced any erosion in the capability of the Communist countries to continue their avowed policies in Southeast Asia and elsewhere. Furthermore, if a split—a real break— were to occur between Moscow and Peking, the task of countering Communist China's aggressiveness in Southeast Asia or the Soviet Union's effort to reattain paramountcy in the area, would most probably prove to be a greater burden on all anti-Communist forces, our own included.

7

UNITED STATES DIPLOMACY

IN SOUTHEAST ASIA:

THE LIMITS OF POLICY

JOHN M. ALLISON

ANY DISCUSSION OF UNITED
States diplomacy in Southeast Asia must begin by defining
what such diplomacy is supposed to do. What, in other
words, are the objectives of the United States in the area
which diplomacy is supposed to advance? It may be useful
to restate briefly what these objectives are and what they
have been over the years.

In an article in the *Foreign Service Journal* for July 1962,
Deputy Under Secretary of State U. Alexis Johnson gives
what must be considered an authoritative statement:

It has been recognized as never before that what we in
the United States are seeking in the less-developed world
is not the building of military forces for their own sake,
or economic development for its own sake, or pro-American propaganda for its own sake, but rather the use of all
of the available resources for assisting these new nations

in building the kind of society and government that can maintain itself, develop in step with the modern world and, above all, remain free from domination or control by Communist forces hostile to us. United States interests do not require satellites, colonies, or subservience to all of our ideas. I am convinced that our interests are well served if foreign peoples and lands are truly independent, and if that remains the objective they seek for themselves. Thus we have a basis for truly mutual cooperation.[1]

Mr. Johnson's statement is doubly interesting when we realize that it is a modern affirmation, attuned to modern conditions and problems, of a United States interest which goes back many years. Almost forty years ago, before there was any Communist threat in Asia of any significance, an American scholar, Tyler Dennett, concluded his famous work, *Americans in Eastern Asia,* with the following statement:

> . . . the United States is so situated that American interests in Asia are best promoted by the growth of strong, prosperous and enlightened Asiatic states. Indeed it is difficult for an American to believe that the repression or weakening of any part of Asia is a benefit to any power. The United States is committed to its policy by geographical, economic, and political facts, and in the same measure is also bound to a policy of cooperation with all powers which sincerely profess a similar purpose.[2]

As we shall see later, one of the limitations on the effectiveness of American diplomacy in Southeast Asia has been the tendency from time to time of American leaders and publicists to narrow the scope of our objectives as set forth in these two statements and to express them in such a way as to weaken the basis for the "truly mutual cooperation" mentioned by Mr. Johnson.

[1] Johnson, U. Alexis, "Internal Defense and the Foreign Service," *Foreign Service Journal,* Vol. 39, No. 7, July 1962, p. 20.
[2] Dennett, Tyler, *Americans in Eastern Asia* (New York: Macmillan, 1922), p. 680.

While the scope of diplomacy today has expanded far beyond the range of activities contemplated by those who set up the first codification of diplomatic rules of procedure and protocol at the Congress of Vienna in 1815, it is useful to remember that the original function of the diplomat remains. In spite of all that has been added to his task, diplomacy is still, as the *Oxford English Dictionary* says, "the management of international relations by negotiation." A somewhat broader definition has been given by Sir Ernest Satow when he says that diplomacy is "the application of intelligence and tact to the conduct of official relations between the governments of independent States." [3]

Satow's definition contains factors which are often forgotten and which, when forgotten, often cause confusion. The task of the diplomat is to conduct *official* relations between *governments* of *independent* states. In other words, the diplomat is trying to persuade an independent government to take action in line with American objectives or to refrain from taking action detrimental to those objectives. Today we realize that in performing this function he uses a variety of tools and methods never contemplated by the diplomat thirty years ago. He makes much greater effort to make American policy and objectives popular among the people of the country to which he is accredited, for today, in the final analysis, power and decision often rest with the masses. But nevertheless, in the end it is a government which must act, whether solely as a result of its own determination or as a result of mass pressure. The diplomat who forgets that his primary task is to influence governments takes great risks.

But the diplomat who interprets "government" too narrowly, or who makes no attempt to understand the forces which move governments, or who, because he is too traditionally minded, fails to use all the tools available in the

---

[3] Quoted in Nicolson, Harold, *Diplomacy*, 2nd ed. (London: Oxford University Press, 1950), p. 50.

modern diplomatic kit bag, also takes great risks. Perhaps his are the greater.

While the modern ambassador must remember that the traditional diplomatic functions of reporting, negotiation, and representation remain of great importance, he must be prepared to cope with the comparatively new instruments of diplomacy. Economic aid and technical assistance, information services, and educational and cultural exchange programs are the diplomatic instruments with which he will probably be most directly concerned. However, in many areas, particularly in the troubled, transitional region of Southeast Asia, he may well be concerned also with military aid programs, counterinsurgency activity, and even the problems of psychological warfare. In addition to all this, the ambassador in Southeast Asia must be aware of his own country's monetary policies and trade programs and how they affect the economies of the emerging nations of Asia, which are so dependent upon world prices of the raw materials that make up their principal export resource.

In considering how the modern ambassador and his staff use these new tools of diplomacy as well as the older ones, it is well to think for a moment of the one great limiting factor with which all diplomats of all countries are faced, whether in Europe, Latin America, Africa, or Asia. This is the fact, often forgotten or not sufficiently realized, that foreign affairs are, as Sir Harold Nicolson, the British diplomat and author, has so often stressed, *foreign affairs*. Americans seem to be more prone than others to overlook this vital factor. During the settlement and development of our own continent over the past two centuries, we have become so accustomed to solving difficult problems by our own efforts and our own decisions that we find it difficult to believe that there are areas of the world where our writ does not run. The facts that other nations have their own ideas of what they want to do and how they want to do it, and that we cannot order them around, are often frustrating to the zealous American who is certain he knows best what needs to be done. This factor is particularly important in dealing with the new nations of Southeast Asia. At a time in world development when the older nations of the West are beginning to realize that in the modern world *interdependence* is of at least equal importance to *independence,* the newer nations, which have but recently emerged from colonialism, are keenly sensitive to their independence and extremely suspicious of any acts of Western nations which could even remotely be considered as limiting it.

It is in such areas that the Western diplomat does well to remember Sir Ernest Satow's definition of diplomacy as the conduct of relations "between the governments of independent States." This desire of the Southeast Asian nations to be independent is, I believe, the root reason why so many of them insist on following a policy of neutralism or non-alignment. The United States has learned from two world wars that neutrality is impossible, but the new nations of Southeast Asia have not had the same experience. The two world wars, which taught us the folly of neutralism, in the eyes of many Asians made possible the success of their struggle for independence; and they have no intention of reversing the process by becoming involved, directly or indirectly, in the power blocs of their former masters. Even those Asian nations, such as Thailand and the Philippines, which have allied themselves with the West, have their own ideas about how the alliance should be conducted and are jealous of their own independence.

This is a deep-seated feeling which we ignore or harshly criticize at our peril. At one time the United States seemed to understand this Asian feeling, and we began to reap the rewards of this understanding. During the last year of President Truman's administration, in my capacity as Assistant Secretary of State for the Far East, I visited the capitals of all the nations of Southeast Asia, stopping first in Manila. This was at a time when the late President Elpidio Quirino of the Philippines was strongly urging the formation of a Pacific pact along the lines of the North Atlantic Treaty.

Some of our newspapers and public men supported this idea as a great barrier to Communist expansion in Asia. On the other hand, we knew from our experience while negotiating the Japanese peace treaty, and from more recent reports, that there was considerable opposition to this among the newer nations of Southeast Asia, particularly Indonesia and Burma, and great fear that the United States would use high-pressure methods to get them to join such an alliance.

Prior to leaving Washington I had an interview with President Truman, during which he gave me authority to tell the governments and peoples of Indonesia and Burma that the United States fully understood their desire to be neutral and to build up their own strength and settle their own internal problems before getting involved in international problems. Mr. Truman went even further. He exclaimed, "We did exactly the same thing when we were young!" I was able to use Mr. Truman's statement to good effect in press conferences and private talks throughout the area. An article in the Rangoon newspaper, *New Light of Burma*, on October 14, 1952, typifies the reaction to this attitude. The paper said:

> We are much heartened because of the statement made by the U.S. Assistant Secretary of State clarifying the U.S. Government's attitude in regard to the neutral policy adopted by most Asian nations. . . . We are much encouraged because the Americans now seem to understand more of the real aspirations of the Asian peoples.[4]

Unfortunately, in the following years a more aggressive and less tolerant attitude toward Asian neutralism was adopted in Washington, and much of the previous good will was replaced by a renewal of deep suspicion of our motives.

If United States diplomacy is to succeed and have real influence among the emerging nations, we must recognize the limiting factor of this jealous guarding of their inde-

[4] *New Light of Burma* (Rangoon), October 14, 1952.

pendence with its resultant neutralism. Instead of railing at such an attitude and charging that it plays into the hands of the Communists we should, I believe, do everything possible at this stage in the development of these nations to strengthen real neutrality. It is encouraging that our government is at present apparently aware of this, and that Deputy Under Secretary Johnson, in the statement quoted in the beginning of this essay, also recognized that "our interests are well served if foreign peoples and lands are truly independent." While keeping this in mind we must at the same time not neglect the interests of Thailand and the Philippines, which have gone beyond neutralism and have shown a willingness to take risks for the free world.

When the new nations of Southeast Asia opposed a Pacific pact in 1952, it was not alone from their fear that it would compromise their independence. It was also the result of the ignorance and often the indifference of the nations of the area concerning each other. I found that the people of Rangoon knew more about and often had greater understanding of what was happening in London, halfway around the world, than they did of Bangkok, thirty minutes distant by air. Much has been done to remedy this situation during the last ten years, but much remains to be done. Regionalism as yet has little hold on the area. This again is a limitation on what the United States can do in the diplomatic field, and suggests that grandiose plans for the area as a whole are premature, or at least must be approached with great caution. It also suggests that our aid programs, both economic and military, should be tailored to fit individual nations, and that just because something has proved good in Indonesia does not mean that it will be equally good in Thailand or Burma.

The difficulties inherent in a regional approach, while real and of great importance, do not necessarily mean that no progress can be made in this direction. The United States has never concealed its hope that eventually the nations of Asia would recognize the value of some form of collective security. It was hoped at the time the Japanese peace treaty was negotiated, that it might be possible to develop an over-all Pacific security system. However, for the reasons mentioned earlier, this proved impossible. In place of such an alliance there were negotiated separate bilateral mutual security and defense agreements with Japan and the Philippines, and a tripartite pact with Australia and New Zealand, all of which were signed on or about the same time as the Japanese peace treaty. President Truman referred to these arrangements as "initial steps" in the development of a Pacific security system.

Since that time the only progress that has been made has been the formation in 1954 of the Southeast Asia Treaty Organization. SEATO is discussed at length elsewhere, but it can be said here that it is by no means a forerunner of an over-all Pacific pact. The three potentially most important non-Communist nations of Asia, Japan, India, and Indonesia, are not members, and there is little or no likelihood of their becoming members during the next few years, if ever. SEATO has undoubtedly served useful purposes, particularly in restraining overt, large-scale aggression, and should not lightly be discarded. It would seem, however, that United States diplomacy would do well to recognize its limitations, and not attempt to build up its strength and prestige if this must be done at the expense of increasing mistrust and suspicion of American motives among those Asian nations which look upon any form of military alliance as a threat to their independence and sovereignty.

If United States diplomacy cannot for the present look forward to the early formation of an over-all Pacific security system, it can continue to help promote "the growth of strong, prosperous and enlightened Asiatic states" as advocated by Tyler Dennett. In doing so it will find that, while there is still only an embryonic regional consciousness, there are certain factors common to much of the area of Southeast Asia which largely determine what can and cannot be accomplished. The one factor that I believe most significant is that since the end of World War II, none of the nations of Southeast Asia, with the exception of Malaya and the Philippines, has developed democratic, representative governments such as we know and such as many of our leaders had expected.

What do we see throughout the region? Thailand has a military dictatorship again. For the second time in recent years, Burma has discarded a parliamentary government in favor of rule by the army. Indonesia has what President Sukarno calls a "guided democracy," with elections proscribed and political parties thrust into the background. In the three non-Communist states of former French Indochina there are varying degrees of representative government, but considerable progress needs to be made before they can be considered to possess what we normally think of as the essentials of modern, democratic government.

Not only do these countries not have our style of democratic government, but most of them are deeply suspicious of the free enterprise democracy of the West. In many countries the most conservative leaders are socialists. This is caused, as the television commercials say, by "a combination of ingredients." The free enterprise, capitalist system of the West is equated with colonialism, and hence is considered a threat to freedom and independence. The weak, unbalanced economies of the area require a large measure of government planning and guidance, if not control, and private enterprise capitalism seems to be opposed to this. And then, many of the leaders of these new countries are men who are much better at leading revolutions than at carrying out the thousand and one dull, unromantic tasks necessary to building a modern state. They often appear to think of themselves in the role of the "god-king" as it existed in the early history of many Southeast Asian nations. As Lucian Pye has pointed out:

> Once the primary objectives of state action were established . . . men did not have to spend their time looking for new problems to be solved or disagreeing over what

173

new policies might be needed to ensure a better world; they could devote their energies to seeking prestige and power.[5]

Anyone who has spent any time in Southeast Asia could easily name more than one contemporary leader whose actions, consciously or unconsciously, follow the old traditions. Modern, private enterprise capitalism, with its emphasis on efficiency and progress, is not in tune with the old ideas. When efficiency and tradition clash, it is often efficiency that is the loser. The state has been established; independence has been gained. The search for and maintenance of prestige and power are now the important objectives, not the creation of an economically viable state.

It is only recently that United States policy has seemed to take into account the effect of historical and cultural factors on the modern development of these emerging nations. We have too often assumed that the leaders as well as the masses would be enamored by our success in building the world's most prosperous country and would, at least in broad outline, wish to follow our example. We have often misjudged the interests as well as the capabilities of the leaders. There is danger that in our commendable desire to build a better and a more stable world as quickly as possible, we shall also misjudge the masses.

In our efforts to help build strong, economically viable, and truly independent states in Southeast Asia, we have been greatly influenced by the increasingly articulate leaders of these countries, and we have noted the rush to the larger cities of the country people. We are constantly being told of the "revolution of rising expectations," and that the peoples of the ex-colonies are on the march. But those of us who have lived and worked among these people for any length of time know that the social organization of their nations is still largely based on the family and the village.

[5] Pye, Lucian, "The Politics of Southeast Asia," in Almond, Gabriel A., and Coleman, James S., eds., *The Politics of the Developing Areas* (Princeton: Princeton University Press, 1960), p. 79.

We know that in all countries of Southeast Asia, agriculture is still the major or sole source of income of at least 50 per cent of the people and, in some countries, 90 per cent. We know that the "rising expectations" are, in the main, confined to a small stratum of the population at the top, the elite who have had an opportunity to get a Western or semi-Western education and to observe the progress of more modern nations. And while many of the people may be "on the march" to a more modern world, an equal if not great number are "on the march" back to what they have always known and away from the strange new ideas from abroad.

What we can hope to accomplish in building stable societies in this part of the world is strictly limited by these facts. Too often we have ignored or not given sufficient thought to the kind of society we were working in. We have initiated programs which were far too advanced to be successful. With what result? For example, in Indonesia, which has received more than $2 billion in international aid in the last twelve years, we find that central Java, once a great rice exporter, is now dependent upon surplus American agricultural products, and that while the official foreign exchange rate is 45 rupiahs to the dollar, the unofficial rate is more than a thousand.

There is some evidence that this situation is coming to be more fully understood. Certainly there have been plenty of warnings. Ambassador Galbraith in his short but suggestive book *Economic Development in Perspective* cogently states the case:

> In short, on even the most preliminary view of the problem, effective government, education, and social justice emerge as critically important. In many countries, in diagnosing the barriers to advance, it is lack of these that is of critical importance. And it follows that until these barriers are removed little will come from capital investment and technical assistance. While plans may be big on paper they will be small in result.[6]

[6] Galbraith, John Kenneth, *Economic Development in Perspective* (Cambridge: Harvard University Press, 1962), pp. 9–10.

Too often American diplomacy has started at the wrong end in using these new tools of technical assistance and economic aid. In most cases, while money, foreign technicians, and foreign products are needed, the greatest need is trained men. The beginning of effective aid is often schools and teachers, and if they are not forthcoming in sufficient quantity, anything else supplied from abroad may well be wasted.

And it will not be sufficient for the schools and the teachers merely to turn the local peasants into modern technicians. If progress is to be made in the field of economic development, the building of a modern free society, changes will have to be brought about, as Kenneth Neff, Southeast Asian specialist in the United States Office of Education, says, "in the behavior patterns and attitudes of the people." [7] Technicians will not be effective if they do not have a position of honor and respect in their community. If the only people with status are the lawyers and politicians and army officers, it will be hard to get young men to become mechanics or electricians. Vocational schools must approach the same prestige as academic schools in the developing countries. What this means for American diplomacy is also revolutionary. As Mr. Neff has pointed out:

Any thought the United States might have of influencing and assisting the economic growth of a country without altering the social and political structure is wishful thinking.[8]

This is difficult medicine to swallow. It goes against one of the most cherished precepts of international conduct, that we shall not interfere in the internal affairs of other nations.

Having spent over thirty years in the more traditional avenues of the conduct of international relations, I have considerable sympathy for the conventional diplomat who has been trained from youth to keep "hands off" the internal

[7] Neff, Kenneth, "Education and the Forces of Change," *International Development Review*, Vol. 4, No. 1, March 1962, p. 23.
[8] *Ibid.*, p. 22.

problems of other nations. Certainly a heavyhanded interference accompanied by a "father knows best" attitude will
do more harm than good. But in the transitional world of
Southeast Asia the mere fact that the United States is there
at all, with its economic and military aid programs, constitutes interference in one form or another. It would be
better to recognize this fact and make certain that our interference is wisely directed, is sensitive to the customs and
egos of the peoples involved, and is kept to the minimum
necessary to accomplish its objectives. It will also be well to
remember that while some interference is inevitable and
probably necessary, there are limits beyond which it cannot go. These limits will differ in each country and in the
different fields of economic aid, military aid, and cultural
and social change. Here again it must be remembered that
foreign affairs are *foreign* affairs. John D. Montgomery has
well expressed the problem:

> The true independence of countries receiving U.S. aid is
> nowhere better shown than when the United States tries
> to insist upon some well-meant reform. There are no means
> of forcing governments into efficiency and few means of
> persuading them. Withdrawing aid from any basic joint
> program is self-defeating, and below the level of with-
> drawal sanctions scarcely exist.[9]

In the field of cultural and educational exchange we often
see examples of effective interference in internal affairs, and
at the same time examples of the limitations surrounding
this field. Every American embassy educational officer has
experienced the frustration of picking well-qualified, able
young people for special training in the United States, only
to have them turned down because they were politically
suspect by an ultrasensitive regime, or because some cabinet
minister's favorite nephew was considered by the government a more acceptable recipient of the award. If progress
is to be made, even in this vital and supposedly nonpolitical

[9] Montgomery, John D., *The Politics of Foreign Aid* (New York:
Praeger, 1962), p. 148.

field, compromises will have to be made. The number of able and dedicated people to whom it is possible to give advanced training will for some time to come be limited by the number of the "specially privileged" we deem it expedient to accept. Again we must remember our object is to influence governments.

These problems can be overcome, at least in part, if our diplomats of all kinds, Foreign Service officers, aid and information officers alike, remember the necessity of considering the problems of the local officials they are dealing with. Often the local official will understand and be sympathetic to American objectives, but he has to contend with his superiors who may not be as advanced as he is. The American must make it as easy for the local official as possible. In a recent conversation with a young, American-educated Thai official who has had much to do with American officials in his country, he maintained that not once in all his experience had an American official said to him, "We wish to do so and so. How can this be done with least embarrassment or difficulty for you?" Instead, the usual approach was, "If such and such is not done, we will have to report to your superiors that we are not getting cooperation," or, "Congress will make us withdraw the money." I submit this is not the way to win friends and influence people. The local official has to live with his people and his government; his way of doing things may not be our way, but with good will and flexibility it should be possible to work matters out, perhaps not perfectly, but well enough. Our officials might well remember that the perfect is often the enemy of the good.

In great degree, this situation is but one facet of a problem which exists in many countries, but which is particularly acute in the nations of Southeast Asia. That is the great suspicion and distrust felt by the regime or the man in power for those who have any but the most formal and distant relations with members of the opposition. American diplomats are often criticized for concentrating too much attention on the government in power, and knowing nothing of the "next government." In countries with well-established governments of long standing, it is possible for a diplomat to know not only the present government leaders but also many of their potential successors. Certainly the American ambassador and his staff in London should and do have cordial relations with many members of the Labour Party, now out of power. They can do this without the present Conservative government thinking that they are plotting its overthrow.

In Southeast Asia it is not so simple. The leaders of practically all of these nations, with the exception of Malaya and the Philippines, have come to power through revolution or some form of extralegal activity. They hold their positions by, at best, semi-police-state methods. The tradition of a loyal opposition does not exist. It is in these countries that the diplomat must continually remember that his job is to conduct "relations between governments." If he is to have influence with the existing government and any degree of success in advancing American objectives, any action which even remotely could be construed as flirting with the opposition could be fatal.

An article in the Western Edition of *The New York Times,* datelined Saigon, February 14, 1963, gives a concrete example of the problem American officials are up against even in dealing with a country in which they are actively helping the regime in power. The article points out that American civil and military officials have become increasingly involved in a behind-the-scenes role in the outlying districts of Vietnam in an attempt to strengthen and make more effective the Ngo Dinh Diem government. The writer of these articles details some of the successes of the Americans, but reports that the processes of change they have brought about are just beginning, and that continuing progress will not be easy. He attributes this fact to the "basic uneasiness between the two allies in this joint effort." He then says:

The South Vietnamese Government remains in part suspicious of the American presence and motives here and extremely wary of a possible American-inspired coup.[10]

American policy in Indonesia will suffer for some time to come, in spite of recent changes for the better and visits of such prominent Americans as the President's brother, because of the conviction held, rightly or wrongly, by Sukarno and many other prominent Indonesian leaders, that certain agencies of the United States government gave encouragement and material support to the rebels who in 1957 and 1958 attempted to take over the government.

This does not mean that the American diplomat should make no effort to know what he can of the opposition and to be in a position to predict with some accuracy its future actions and prospects. It only means that action in this field is among the most sensitive and delicate the diplomat will be called upon to perform. He must constantly be aware of the dangers and be certain that the results he may obtain are fully worth the risks involved. A diplomat who knows the people and the country where he is working, and who has the necessary sensitivity, should be able to evolve means of achieving this objective, providing he keeps from becoming emotionally involved in the feuds and rivalries surrounding him.

In attempting to learn what is going on in outlying districts and keep in close touch with "grass roots" opinion, some diplomats may be tempted, where possible, to make use of that newest instrument of American foreign policy, the Peace Corps. I believe this temptation should be avoided like the plague. While the Peace Corps is certainly an arm of American foreign policy, it is not, and should not, be involved in the "official relations between governments," which is the proper function of the traditional Foreign Service. After considerable initial skepticism, I have come to the conclusion that there is a real and worthwhile role

[10] *The New York Times,* Western Edition, February 15, 1963, p. 3.

for the Peace Corps to play. The traditional Foreign Service must, because of the nature of its responsibilities, deal primarily with officials and the leading members of the community who influence officials. They have little time or energy left, if they properly carry out their normal duties, for the type of "people-to-people" activity which has now become so popular. The Peace Corps can and does perform this function with considerable success. Their work complements the work of the regular Foreign Service, and the two together make a rounded whole of foreign relations activity such as we have never had before. But because of the great sensitivity of the leaders and governments of the nations of Southeast Asia, which has just been discussed, any attempt to make use of the Peace Corps outside its normal functions could be fatal.

Before passing on to what might be called self-imposed limitations on our diplomacy, there is one other factor to be mentioned. We must not forget that in Southeast Asia, as in many other areas, what we wish to do in one country may be strictly limited by what we hope to accomplish in another. The United States, for example, was strongly in favor of the proposal to set up the new Federation of Malaysia. But for some time the extent and manner of its support for this new concept was conditioned and, to some extent, limited by the attitudes of Indonesia and the Philippines toward the new state. Both Indonesia and the Philippines, for their own reasons, initially opposed the formation of Malaysia; both countries are also of great importance to the United States. To the extent that we backed the formation of Malaysia we came into conflict with Indonesia and the Philippines, and our influence with them on other matters of importance to us was reduced.

Let us now turn to the self-imposed limitations on our policy just mentioned. The main point here is that the effectiveness of American policy in Southeast Asia, and elsewhere as well, can be and often is strictly limited by the actions and attitudes of our policymakers and leaders in Washington and throughout the United States.

The good effect of many of our generous aid programs in the less-developed countries has often been weakened by the context in which these programs have been placed by American leaders in both the executive and legislative branches of government. As a result of the great material and psychological shock of the Korean war, the American people, particularly as reflected by their representatives in the Congress, have become extremely security conscious, and the tendency has been to interpret security in strictly military terms. A parallel development has been what I call an upsurge of neoisolationism. The American people are tired of crises, they are weary of saving the world, but they have reluctantly accepted the decision of their leaders that the crises and the aid programs will have to continue for some time. However, if this is so, the Americans are going to call the tune and make certain that what is done contributes directly to their security. This attitude finds great favor in the American press which, in reporting on foreign policy and aid matters, usually stresses the hardboiled or tough approach.

This is not unnatural. It is also based upon a sound principle that the first obligation of any government is to further the welfare and security of its own people. But a too narrow definition of security and too great insistence that our ways are always best can and often does operate against our true long-term interests. A recent example appears in the January 31, 1963, issue of the Western Edition of *The New York Times,* in which Felix Belair, Jr., reports from Washington on the initial findings of the Presidential study group, headed by General Lucius Clay, on our foreign aid program. The group states, according to the press report, "that there is need to relate military and economic aid more directly to the paramount security interests of the United States." At a later point the committee is reported to feel that there may have been too much emphasis in the past on economic development for its own sake and without adequate consideration of the political importance of a given area to this country's security interests.[11]

From the American point of view this is fine, but one wonders what sort of impression such a report makes in Rangoon or Djakarta or even in Bangkok, the headquarters of SEATO. Are the leaders of Southeast Asia cheerfully to accept aid programs designed primarily to bolster American security interests? And if some official or senator in Washington insists that these interests have suddenly changed, what becomes of the local money and effort put into an aid program which is presumably dropped because that country is no longer politically important to American security interests? And if Southeast Asian leaders accept aid under such circumstances, what effect does this have on their desire to remain neutral? Or are neutrals again to be banished to the outer regions?

I am afraid America is in danger of forgetting the fact that if we are to lead a world alliance, or even hope to have effective influence in such an area as Southeast Asia, the other nations must believe we have their interests at heart as well as our own. As far back as 1907, Sir Eyre Crowe of the British Foreign Office pointed this out to his chiefs in a memorandum directed to British relations with Germany, but which gives guidance on the principles that must govern the foreign policy of any strong state in a leading or dominant position in world affairs. Crowe was speaking of a nation that was the leading maritime power of the day, but his remarks are equally applicable to a nation that aspires to be the leading nuclear or space power. He says:

It would, therefore, be but natural that the power of a State supreme at sea should inspire universal jealousy and fear, and be ever exposed to the danger of being over-

[11] *The New York Times,* Western Edition, January 31, 1963, p. 1.

thrown by a general combination of the world. . . . The danger can in practice only be averted—and history shows that it has been so averted—on condition that the national policy of the insular and naval State is so directed as to harmonize with the general desires and ideals common to all mankind, and more particularly that it is closely identified with the primary and vital interests of a majority, or as many as possible, of the other nations.[12]

This does not mean that aid programs should be carefree handouts with no controls. It does mean that we recognize, as Tyler Dennett and Deputy Under Secretary Johnson have pointed out, that American interests require the development of strong, independent states in Asia, and that our interests are their interests. Only when we make this sufficiently clear can we hope to inspire confidence in us and our world objectives among the governments and peoples of the underdeveloped nations.

It is significant that while the press played up the tough or negative aspects of the Clay Committee report, it gave scarcely any attention to those portions of the report that recognized the need of an aid program even if the cold war were ended. In particular, no effort was made by the press to tell the uncommitted nations that in its concluding paragraph the Clay Committee report also stated:

We would point out that the need for development assistance and an U.S. interest in providing it would continue even if the cold war and all our outstanding political differences with the Communists were to be resolved tomorrow. This is so not merely because it is part of the American tradition to be concerned with the plight of those less fortunate than ourselves. This is so not merely because it is in our national self-interest to assure expanding markets for our production and reliable sources of supply of necessary raw materials. It is because the people of the United States hope to see a world which is prosper-

[12] Quoted in Morgenthau, Hans, and Thompson, Kenneth W., *Principles and Problems of International Politics* (New York: Knopf, 1950), p. 248.

ous and at peace that we believe those nations which are seriously striving to promote their own development should be helped by us and by our partners to create and maintain the conditions conducive to steady economic progress and improved social well-being within the framework of political freedom.[13]

This, I submit, is a much better description of the true American attitude than the more negative portions of the report which the press chose to emphasize. Again the appeal and the effectiveness of our foreign policy has been limited by our own action.

During an excess of partisan enthusiasm in the election campaign of 1952, John Foster Dulles charged that the Truman administration was treating Asians as second-class expendables. As the person directly in charge of our Far Eastern policy at that time, I went to some lengths to demonstrate that he was wrong, and I think I succeeded, even to Mr. Dulles' satisfaction. At least, we continued good friends. However, I have since sometimes wondered whether or not Mr. Dulles was at least partially right. In the succeeding years, it has seemed on occasion that the treatment of Asians not as second-class expendables but as second-class allies or partners, as compared to Europe, was characteristic not of a single political party or administration but rather of the American government as a whole, under the control of whatever political party.

This has happened, at least in part, I believe, because over the past several years there has been no one in the highest councils of the government in Washington with a real visceral understanding and appreciation of Asia, particularly Southeast Asia, and its importance to our country and the future peace of the world. While in recent years there has been a great increase in the number of Asian ex-

[13] The Committee to Strengthen the Security of the Free World (the Clay Committee), *The Scope and Distribution of United States Military and Economic Assistance Programs* (Washington, D.C.: Department of State, March 1963), p. 22.

perts in the ranks of the State Department and other government agencies in Washington, it is still questionable whether their opinions and advice are often decisive in government councils. Too often in the past, our Asia policy has been cut to fit the European cloth of our world policy. I do not mean that we should weaken our European allies merely for the sake of our Asian friends. But I have seen us fail even to attempt to persuade our NATO partners to adopt somewhat unwelcome policies in Asia that would, in the end, actually strengthen them.

For example, back in 1957, before the Indonesians expelled all the Dutch from their country, a proposal was submitted to the State Department by the American embassy in Djakarta that was designed not only to solve the problem of West New Guinea but also to bring about a settlement of the economic and financial differences between the Dutch and the Indonesians. Safeguards were included to protect the security interests of all, including the Australians. No one at the embassy believed this to be a perfect plan. We did believe that it offered a basis for negotiation which would prevent early and extreme action. And responsible Indonesians with whom the proposal was informally discussed agreed that it was acceptable as a basis for talks, although they had reservations about certain details. No real effort was made by Washington to persuade the Dutch and the Australians that this was something worth trying. I am convinced that if it had been tried, there is a real possibility that Dutch business and financial interests would still be in Indonesia. Not, certainly, in their former monopolistic manner but in a modern, progressive relationship which would be to the benefit of both the Indonesians and the Dutch. It would also, I believe, have greatly contributed to the political stability and security of Southeast Asia.

This proposal was not rejected in Washington by ignorant, evil men but by intelligent, patriotic Americans who honestly believed they were acting in the best interests of the United States and its allies. They were, however, men who from youth had been conditioned to look toward Europe and not Asia. They had considerable knowledge of Asia, but many of them felt that work on Asian matters took them away from the main stream of foreign policy. They did not have the deep understanding and sympathy which would have made it possible for them to place the Asians more nearly on an equal footing with our Western allies. So nothing was done, and the Dutch are now out of New Guinea as well as Indonesia. That this attitude still prevails, perhaps unconsciously, was aptly illustrated recently when one of the most able and dedicated officials in the State Department, Under Secretary of State W. Averell Harriman, in his remarks to the American Society of Newspaper Editors, said:

> Perhaps some of you know I have been in the last year and a half exiled in the Far East but recently I have been reprieved and I am back in general circulation.[14]

There are one or two additional points I wish briefly to touch upon. I have not dwelt on the Communist menace or its direct influence upon our policies. It is treated in another chapter. And also, many, if not most, of the problems with which we are confronted in Southeast Asia would be with us if there were no Communist threat. But I do wish to urge that we take Southeast Asia as seriously as do the Communists. Whatever position Stalin may have today in the Communist hall of fame, most Communist leaders, I believe, still agree with his statement in *Problems of Leninism:*

> The road to victory of the revolution in the West lies through the revolutionary alliance with the liberation movement of the colonies and the dependent countries against imperialism.[15]

When we talk of partnership with Asians we must see to it that we mean it and that it honestly means more to the

[14] Department of State Press Release No. 204, April 19, 1963.
[15] Stalin, Joseph, *Problems of Leninism* (Moscow: Foreign Languages Publishing House, 1960), p. 52.

Asians than the spurious partnership offered by Moscow or Peking.

I also wish to make clear I am assuming that in the confused, transitional world of Southeast Asia it is of vital importance that the United States maintain and properly use a military supremacy behind which the constructive efforts to build stable, independent states can go forward without hindrance. I also plead that our military policy and our economic, social, and political policies not be kept in watertight compartments. As Oskar Morgenstern of Princeton has pointed out, our military operations "must fit into our political plans and schemes. By themselves they would be meaningless." [16] We are doing much better in this respect than we did during World War II, but there is still room for improvement. The details of how this should be done I leave to those with special competence in the field.

In conclusion, let me emphasize two points. Our policies toward Asia must truly have Asian interests as well as our own in mind, and must not always be at the mercy of shortsighted concerns about Europe. In this connection, I commend to our leaders the words of Thomas Finletter in his book *Foreign Policy: The Next Phase:*

> The problem is not to weaken the Grand Alliance in order to please Asia. It is how to develop good policies in the Grand Alliance which will command the respect of Asia.[17]

And finally I urge that in developing our Far Eastern policies a stronger voice be given to those who have lived long in Asia, who have the feel of the area in their bones, and who have the sympathy, understanding, and sensitivity that will make them readily acceptable among Asians as leading

[16] Morgenstern, Oskar, *The Question of National Defense* (New York: Random House, 1959), p. 266.

[17] Finletter, Thomas K., *Foreign Policy: The Next Phase,* 2nd ed. (New York: Harper, 1960), p. 83. In addition to the readings already referred to, I would also call particular attention to the following: Thayer, Charles W., *Diplomat* (New York: Harper, 1959); and Marshall, Charles Burton, *The Limits of Foreign Policy* (New York: Holt, 1954).

partners in the common task of building "strong, prosperous and enlightened Asiatic States." There need be no fear that such men will follow policies beamed only to Asia. There will always be in Washington sufficient men who look first and foremost toward Europe and who will serve to maintain the balance.

8

ANOTHER LOOK AT SEATO

RUSSELL H. FIFIELD

T HE MANILA TREATY AROSE
from the circumstances of the Indochina war and the Geneva settlement of 1954.[1] It was signed at a time when international communism was making strong inroads in Indochina and when anticolonialism was rampant. The common
denominator for membership was an evaluation of international communism as a threat to national security coupled
with a conviction that collective defense was the best way
to deal with the menace. Contrary opinions were held by
many South and Southeast Asian states which preferred to
pursue a policy of nonalignment. At the same time a
multiple motivation was found in the attitudes of both the
signatories and nonsignatories of the pact.

[1] Literature on SEATO is limited but growing. Especially helpful
is *SEATO Record,* published every two months at Bangkok, the
headquarters of the organization. Still valuable, although dated, is
Collective Defence in South East Asia (London: Royal Institute of
International Affairs, Oxford University Press, 1956), which represents
the findings of a Chatham House study group. George Modelski has
carefully edited *SEATO: Six Studies* (Melbourne: F. W. Cheshire,
1962). Also noteworthy is Norman J. Padelford's "SEATO and
Peace in Southeast Asia," *Current History,* Vol. 38, February 1960, pp.
95–101, 109.

RATIONALE

It is important at the outset to recall the essential terms of the Southeast Asia Collective Defense Treaty signed September 8, 1954, by three Asian states, the Philippines, Thailand, and Pakistan, and by five Western countries, Australia, New Zealand, France, the United Kingdom, and the United States. In Article IV, paragraph 1:

> Each Party recognizes that aggression by means of armed attack in the treaty area against any of the Parties or against any State or territory which the Parties by unanimous agreement may hereafter designate, would endanger its own peace and safety, and agrees that it will in that event act to meet the common danger in accordance with its constitutional processes. Measures taken under this paragraph shall be immediately reported to the Security Council of the United Nations.[2]

In an understanding approved by the other signatories, the United States declared that its obligations under the article applied only to "Communist aggression."

Despite the other provisions of the Manila Treaty and the evolution of SEATO, Article IV, paragraph 1, represents the rationale of the pact and the chief basis for judging its success or failure since 1954. Vague indeed were the provisions aimed at coping with subversion directed from outside; here, if a signatory was convinced that the political independence or territorial integrity of any other signatory in the treaty area, or of any designated state or territory was menaced by other than an armed attack or by "any fact or situation" that might threaten the peace of the area, immediate consultations on steps for the common defense would occur. The United States significantly agreed to the

---

[2] "Southeast Asia Collective Defense Treaty and Protocol between the United States of America and Other Governments," *Treaties and Other International Acts Series*, No. 3170 (Washington, D.C.: Department of State, 1956), p. 3.

consultation formula if armed attack or aggression other than Communist took place. The "treaty area" was defined as the "general area" of Southeast Asia and the Southwest Pacific, embracing all the territories of the Asian signatories but omitting Taiwan and Hongkong, although not by name. In a protocol, Laos, Cambodia, and the "free territory under the jurisdiction of the State of Vietnam" were designated as areas where the provisions of Article IV, paragraph 1, were applicable.

The special motivations of the different signers of the Manila Treaty merit particular attention, for the rationale of an alliance is weakened if the community of interests among them is not sufficiently binding. Thailand, worried over developments in Indochina and concerned about its Chinese and Vietnamese minorities, saw in the pact the means of an alliance with the United States, which it had been seeking since 1950. Pakistan believed that the Southeast Asia Collective Defense Treaty would strengthen its position with reference to India and bolster its stand in a dispute with Afghanistan over "Pushtunistan." The Philippines, already an ally of the United States and influenced by a strong pro-American policy under President Ramon Magsaysay, was willing to join Washington in a multilateral security pact.

Australia, whose interests in Southeast Asia or the "Near North" were clearly demonstrated by Japan's conquest of the area during World War II, was eager to enter into an alliance with the United States, Great Britain, and other powers as a deterrent to future Communist aggression in the region. Canberra was particularly interested in the extension of Washington's commitments in the "general area" of Southeast Asia. New Zealand also was chiefly influenced by security considerations. Wellington had been concerned about the absence of Great Britain from ANZUS, an alliance signed in 1951 by the United States, Australia, and New Zealand, but it saw in the Manila Treaty its three closest friends, Great Britain, Australia, and the United States, united in a common pact for the security of the "Near North."

The United Kingdom considered the Southeast Asia Collective Defense Treaty an important vehicle for maintaining the British presence in Southeast Asia. At the same time, it viewed the Geneva settlement on Indochina in 1954 as an essential element in the future peace of the area. Foreign Minister Anthony Eden had even considered a Locarno-type arrangement, but this project had run into widespread opposition. At the time of the Manila Conference, France believed it could keep a major part of its economic, cultural, and even political stake in Indochina. Paris, not being able to look into the future, saw in the prospective Southeast Asia Treaty Organization a means of defending its interests in the area.

As for the United States, the Manila Treaty reflected the basic security approach of Secretary of State John Foster Dulles. He firmly believed that the best way of deterring the Communist powers was by letting them know ahead of time that if they attempted aggression in certain defined areas, they would have to face the collective action of a number of countries united in a formal, open alliance. In his words at the Manila Conference, it should be made clear that the reaction to "an attack upon the treaty area" would be "so united, so strong and so well placed" that a potential aggressor would realize it "would lose more than it could hope to gain."

CHANGING ENVIRONMENT

In any evaluation of SEATO, the climate under which it operates is a primary consideration. By mid-1963, international developments quite different in many respects from those in 1954 were affecting the outlook of member and nonmember states. In addition, decolonization was almost a page in history, for independence had come to most of Southeast Asia by late August 1957. Anticolonialism was losing much of its intensity, although the degree varied from country to country. In Indonesia, for instance, the controversy over Netherlands New Guinea aroused for many years Djakarta's nationalism against the West.

Significantly, friction between an openly militant People's Republic of China and a basically cautious Soviet Union on the most effective ways of promoting communism has destroyed the image of international solidarity in the movement. The Communist parties of Southeast Asia as well as the Democratic Republic of (North) Vietnam are experiencing the effects of this dissension. If they were actually forced to choose as the result of an absolute break between Peking and Moscow, the consequences might be even more serious for the peace of Southeast Asia. Communist China would probably gain their full allegiance. The Chinese invasion of India in 1962, moreover, dealt a mortal blow to the Five Principles of Peaceful Coexistence as the basis for relations between these two Asian giants. The countries of Southeast Asia which endorsed the Five Principles have every reason to question privately, if not publicly, their validity. At the same time, unless a viable alternative to accommodation with Communist China is considered to exist, not only the neutral states but also the pro-Western nations will bend like bamboo in the wind to pressures from Peking.

The attitudes of both members and nonmembers toward SEATO have changed over the years. It has become less an element of discord among Asians, for many now have a better understanding of the nature of Communist objectives, while the organization has not served to provoke Communist China, as was once widely predicted. In fact, the Asian members are convinced that SEATO has not been sufficiently united and forceful, especially in the Laotian crisis of 1960–1962. Changes in national interests or accentuation of local controversies have affected the viewpoints of some signatories.

COMPETENCE

A number of questions should be raised and answered about the competence of SEATO in the international environment of Southeast Asia today. Just what are its limitations and opportunities? In some instances the time element should be introduced in terms of past performance and future contingencies.

First of all, has the organization succeeded in serving as a deterrent to overt Communist aggression on the model of the Korean war? As the record clearly indicates that the Communist states have not resorted to such warfare in Southeast Asia, despite the existence of opportunities, SEATO can claim at least some of the credit. It may well be a factor in the current stress of the Communists on so-called wars of national liberation. If Peking or Hanoi should openly invade a member or protocol state in Southeast Asia, Article IV, paragraph 1, of the Manila Treaty would in all probability be honored by all the signatories. The strong criticism of SEATO in the Communist press indicates that it is considered something more than a "paper tiger." The military training exercises and the experience in defense planning, notwithstanding their limitations, do serve as a brake on open Communist aggression. Bilateral programs of military assistance, especially on the part of the United States to Asian signatories, add to the military strength of the latter.

When Communist China acquires a nuclear capability in terms of an atomic arsenal and delivery facilities, its impact on Southeast Asia will be even greater than today. Moreover, Peking will no longer be as dependent upon the atomic shield of Moscow and will thus be less subject to leverage in certain contingencies. The deterrent to overt military aggression by Communist China may need to be maximized.

Under the circumstances of today, how effective has SEATO been in coping with another grave threat, namely, indirect aggression in Southeast Asia? Here guerilla warfare is the military component of wars of national liberation; international sanctuaries are systematically exploited by the Communists; and the level of provocation is deliberately kept low in order to confuse the issue of aggression and to sow dissension among allies. Communist insurgency in Laos during the crisis of 1960–1962 reached a point where the Pathet Lao, with support particularly from North Vietnam and the Soviet Union, would have been able to overthrow the royal government unless a negotiated settlement favorable to the Communists was reached, or unless direct military aid by Western and pro-Western powers was provided. As the members of SEATO could not agree on military measures to cope with indirect aggression, Communist successes inside Laos raised serious questions about the future of the organization. Although the Laotian crisis did not have the effect of torpedoing SEATO, it indicated clearly the need for a re-examination of SEATO's role in dealing with Communist-inspired subversion.

The Geneva settlement on Laos in 1962 left South Vietnam as the chief country in Southeast Asia where the Communists were actively engaged in indirect aggression. The offensive of the Vietcong, which was mounted, guided, and supplied in part from North Vietnam, would probably have succeeded in its goal of overthrowing by force the government of President Ngo Dinh Diem and ultimately unifying Vietnam under Ho Chi Minh if the United States had not decided to make a major effort to prevent a Communist victory. More than 12,000 Americans in uniform from the army, navy, marine corps, and air force are engaged in widespread training and support functions in South Vietnam, while the dividing line between combatants and non-combatants is narrowing. Some time ago Washington moved beyond the point of disengagement. The counterinsurgency efforts of the Americans and South Vietnamese extend across a wide spectrum, from day-to-day military operations against guerillas to the establishment of strategic hamlets, a rehabilitation program for the mountain tribesmen, and support for economic development. The Communists, to their great advantage, are able to use as a sanctuary not only North Vietnam but also Laos and to some extent Cambodia.

SEATO has not yet been involved in the effort to defeat the Communists in South Vietnam. As in Laos, the military threat is not posed in terms of direct aggression. However, some of the individual members of SEATO, such as Australia, are cooperating with the South Vietnamese and Americans. A special assistant to the secretary general of the organization was appointed in 1962 to furnish advice on how to increase its effectiveness in countersubversion. Seminars had previously been held on the subject while the Committee of Security Experts continues its work. Communist-inspired indirect aggression may well spread to other parts of the treaty area. The northeast region of Thailand is already considered an example of incipient insurgency.

In a related aspect, what can SEATO do if the local Communists come to power through victory at the polls? Neither the members nor the organization itself are able to take effective action in such circumstances. On the other hand, individual members of SEATO can take preventive steps before the elections which may have an influence on the results. Quite often rising Communist pressures in a country arouse counterpressures in the body politic. Support through various programs of foreign assistance can be given to anti-Communist or non-Communist forces. This approach, of course, requires the most careful application of skills and resources, for the local Communists can capitalize on what could easily become foreign intervention. But even if they win at the polls and set up a government, its exact international posture would be hard to predict. The polycentrism in the Communist world and the degree of independence of the local Communists are important elements in the equation. Tito's relations over the years with Moscow and Peking provide considerable insights. If SEATO is properly utilized, its very existence in the background can be an element of stability.

Another important question centers around the attitude of SEATO toward neutralism in Southeast Asia. Burma, Cambodia, Laos, and Indonesia constitute the uncommitted states of the area, although their exact posture varies with time and circumstance. India in South Asia is still formally nonaligned, but the Chinese Communist attack in the last quarter of 1962 pushed it very much toward the West. Thailand is almost surrounded by three neutralist countries, Cambodia, Laos, and Burma, while the Philippines has neutralist Indonesia as its neighbor to the south. South Vietnam has a common border with Cambodia and Laos. In recent years Burma under the second government of General Ne Win and Cambodia under Prince Norodom Sihanouk have given indications of a desire to accommodate themselves to Communist China as the key power of the future in Southeast Asia. The Geneva settlement on Laos in 1962 reinforced their evaluation, for the domestic and international aspects of the arrangement did not augur well for the future of that kingdom outside the Communist world. The neutrals of Southeast Asia, moreover, did not rally behind India when it was under attack from Communist China in late 1962, although Indonesia, Cambodia, and Burma joined Ceylon, Ghana, and the United Arab Republic in an effort to find a peaceful settlement to the controversy.

The Communists, it should be pointed out, consider neutralism advantageous under certain conditions for tactical reasons, but they do not look upon it as a permanent alternative to Communist victory in a neutral state. Their tactics toward neutralism vary with the circumstances; they support the 1962 settlement in Laos pending future world developments, approve the neutralism of Cambodia and Burma as a posture oriented in the correct direction, and woo neutralists in the pro-Western states of Southeast Asia in an effort to change the orientation of the latter. SEATO obviously is not able to oppose neutralism *per se* in the treaty area, but it can, under favorable circumstances, provide an alternative to an accommodation on the part of several countries to Peking.

In another aspect, what role can the international organization play in non-Communist local disputes involving or affecting a member or members in Southeast Asia? Some of these controversies have a potential for trouble far beyond the immediate circumstances. The recent West New Guinea dispute between Indonesia and the Netherlands greatly disturbed some of the SEATO members, but it was not officially placed on the agenda of the SEATO Council of Foreign Ministers. For one reason, neither of the two contestants was a member of the international organization. The settlement of the dispute, basically in favor of Indonesia, extended the boundary of the island republic to Australian New Guinea. It should be stressed that an Indonesian attack on this territory would automatically lead to Canberra's invoking Article IV, paragraph 1, of the Manila Treaty.

The plan to establish a Federation of Malaysia—embracing Brunei, Sarawak, British North Borneo, Singapore, and the Federation of Malaya—stirred up considerable international turmoil. The Philippines strongly pressed a claim to British North Borneo, coming into opposition with both the United Kingdom and the Federation of Malaya. Since the Philippines and Great Britain are associates in SEATO, the controversy affected the solidarity of the alliance. Moreover, as the Federation of Malaya, Thailand, and the Philippines are members of the newly organized Association of Southeast Asia, the cooperation of the three participants in economic and cultural activities through this grouping was given a setback.

Djakarta's interests in British Borneo, clearly manifested

as a consequence of the revolt against the Sultan of Brunei in December 1962, have a highly explosive potential. If Indonesia had attacked British Borneo prior to formation of the new Federation of Malaysia, the United Kingdom could have invoked SEATO, as the area was covered by Article IV, paragraph 1, of the Manila Treaty. Now that the Federation of Malaysia has come into existence, Sarawak and North Borneo are no longer protected by the Manila Pact, for the Federation of Malaysia is not a member. Brunei, on the other hand, which opted to remain outside the new Federation, is still covered by the treaty. At the same time, an Indonesian attack today on the Bornean members of the new Federation could lead to invocation of the United Kingdom–Federation of Malaya defense pact, the terms of which have been extended to embrace the new Bornean members of the Federation.

In peninsular Southeast Asia the serious disputes between Cambodia and Thailand, and between Cambodia and South Vietnam, have been a source of concern to SEATO, but they have not produced action. Precolonial rivalries have emerged to poison relations between the countries, while boundary controversies and minority problems have added fuel. Personal animosity between Prince Sihanouk and President Ngo Dinh Diem, and between the former and Premier Sarit Thanarat of Thailand, plays an important role. As South Vietnam and Thailand are associated with the United States and the Western grouping, Phnompenh is prone to blame Washington for not restraining Saigon and Bangkok in what it considered provocative action on their part. SEATO is often accused of duplicity in an attempt to force Cambodia into the alliance. In a crisis with one or both of his stronger neighbors, Prince Sihanouk usually moves closer to Communist China in an effort to put pressure on them and the United States. SEATO does not provide the proper facilities for dealing with controversies between Cambodia and Thailand or South Vietnam.

Since the Southeast Asia Treaty Organization is involved

in a number of economic and cultural activities not directly related to its security role, what are the opportunities provided by them? Do they afford an avenue for widening SEATO contacts among member and nonmember states? Should the activities be minimized or maximized? In its cultural relations program the organization has undergraduate and postgraduate scholarships, research fellowships, and professorships. Its medical projects are a General Medical Research Laboratory in Thailand and a Cholera Research Laboratory in Pakistan. A SEATO Graduate School of Engineering has opened its doors in Bangkok. Among the Skilled Labor Projects of the organization are 18 vocational training centers in Thailand, two in Pakistan, and one in the Philippines. In addition, there are a Military Technical Training School and a Teacher Development Centre in Bangkok. Although various activities of SEATO attract a number of Asians whose countries are not members of the organization, the figure to date has not been very impressive. At the same time, the potential for the future should not be ignored. For instance, it will be interesting to watch the attitude of Indians in the years ahead.

SEATO efforts in the cultural and economic fields are very modest compared to the extensive bilateral programs of the United States and to the significant programs of other Western partners with Thailand, Pakistan, and the Philippines, as well as with the former and present protocol states. Comparable efforts would undoubtedly have been made even if SEATO had never existed, but they tend under the circumstances to reinforce the efforts of the organization. Nevertheless, the restricted membership of SEATO prevents it from being a channel *per se* for extensive economic aid and cultural cooperation. Economic development and cultural exchange in Southern Asia need as broad a geographic and political base as possible.

Related to the over-all activities of the Southeast Asia Treaty Organization is the question of whether its structure, personnel, and procedures are adequate to meet the objectives of the Manila Pact. The current organization of SEATO is the product of its evolution since 1954. At the apex is the Council of Foreign Ministers, usually meeting once a year; at the next civilian level are the Council Representatives, in most cases ambassadors to Thailand from the member countries, convening periodically in Bangkok; below them is a Permanent Working Group doing the spade work for the sessions of the Council Representatives. Three expert committees meet periodically to handle relevant matters. The Secretary General of SEATO personifies the organization; his secretariat is divided into six offices. As of January 1, 1961, the staff numbered 132. At the military level is the Military Advisers Group, meeting twice a year and reporting to the SEATO Council of Foreign Ministers. In the headquarters of the organization in Bangkok is a Military Planning Office, with a chief who reports to the Military Advisers Group.

It would be a mistake, however, to judge the effectiveness of SEATO by a table of organization. Although a comparison of the table at different times over the years clearly indicates an effort to respond to new pressures and needs, actual use of the machinery has left much to be desired. SEATO does not have a career civil service like that of the United Nations; loyalties in the "international" secretariat of the former are basically to the home countries of the participants, who are usually assigned to SEATO on a temporary basis. There has also been frustration among members of the secretariat over the effectiveness of the organization in a number of instances.

The general rule that SEATO's decisions must be unanimous has led to more than one controversy. The Laotian crisis of 1960–1962 brought to a climax the question of unanimity. In an effort to get around the issue, the United States and Thailand, in a joint communique issued on March 6, 1962, stressed that the obligations of the Manila Treaty were both collective and individual. Other signatories accepted the interpretation as sound procedure. When the

United States at the request of Thailand sent combat forces into the kingdom the following May as a result of the breaking of the cease-fire in Laos by the Pathet Lao and the advance of Pathet Lao forces to the Thai border, the Council Representatives were informed of the action. Australia, New Zealand, and the United Kingdom sent token forces into Thailand as an indication of SEATO solidarity. The fact that four members of the organization ordered military units into Thailand at its request, and two others, the Philippines and Pakistan, expressed willingness to take comparable action, bolstered SEATO's posture in Southeast Asia.

At the same time, a basic question remains on the best means of consulting and reaching decisions in the organization. Involved are relations between the three major Western powers, the United States, the United Kingdom, and France; between the Asian and Western members; and between the great powers and the weak allies. Various issues lead to different positions by the eight participants. This situation should not be considered unique, for peacetime alliances usually lack the motivation that comes from wartime conditions. The conflicting interests now rampant in the North Atlantic Treaty Organization are a matter of public record. As SEATO is no stronger than the attitudes of its eight members toward it, national interests will continue to dictate the role of each in the alliance. The Asian members, for instance, which have committed themselves to alignment, will continue to press for more military and economic aid from the Western powers than the nonaligned states of South and Southeast Asia receive.

Perhaps the best solution to the controversy over consultation and decision-making would be found in altering the membership of SEATO to include only those countries which still have vital or relatively vital interests in Southeast Asia, and which are willing to take effective action in certain critical areas. Today Australia, New Zealand, the United Kingdom, the Philippines, Thailand, and the United States are the SEATO powers who meet these qualifications. The French position has declined to the extent that Paris has only peripheral interests in the region. On balance, French withdrawal from SEATO would strengthen it. Pakistan, whose foreign policy is primarily related to its difficulties with India, may well consider that it does not have vital interests in Southeast Asia. On the other hand, Pakistan has been willing on occasion to commit forces to the area, is a member of the Central Treaty Organization, and might well be a better member of SEATO if the Kashmir dispute with India were settled on mutually acceptable terms.

It would be desirable if the Federation of Malaysia would become a SEATO member, but the defense arrangement between it and the United Kingdom, along with the continued stationing of the Commonwealth Strategic Reserve of British, Australian, and New Zealand units in the country, provides a significant alternative. The detachment, in effect, of Laos as a protocol state under the Manila Treaty by the Geneva settlement of 1962 removed an area where the members of SEATO in a previous showdown revealed that they were not prepared to take effective military action, except possibly in the circumstances of an open invasion on the model of the Korean war. On the other hand, South Vietnam should remain a protocol state. Saigon is sympathetic to the Southeast Asia Treaty Organization and profits from the protection of its mantle.

ALTERNATIVES

Some alternatives to SEATO should be considered before any suggestions are made about its future. A system of bilateral defense agreements, a Southeast Asian NATO, or an arrangement along the lines of the Locarno Pact might be substituted. The issuance of a Monroe Doctrine or Eisenhower Doctrine by the United States, or stress on genuine neutralism or neutralization, or emphasis on the develop-

ment of regionalism are other possibilities. A community
on the model of the British Commonwealth of Nations might
be considered; and reliance on the United Nations should
also be mentioned.

Considerable discussion has centered on the idea of a bilateral defense system in Southeast Asia. The United States
has a mutual security pact with the Philippines and, in
effect, comparable arrangements with Thailand and South
Vietnam. As indicated, Great Britain has a defense pact
with Malaysia with which Australia and New Zealand are
also associated. Thus the countries of SEATO with vital or
relatively vital interests in Southeast Asia are already committed in various ways to maintaining security in parts of
the area. Omitted from such arrangements are neutralist
Laos, Cambodia, Burma, and Indonesia, and the present
SEATO members, France and Pakistan.

Since the basic purpose of a military alliance is to deter
a potential aggressor, does a piecemeal effort through various bilateral pacts which are often different in scope carry
more weight than a multilateral security treaty? If SEATO
were disbanded and the current bilateral arrangements were
left, an open armed attack on South Vietnam would find it
with no formal allies, but only the deep commitment of the
United States. Moreover, it cannot be taken for granted that
Great Britain, Australia, New Zealand, the United States,
Thailand, the Philippines, and South Vietnam would in all
instances be prepared today to enter into defense arrangements on a bilateral basis comparable to the obligations of
SEATO. The advantages of the multilateral approach are
clear-cut, for instance, in the inter-American and North
Atlantic communities. Even the Soviet Union thought it
preferable to form the Warsaw Pact rather than rely exclusively upon bilateral defense agreements. The evidence
indicates that bilateralism is not an adequate response for
the West to a challenge as total as that of international
communism today.

A Southeast Asian NATO would represent an effort to

put more teeth in SEATO. The Manila Treaty might be amended so that an armed attack on one participant would be considered an armed attack on all the signatories. In addition to more precise obligations, specific allied units might be permanently stationed in Southeast Asia and a joint headquarters and supreme commander instituted. The United States, however, does not desire to get involved again in the constitutional issues between the President and Congress that would arise if a NATO-type defense commitment were applied to SEATO. And Washington still believes in maintaining mobile striking power, chiefly of sea and air composition, equipped with conventional and nuclear weapons, instead of tying down committed forces in specific areas. Moreover, the problems of defense in NATO are quite different from those in SEATO where, for instance, none of the Asian member states are contiguous and where there is greater disparity in the general distribution of power.

A Monroe Doctrine for Southeast Asia by the United States or a variation of it, an Eisenhower Doctrine, would put Washington more in the background, and emphasize the role of Southeast Asian countries themselves in providing for their defense. On the other hand, such a basically unilateral policy by the United States would be largely ignored or considered presumptuous in the capitals of the area. The bilateral or multilateral approach to security takes into better account the sensitivities of nationalistic governments.

The encouragement of genuine neutralism for Southeast Asia has been suggested as an alternative to SEATO. Here an attempt is made to take advantage of one of the current forces in the newly independent, developing countries. There are some who have advocated the creation of a nonaligned bloc under the leadership of India. If it were possible to establish a truly neutral Southeast Asia, one immune from the pressures and conflicts of the outside world, this model would be ideal. But the world of the twentieth century is shrinking, and no region can be isolated from the actions of its neighbors. Moreover, as already noted, international communism does not accept neutralism as a long-range alternative. A variation is the proposal that some states might be neutralized along the lines of Switzerland. Here Cambodia and Laos have been most often mentioned as a potential cordon sanitaire. Occasionally Burma and other states have been added to the list. It does not seem at all likely, however, that all the outside powers interested in these countries would be willing genuinely to apply the Swiss model to them. Laos under the Geneva settlement of 1962 is a living testament to the limits of "neutralization" in Southeast Asia.

In another direction, regionalism might be considered the foundation upon which a framework of security could be built. The countries of the area have shared many common experiences and have basically similar aspirations. Together they could have considerable influence in world politics. But the differences that separate them are greater than the factors that unite them. If regionalism begins with a good neighbor relationship, many of the states of the area have considerable work cut out for them. Furthermore, regional consciousness is in a very early stage, for colonialism, among other considerations, tended to divide the dependent areas into compartments oriented almost exclusively toward the metropolitan power. Perhaps joint cultural and economic activities offer the best approach to developing regionalism at the present time. The process, however, is certain to be slow, while the imperatives of security are immediate.

An alternative to SEATO that is sometimes seriously argued is reliance upon the peacekeeping machinery of the United Nations. It is contended that the world body has the best resources for settling disputes, especially if the United States and the Soviet Union are not in confrontation. The United Nations has been able to play a role in resolution of the controversy over West New Guinea and over the Kuomintang forces in Burma. But it was not active in the

Laotian crisis of 1960–1962, nor is it in the South Vietnamese conflict today. In any issue involving Communist aggression, the Soviet Union could use the veto in the Security Council as it saw fit; and it would be difficult to assemble a two-thirds majority for an effective resolution against the Communists in the General Assembly, given the current membership of the United Nations, apart from the circumstance of a clear-cut, open Communist aggression. The world organization, furthermore, does not have military resources at its disposal on a standby basis to cope with a serious case of aggression in Southeast Asia.

When all is said and done, it may be that the alternatives to the Southeast Asia Treaty Organization raise more questions than does SEATO itself.

THE FUTURE OF SEATO

As the record clearly indicates, SEATO has certain elements of strength and many of weakness. In certain respects its limitations, if they remain, seriously curtail its future opportunities. Yet some of the criticisms are inherent in any alliance system. Given the divergence of interests among its members, it is perhaps surprising that SEATO has been able to accomplish what it has. Too much is expected of alliances in the context of the world of 1963; indeed, both the Communist and Western groupings are facing somewhat comparable difficulties.

The following basic premises involving the future of SEATO may be presented:

a. A deterrent will be needed to overt Communist aggression in Southeast Asia for some time.

b. The multilateral approach to deterring overt Communist aggression in the area is preferable to any bilateral or unilateral formula.

c. The cooperation of Asians and Westerners in such a

common effort is desirable and essential in contemporary Southeast Asia.

d. At the same time, the United States will continue for the foreseeable future to provide the main military sinews of deterrence.

e. All non-Communist countries of the area will continue to prefer an alternative to accommodation with Peking, providing the alternative is credible.

f. In coping with insurgency, unilateral efforts on a cooperative basis with those of other states are generally best suited to meet the needs of the situation. At the same time, an international security organization can serve in various ways to bolster such efforts.

g. As long as a security pact in Southeast Asia has only a limited number of adherents, the channels of economic aid and cultural cooperation should and will continue to be on a much broader geographic basis.

In the future, the United States can seek to end SEATO abruptly or gradually, or at the other extreme, the United States can try to maximize it. Other courses of action for Washington would be to seek to keep SEATO as it is, or moderately to strengthen it. At the same time, the United States must bear in mind the effects of any policy decisions on its allies in the organization, on the neutralist countries of Asia, and on the Communist bloc.

The abrupt abrogation of the Manila Treaty and disbandment of SEATO without a credible substitute would greatly weaken the position of Washington in the entire Far East, and would be received with marked rejoicing in Hanoi, Peking, and Moscow. It would be widely interpreted as a step toward disengagement on the part of the United States in the Western Pacific. In fact, it would start a chain reaction that would make the position of Washington difficult wherever it wanted to stay in the Far East. Fortunately, the abrupt termination of SEATO is not at all likely. But the gradual ending of its role is within the realm of consideration. A policy directed toward the withering away of SEATO would raise a number of complex problems. In the first place, steps to lessen SEATO's role would soon become evident and the organization would quickly die without benefit of gradualism. Moreover, in such an important matter, the United States could not afford not to consult its allies, who obviously do not want to be victims of duplicity. The Communist world would leap at any evidence of the adoption of a withering-away policy. It has already noted the absence of a formal meeting of the Council of Foreign Ministers in 1962. Certain activities of SEATO can be graded downward and others can be graded upward, but a deliberate policy of allowing it to wither away may have more unfavorable aspects than one of abruptly disbanding it.

An attempt to maximize SEATO under current conditions would not be fruitful unless all or almost all the non-Communist countries of the treaty area were willing to join it. Since this is unlikely today, maximizing the international organization would create a marked imbalance between the members and nonmembers in the treaty area, while under certain conditions the alliance might seem really provocative to Peking. It is not in the interests of the United States, with its world-wide commitments and responsibilities, to maximize SEATO at the present time. And other members of the alliance, like Great Britain and France, would not want to use SEATO as the chief instrument of policy in Southeast Asia.

Another course of action would be to leave the organization as it is today without trying to strengthen or weaken it. This policy would have the advantage of watchful waiting. Developments on the local and world stage would to a large extent determine the future direction of SEATO. The weakness of this alternative is in the assumption that SEATO, apart from being a steadying force in the background, would make no dynamic effort to influence the course of events. On the other hand, given its present membership and role, the organization may well be functioning to the maximum extent of its capabilities at the present time.

A desirable policy for the United States to follow with respect to SEATO would be to strengthen it on a moderate scale without prejudicing any alternative approaches to security that might emerge in the decade ahead. It has been indicated that the organization may represent the best alternative today, for its demise would, in many respects, leave a vacuum that could not be as adequately filled. A moderate strengthening of SEATO would include better military training exercises and defense planning with a higher degree of readiness and consequent credibility; more effective measures to cope with subversion on the basis of further experience and research; development of SEATO headquarters as a genuine regional center for collecting information and planning projects; exploration of better ways to reach a consensus on various matters among the SEATO participants; and development of additional activities that might stimulate the interest of the nationals of nonmember states. As already indicated, the organization might profit by restricting membership to countries with vital or relatively vital interests in Southeast Asia. The deterrent to limited war in the area should certainly be strengthened, while the deterrent to total war is obviously associated with the over-all might of the United States and its allies. SEATO cannot and should not become the sole instrument of American policy in Southeast Asia, but to strengthen it moderately is in the national interests of the United States, most of its allies under the Manila Treaty, and the Southeast Asian countries as a whole.

9

UNITED STATES FOREIGN ASSISTANCE

IN SOUTHEAST ASIA

ဆသမဆသမဆသမ

AMOS A. JORDAN

INTRODUCTION

The United States has poured almost $8 billion in aid into
Southeast Asia since World War II, and the flow of assistance funds shows little sign of slackening. All eight countries in the region have been recipients; the amounts vary
from $23 million to Malaya to about $2.5 billion to the
Republic of (South) Vietnam, as shown in Table 1. The full
range of possible aid situations is present within the area:
recipients vary from neutrals to fully committed allies, from
nations barely started on the road to economic development
to others well along that road, from those enjoying domestic
tranquillity to those undergoing violent internal war.

It is not feasible in a brief essay to deal with the details of
past, present, and projected aid programs to each of the
eight countries in the region; accordingly, this essay general-
izes along regional lines as far as possible, although it will
from time to time deal with country-level programs. Only
general principles and guidelines can be derived from such

TABLE 1

UNITED STATES AID TO SOUTHEAST ASIA
(Millions of dollars) *

Country	Military Aid		Economic Aid		Total Aid	
	FY 1962	FY 1946– 1962	FY 1962	FY 1946– 1962	FY 1962	FY 1946– 1962
Burma	—	—	0.8	93.3	0.8	93.3
Cambodia	9.4	84.9	31.2	250.7	40.6	335.6
Indonesia	—	—	82.9	681.5	82.9	681.5
Laos	74.6	169.8	27.0	290.9	101.6	460.7
Malaya	—	—	9.9	23.2	0.9	23.2
Philippines	28.3	402.9	49.9	1,334.3	78.2	1,737.2
South Vietnam†	176.5	742.4	143.2	1,687.5	319.7	2,429.9
Thailand	81.0	428.6	47.7	338.1	128.7	766.7
TOTAL	369.8	1,828.6	383.6	4,699.5	753.4	6,528.1

* Sources for data are Department of Defense, *Military Assistance Facts,* May 1, 1963, and March 1, 1962, and *United States Foreign Assistance,* June 30, 1962. In these data, "economic aid" includes United States subscriptions to international organizations, Development Loan Fund and Export-Import Bank loans, and surplus commodity loans-and-grants, as well as ordinary economic and technical assistance programs. It should also be noted that, while the United States does not have a program of grant military aid to Burma, it does have a sales program.

† For the period 1955–1962. In addition, the United States gave $1,535.2 million in aid to Indochina prior to its partition.

regional analysis. Specific foreign aid policies must be derived country by country; this is a point made by the 1962 Senate Study Mission to Southeast Asia, which stated that "the group is unanimously agreed that there can be no common solution or standardized procedures for carrying out our foreign assistance program in these lands." [1]

In a celebrated article on foreign assistance, Hans Mor-

[1] See Jordan, Amos A., *Foreign Aid and the Defense of Southeast Asia* (New York: Praeger, 1962), pp. 6–10, for a discussion of this point. The Senate report cited is Senators McGee, Gale W.; Church, Frank; and Moss, Frank E., *Study Mission to Southeast Asia, November–December 1962,* 88th Congress, 1st Session, Washington, D.C., 1963. The quotation is from p. 1.

genthau has noted that it is pointless to ask whether the United States should have a policy of foreign aid. "We have interests abroad," he wrote, "which cannot be secured by military means and for the support of which the traditional methods of diplomacy are only in part appropriate. If foreign aid is not available, they will not be supported at all." [2] He went on to observe that Americans wrongly but customarily argue about the proper size of aid programs and the efficiency with which they are administered without being clear about the purposes they should serve.

Let us begin, then, by asking what the purposes of our aid program in Southeast Asia are. A recent, and succinct, statement is that of the Committee to Strengthen the Security of the Free World, the so-called Clay Committee: "If our assistance strengthens the will and capacity of a country to remain independent and helps it move toward political and economic stability, our money will have been wisely spent." [3] As applied to Southeast Asia, these purposes can be paraphrased as follows: to assist the countries of the region to achieve (a) an adequate defense against external threats, (b) internal stability, and (c) economic development. Other aid purposes could be and have been adduced, such as the securing of United States military bases, preclusion of Communist aid, consolidation of alliances, safeguarding of strategic sources, expansion of United States markets, and encouragement of cooperation in a range of mutual concerns. In part, these objectives can be subsumed under one of the three essential purposes listed above. To the extent that they cannot, they are at most secondary purposes. As an example, we can analyze the first of these other purposes, securing American bases. The only major United States bases in Southeast Asia are in the Philippines. But these

[2] Morgenthau, Hans, "A Political Theory of Foreign Aid," *The American Political Science Review*, Vol. 56, No. 2, June 1962, p. 301.

[3] The Committee to Strengthen the Security of the Free World (the Clay Committee), *The Scope and Distribution of United States Military and Economic Assistance Programs* (Washington, D.C.: Department of State, March 1963), p. 5.

are not purely for defense of the American homeland; they serve as a means of strengthening the defenses of the whole of Southeast Asia. Accordingly, the Philippine contribution of base rights is simply its contribution to mutual security in the area; its reward should be the gain in its own security, not a claim on additional aid from the United States. As one further example of many possible ones, the preclusion of Communist assistance is questionable as a basis for granting United States aid, since it tends to invite recipients to flirt with the Communists and builds an escalation factor into our aid.[4]

Before turning to a discussion of ways American assistance programs in the area promote the defense, stability, and development purposes just set forth, we should note three difficulties of our analytical approach. First, data on foreign assistance are normally available either in terms of the form of aid or the legislative program under which such aid is provided. While there is some relationship between forms and purposes of assistance, there is no clear correlation between them. Accordingly, an analysis in terms of aid purposes requires a careful division of the various aid programs according to their several purposes and then a regrouping of the data. The second difficulty stems from the internal flexibility of aid recipients, who can, if they so desire, alter the uses of their own resources in such a way as to offset or bend our purposes to their own. Although this might be a serious problem in some cases and areas, the limited size and flexibility of the economies of the various Southeast Asian recipients of American assistance generally preclude shifts of internal resources on a scale such as to vitiate our purposes. Moreover, to the extent that our purposes and those of our Southeast Asian friends run parallel, this type of difficulty does not arise.

The third difficulty arises from the fact that some forms of assistance, under some conditions, can simultaneously serve more than one purpose. In such cases, only an arbi-

[4] See *ibid.*, p. 6, and Jordan, *op. cit.*, pp. 27–38.

trary division of the aid input between the multiple goals
can be made. While this is a theoretically difficult obstacle
to sound analysis, in practice aid can be allocated and im-
plementing measures can be adjusted to take account of
multipurpose assistance.

It might appear that the foregoing difficulties are sufficient to warrant abandoning the notion of analyzing foreign
assistance according to donor purposes. A similar hard look
at other analytical approaches will show, however, equally
serious difficulties. And, of overriding importance, purpose
is the relevant analytical category for policy analysis, difficult as it may be to disentangle the factors therein.

EXTERNAL DEFENSE ASSISTANCE

The principal security threat to the area comes from Communist China. "It was the hostility of China in Korea which
first projected the United States in depth—via aid programs
—into Indochina. It is Chinese hostility which evokes the
continued flow of the bulk of United States aid and other
activity into Southeast Asia."[5] None of the countries of the
region is entirely immune from this threat, although the
insular position of Indonesia and the Philippines make them
less immediately vulnerable than the peninsular Southeast
Asian states. Although only Burma and Laos share a common border with the Red Chinese, the Thais, Cambodians,
and Vietnamese are under direct pressure from auxiliaries
of the Red Chinese such as the Pathet Lao in Laos and the
Vietminh in North Vietnam. And, despite their comparative
remoteness, even the Malayans cast anxious eyes at Communist China.

None of the Southeast Asian states can realistically expect,
even with massive foreign aid, to develop sufficient armed
forces to stave off determined Chinese Communist aggres-

[5] Senators Mansfield, A. S. Mike; Boggs, J. Caleb; Pell, Claiborne;
and Smith, Benjamin A., *Viet Nam and Southeast Asia,* 88th Congress,
1st Session, Washington, D.C., 1963, p. 19.

sion. (This judgment assumes that the states in the region will neither themselves develop nor be given nuclear weapons.) Countervailing power must, therefore, be supplied from outside the area unless these nations are to rest their long-run security on the fragile base of Red China's good will and self-restraint. If the nations of the region choose to abjure the prospect of calling on such outside power and, instead, elect to meet their security needs by becoming neutrals—as Burma, Laos, Cambodia, and Indonesia have —the most the United States can realistically offer them is assistance in developing light, fire-alarm-type forces to signal neutrality violations. If, on the other hand, the nations of the area choose to align themselves with the sources of countervailing power—as South Vietnam, Thailand, the Philippines, and Malaya have in effect done—they can realistically contemplate an active external defense policy, in conjunction, that is, with the support and defense assistance of the Western world.[6]

In South Vietnam, Thailand, and the Philippines our external defense assistance programs have two central purposes: (a) to strengthen the local forces' capability to deter or meet external threats on their own or in concert with allies, and (b) to help build facilities and arrangements to speed and add weight to allied armed support should support become essential. Furnishing aid for the additional purpose of enabling these nations to contribute forces for checking aggression throughout the region is a theoretical possibility; in practice, however, they are unlikely to provide more than token forces for use outside their immediate security zones.

The kind and scale of assistance required to strengthen another nation's external defense forces depend not only upon the threat confronted but also upon the type of defense strategy to be employed and the respective roles of

[6] Malaya has historically turned to Britain and the Commonwealth for defense help; the other three nations have been relying upon the United States.

the various partners therein. Since the primary dangers of overt aggression facing South Vietnam, Thailand, and the Philippines are limited thrusts—initially perhaps in the form of probes and border flareups which can be expanded if successful or "traded off" if not, and since it is in any case wholly infeasible to support forces in these nations large enough to check massive assaults upon them, the strategy best suited to their needs is one of "unconventional delay-defense." This is a strategy for meeting external aggression with vigorous delaying actions and, if the enemy thrust is more than a probe, for fighting to identify the aggressor, to preserve the nation's existence, and to gain time until allied forces can move into the area. The vulnerable borders of these nations, their small populations, and the rugged terrain in the area all suggest that defensive operations under such a strategy should be carried out by comparatively small, well-trained, and highly mobile contingents. Such an approach would not entail a fortified defense of the classic Western type; rather, the invaded country would depend on forces which, if overrun or cut off by large-scale assault, would use guerilla tactics to delay, harass, and wear down the aggressor.

Following the economist's principle of comparative advantage, each partner in the defense enterprise just suggested should provide those forces and resources for which its unique situation best fits it. Accordingly, the primary American role should be to furnish training assistance, light arms, and equipment for enhancing communications and mobility (while maintaining the capability for the kind of massive intervention which deters the aggressor from a large-scale, unambiguous assault). Although the provision of some comparatively heavy and advanced equipment, such as tanks, artillery, and fighter aircraft, can be justified in some cases, the United States should strictly limit such varieties of aid, and, in general, avoid prestige-type military assistance which wastes both our own and our allies' resources.

Assistance for the second external defense purpose, that

is, to facilitate the intervention of supporting forces, should build or improve airfields, ports, roads, and communication facilities. Not only can such projects multiply the impact of friendly intervention, but they can also be designed to improve the local forces' unilateral capabilities. Moreover, their provision through aid gives tangible evidence of American intentions to both allies and potential aggressors. Because the rationale for this type of defense assistance depends on the availability of allied support, the respective roles of each partner and the conditions under which they will fulfill these roles should be clearly specified, probably to a greater degree than has been the rule in the past. This last consideration reinforces the fundamental fact underlying the whole concept of defense assistance in the region: American armed strength, in appropriate amounts and kinds, and ready for rapid deployment, is the sine qua non of any viable defense and defense assistance strategy for the area.

INTERNAL STABILITY ASSISTANCE

It may seem inherently contradictory for the United States to be espousing the cause of stability at the same time that it is encouraging development with all its destabilizing effects. The apparent contradiction disappears, however, once these terms are carefully defined and the elements of each analyzed. The "stability" sought should not, for example, be that of immobilisme; rather, it should be that which provides for political evolution under comparatively orderly conditions. Stability in a period of increasing popular consciousness implies, further, that there should be a widening base of political participation and an increasing measure of the consent of the governed, explicit and implicit, in the conduct of political life. While a key aspect of stability in this broad sense is the maintenance of internal law and order, the training and equipping of police, the constabulary, or other local security forces is but one part of the problem. Political measures to link villages and capital in a two-way communication process, and economic measures to provide an acceptable minimum of goods and services are also essential parts of the stability problem.[7] Our stability aid has, therefore, two parts: one directed toward improving internal security forces and the other directed toward helping the recipients' governments meet the immediate political, social, and economic demands of their peoples.

None of the countries in the area is immune to internal threats of subversion and guerilla movements sponsored by outside powers. Khrushchev's "wars of national liberation" strategy for the less-developed world, and especially for Southeast Asia, assures that Communist efforts to inspire and support insurgency will continue, and perhaps expand, in the area. By the time insurgency has become overt and widespread ("stage two"), vigorous efforts by a large and well-trained counterinsurgent force are necessary. The main responsibility in such efforts necessarily belongs with the threatened country. Too active a role by an aiding nation is not only resented by the recipient government, but also may serve to discredit it in the eyes of a populace holding memories of colonialism and fears of external domination. Within this basic limit, American training and material assistance can play a key part in building effective counterinsurgent forces.

A basic difficulty confronting the United States in promoting internal stability through foreign aid is the fact that defeating Communist internal war efforts, particularly when they reach the scale found in South Vietnam by 1963, requires the development of efficient, centrally directed forces which can also become instruments of power centralization and domestic repression. Yet the sad experience of the Philippines and South Vietnam when they had weak and

[7] Dankwart A. Rustow has recently made this same point in a different way. See Rustow, Dankwart A., "The Vanishing Dream of Stability," *Aid Digest*, August 1962.

decentralized internal security forces shows that a nation facing serious internal challenges invites chaos and the loss of independence unless it can strengthen its capacity to maintain law and order. To resolve this dilemma between building up forces that are hypereffective or maintaining ones that are ineffective in promoting order, the United States must direct its aid and advice in two ways: first, to motivate the leaders of these security forces toward using them as political integrators as well as military instruments and, second, to encourage more foresighted efforts by these nations to deal with incipient or "stage one" insurgency by political, economic, and social measures designed to meet the basic aspirations and needs of their peoples.

American aid, particularly of a technical and supporting assistance character, can play a key role in inducing recipients to take the political, economic, and social initiatives to cope with insurgency, and in providing them with resources to do so. The bulk of our economic aid to the area, in the form of commodity import programs, has, in fact, been of a stabilization support character. Integrated rural development programs, health and education measures, basic commodity and "Food for Peace" aid, and programs for developing responsible labor union leadership, are further examples of the types of assistance which can help the new and vulnerable nations achieve the base of stability-with-adaptability which is essential for economic development.

It is clear that military and nonmilitary assistance meet and merge in this search for internal stability. Yet, since we lack a clear idea of the nature of political development and the elements of change which must be accommodated to assure continued stability in these states, we cannot easily orchestrate military and nonmilitary means into a comprehensive, integrated program to deal with this problem. But we need not, therefore, stand by helplessly. Since the Southeast Asian states are essentially village-based societies, it is plain that one key to their problem is the development of

viable rural communities, linked by participation in the
political process with the urban and political centers. Building this type of foundation while a nation is under the threat
of incipient or overt insurgency is a task for both the military
and civil leadership of the threatened country. Similarly, it
is a task for both our military and economic assistance.

Aid agencies which are oriented toward economic development *per se* have tended to view rural development in
terms of comprehensive, long-range, integrated programs.
Often quite sophisticated in their conception, such programs
—whether they originated indigenously, or through the
United Nations, or the Agency for International Development—are rightly addressed to the long-range and fundamental disjunction between the autonomous villages of
Southeast Asia and the modern, centrally directed states
emerging in the region. On the other hand, the armed forces
of these countries and the American defense establishment
agencies are largely concerned about the immediate threat
of insurgency, and have tended to view the problem as one
requiring immediate-impact, public-works-type programs
("civic action"). Theoretically, these differing approaches,
requiring differing types of assistance, are complementary.
Unfortunately, the result of trying to implement both approaches simultaneously but separately has been a series of
scrambled and overlapping programs that conflict in timing,
rather than a coordinated and integrated effort.

Perhaps the single most serious gap in American thinking
and practice in aid matters is the lack of an integrated
approach to the internal stability problem. Fresh insights
about the problem itself and new ways to tackle it are
needed. As an example of how we might help these nations
achieve a properly coordinated method of dealing with
incipient or active insurgency, the United States might
sponsor a "rural development and civic action center" in
the Philippines or elsewhere in Southeast Asia. Such a
center would train both civic action and rural development
cadres from the various Southeast Asian nations. Military

and civil officers would work together to analyze the common problem and to develop integrated programs for dealing with it. Instructors would be drawn from both the military and civilian branches of the United States government or other governments having successful experience with this type of problem. (The center should not, incidentally, be tied to SEATO, for such a link would tend to reduce the attractiveness of participation to non-SEATO nations in the area.)

ECONOMIC DEVELOPMENT ASSISTANCE

Only the Philippines, Malaya, and Thailand among the Southeast Asian nations are even approaching "takeoff" into economic development; most are barely moving down the runway. There is considerable evidence that Burma, Laos, and Indonesia have, in fact, been moving backwards in recent years. South Vietnam made considerable progress in the period from 1955 to 1959; perhaps its very success in that period triggered the Vietcong insurrection which has since brought economic development to a virtual standstill.

In the past few years it has become increasingly clear that in most countries the real brakes to economic development are not essentially economic in character but political and social. One knowledgeable writer has recently commented that there are only "between five and a dozen countries in the world" which have reached the point that "with some further addition of capital they will reach a critical proportion of factors . . . and explode into development." [8] It seems unlikely that any of the Southeast Asian nations will so "explode" in the near future. This capability to use capital effectively, which is rooted in noneconomic factors, has been fastened upon by the Clay Committee as the touchstone for determining the size and distribution of American assistance.

The role of development assistance in these nations is

[8] Keyfitz, Nathan, "Can Foreign Aid Be Rational?" *International Journal*, Vol. 17, No. 3, Summer 1962, p. 24.

both to increase absorptive capacity and to exploit existing capacity; that is, development aid fits into two categories: (a) that designed to build the foundation of education, skills, attitudes, and infrastructure essential to further growth, and (b) that which provides the capital investment necessary to increase productivity, create employment opportunities, and set in motion a beneficent circle of production, savings, and investment. It will be noted that the first of these two types of development assistance is similar in character to one part of internal stability assistance, as defined above. This overlap in concept need not trouble us, for the difference between these two varieties of aid is one of intensity rather than identity. Given in amounts just sufficient to allay popular discontent, aid for rural development, health and education, and similar purposes is properly labeled internal stability assistance. Increasing and refining these kinds of programs to the point that additional capital inputs will generate "takeoff" brings us into the realm of economic development assistance. Theoretically, the overlap of these types of aid is troublesome; practically, it is of little consequence.

All the countries in the region need further assistance in building their foundations for economic growth. The problem with this variety of development assistance is not solely in the recipient's absorptive capacity but also in the donor's ability to place skilled technical assistance workers in the field and to plan and administer integrated programs. Since the United States does not yet have the requisite donor capacity to provide the quality and quantity of assistance these nations need, it is encouraging increasing contributions by other nations on both a bilateral and multilateral basis.

The Philippines, Malaya, and Thailand already have sufficient absorptive capacity to use a substantial flow of foreign capital funds. If, as the Clay Committee has expressed it, Indonesia "puts its internal house in order," [9] that nation

[9] Clay Committee Report, p. 9.

could be added to the list. The flow of foreign aid funds for investment purposes can and should be supplemented by a flow of private funds. Moreover, the provision of foreign capital, both public and private, to the Southeast Asian nations should be of concern to all the free world, not merely to the United States. Other nations, particularly Great Britain and Japan, and multilateral agencies are already providing considerable sums. The hundreds of millions of dollars of foreign funds that each of these four nations will need and the smaller sums the other four countries of the region will require in the next decade should be provided by as wide a spectrum of free world countries as possible.

Just as we lack a clear idea of the nature of political development, so, too, do we lack a single, clear concept of the economic development process. Perhaps there are so many different roads to development and so many contributing, interwoven factors therein, that looking for "a" theory is equivalent to the search for the philosopher's stone. Nevertheless, we have a great deal of operational knowledge; we know that political and social institutions which inhibit savings and curb entrepreneurship must be changed; we know, too, that few less-developed countries can, in a comparatively short space of time, generate from internal sources the investment capital needed to fire long-term growth. We know also, although we have not yet acted upon our knowledge, that high rates of population growth virtually preclude development in countries such as these. Population increases in Thailand, the Philippines, and South Vietnam are averaging about 3 per cent annually, largely offsetting the 5 per cent rate of GNP growth in the first two countries and swamping the 2 per cent (or less) rate of GNP increase in South Vietnam. In the four neutral states of the area, population growth of about 2 per cent per year is about as great as their economic growth rates, resulting in static or even declining per capita economic levels.

In short, we know enough about the nature of economic development to proceed with substantial, though empirical, aid programs. It is true that we cannot, as Morgenthau charged, demonstrate the precise causal nexus between our aid and responsible international behavior on the part of the recipients. Yet we have a clear case of enlightened self-interest for providing development assistance of one kind or another to these countries. This case is essentially that "economic development is probably the most significant and lasting aspiration of the newly emerging nations with which the United States can associate itself and make it a firm basis of its long-range foreign policy." [10]

SOME CONCLUDING THOUGHTS

Our interests in forwarding the processes of nation building and internal defense in Southeast Asia demand that we produce integrated assistance programs. Too often in the past our aid programs have been neither internally consistent nor adequately coordinated. The task confronting American policymakers and aid administrators is essentially to devise programs of defense, internal stability, and development assistance which are of sufficient scope and are mutually reinforcing. As John Ohly has written, "the test is not the test of whether military or economic objectives are served, but the test of whether, in the aggregate, various forms of aid or combinations thereof, best serve the total pattern of U.S. objectives, regardless of whether one labels them as 'military,' 'economic,' or 'political.'" [11] We have not yet devised the organizational arrangements or the procedures, or, more importantly, the insight to put our aid programs in Southeast Asia in this perspective.

[10] Committee on Foreign Relations, United States Senate, *Mutual Security Act of 1959, Hearings,* 86th Congress, 1st Session, Washington, D.C., 1959, p. 504.

[11] Ohly, John H., "A Study of Certain Aspects of Foreign Aid," in The President's Committee to Study the United States Military Assistance Program (the Draper Committee), *Composite Report,* Vol. 2 (Washington, D.C.: 1959), p. 283.

10

THE PSYCHOLOGICAL INSTRUMENTS

OF POLICY IN

SOUTHEAST ASIA

PAUL M. A. LINEBARGER
AND
GENEVIEVE C. LINEBARGER

FRAMEWORK OF THE PROBLEM

Although Southeast Asia, as a communications area, used to be lumped with the Sino-Japanese world as "the Far East," its communications patterns and public opinion behavior differ sharply from those of the immense nations to the north. And in Southeast Asia, local particularities far surpass common regional factors. Vietnam can almost be regarded as an extrusion of the Sinitic world into Southeast Asia, because it is so thoroughly Chinese as to resemble Kwangtung more than Cambodia; the Philippines is for most purposes a displaced Hispanic-American republic, rather than an Asian state at all; and the unity of the other Southeast

Asian states is one which can be seen by observers from the outside, rather than one experienced by people living within the region.[1] Regional opinion, as such, is barely beginning to exist; the knowledge of the region as a unit is not yet diffused to the populations which inhabit it. It is significant, for example, that no Southeast Asian has yet achieved an international academic reputation as a Southeast Asian expert. For communications purposes, Southeast Asia must be considered as an aggregate of territories rather than a geographic unit such as Europe, the Middle East, the India-centered world of South Asia, or the Far East.

Not only are the different parts of the area far from one another in terms of local communication; they are uneven within themselves in the sophistication of their communications systems. Saigon, Djakarta, Rangoon, Bangkok, and other cities would show parts of their publics as sophisticated as any in the world; by many scales of measurement, Manila would be rated very high as a communicative city, even if it were compared to the chief cities of Europe or to North America.[2] Yet within a few hundred miles of each of these cities, there are communities which have barely entered the age of metals.

Southeast Asia, like the whole world, is undergoing processes of social and political change so rapid that almost any prophecy, whatever the subject matter, whomever the utterer, and however long the period predicted, is apt to fall short of fact itself. Many of the most dramatic developments in Southeast Asia—the emergence of nationwide idioms, the spectacular growth of cities and city-type communications

[1] Indeed, the name "Southeast Asia" is itself a relative novelty, probably not over thirty years old, except as a rare geographic technicality. In the sense of the "span of time in which men have been aware of this idea," Southeast Asia is by far the newest of the major international regions. Before this name was called into vogue, the area was simply "the Farther Indies" or "the tropical Far East."

[2] A comparative scale of communicativeness would have to take into account not only the existing mass media, but the specialized media which give the advanced civilizations their richness and complexity.

as a model for ways of life,[3] the radical transformations occurring in the marriage relationship or the parent-child relationship, the new paper money economics resulting from the swift disappearance of specie as an actual means of exchange, etc.—are global in character and are by no means confined to the area. One of these factors, the increase in literacy, is apt to be more revolutionary in its long-run effects than the total impact of communism and the cold war.[4] The "regional slice" is a good official or scholastic abstraction, conducive to neater discussion or more pointed conclusions, but it should not blind us to the world-wide nature of the issues with which we deal.

Take, as an instance, the propaganda position of "capitalism." It is easy to equate noncommunism with capitalism. Even intelligent American laymen can suppose that Laos will either be "Communist" or "free," depending on which government is in control. Actually, in terms of thousands of people per million engaging in capitalist managerial or marketing operations, it can probably be said that capitalism has not yet arrived in most of Southeast Asia, having beachheads only in Manila, Hongkong, Singapore, and one or two other entrepôts. Much of the argument about "socialism" and "capitalism" is simply irrelevant to the life situations of most of the peoples of Southeast Asia. Communications which involve irrelevant symbols can be very powerful, but they are not apt to bring out the normative and development potentials of any given society.

THE FRAME OF REFERENCE

The authors of this essay include in the second part, on *The Current Operational Situation,* a scorecard of situations

[3] The authors found that in Taiwan, an area adjacent to Southeast Asia, the peasants were setting up many urban standards of behavior and consumption without physically moving themselves from the rural area into the cities.

[4] A literate man loses humility. He obtains access to the raw material of authority. A Luther once turned to the Bible to attack the overwhelming authority of the pope; newly literate populations become "Lutheran" in their attitudes toward accepted authority.

in the propaganda war, but they venture to submit some redefinitions of the "psychological" or "communications" elements in society which will bring Southeast Asia into sharper definition.

The first of these is a political statement of the day-to-day role of the communications process in the lives of individuals, whoever they are and whatever they may be, which will highlight the intimate connection between communications and identity. In the Southeast Asian areas, the process of revaluation is just beginning; in Japan and China it is in full swing; in the European and North American area, communications have reached such a point that millions of persons are drugged and bewildered by a succession of non-operational communications. An attempt will be made to distinguish the *referential,* the *manipulative,* the *value-giving,* and the *identifying* elements in communication.

As a direct sequel of this, the existing audiences for mass communications will be categorized.

Southeast Asian societies do not have a choice in this matter; they are going to get more and more mass communications, whether they like them or not. Political, social, commercial, and agitational forces beyond local control are pouring a flood of mechanical communications into the area. This is a point, for example, on which neutralists, Communists, and pro-Americans agree unanimously—that there be more print, more radio, more films displayed, more television. The outside powers may disagree with one another about the direction or intent of mass communication; they do not disagree in the least about the process.[5] America and

[5] The processes of mass communications, as seen by American scholars and officials, are well presented in Schramm, Wilbur, ed., *The Process and Effects of Mass Communications* (Urbana: University of Illinois Press, 1954). Neither Schramm nor the other accredited experts in this field pay serious attention to the things that people lose when they obtain mass communication. The man who gets a radio loses the excitement of receiving news from his neighbor; the man who buys a newspaper listens to the opinions of persons unknown to himself, instead of hearing men he knows in the local bazaar. The prime feature of mass or mechanical communication is

Russia are making a concerted assault on traditional forms of privacy, intimacy, warmth, and self-respect. In the name of progress, they replace radio and films for community gossip, bazaar talk, or plain loafing.

The two superpowers, however much they agree on attacking and destroying traditional village society wherever they find it, do differ on the kinds of audience they seek—the "action audience," which takes an input of communication and responds with an output of action; the "response audience," which receives mass communication and responds with letters, purchases, or acknowledgments; and the "communicated audience," which neither responds nor acts, but merely hears. In general, the Communists seek the first group and a portion of the second; the Western powers try to reach the third group, with occasional reference to the second, and are distressed if they reach the first and do not know what to do about the action which their own communication has provoked. (General Kong Le, for example, is an almost perfect instance of a man precipitated into the twentieth century by American communications and training who then, subsequent to his modernization, found that Americans regarded talk as an end in itself and who had to swing to the left in order to find something to do with his life.)

Finally, the institution of language is a very powerful one, working as much on the unconscious personality as on the conscious. One need not go to the challenging extremes posited by the late Benjamin Whorf in order to suppose

the fact that the recipient cannot respond to it at the moment of reception, except through the negative device of turning the radio off or putting the newspaper down. He ceases to be a whole man in communication with other human beings, and he becomes a fractional man deprived of the full range of the communications relationship that physiological communications offer. If the Western peoples are not aware of the harm they are doing by the creation of noise-filled loneliness, they are in no position to set an example to the Asian peoples, now tempted by the same gigantic vices. There are few studies of what it is that mass communications replace, but since there are only 960 minutes in a waking day, it is obvious that an input of mass communications must be replacing some other activity.

that language is itself one of the prime determinants of culture.[6] Political changes in the extent and range of language are among the crudest and most powerful political forces of our time. The obsolescence of a previously accepted language downgrades all its speakers; the arrival of a new language, or an old language in a new form, is itself a social and geographical revolution of the first importance. The Southeast Asian "nations," which are—with the exception of Vietnam, Thailand, and the Philippines—nations only by courtesy today, may well become nations as real as Bulgaria or Italy within the next twenty or thirty years, that is, linguistic monoliths possessing conditioned, uniform political responses through most of the politically active strata of their populations.

THE APPEARANCE OF SOCIAL NOISE

For reasons which the present writers have not been able to isolate or to explain in a scientifically acceptable sense, it seems to be almost universally true that mass communications have an initial entertainment and shock value in almost every kind of culture. The *first* appearance of repetitive signposts, radio reception facilities, or motion pictures, once the getting-acquainted process has been crossed, seems to be stimulative in almost all areas that had previously used a predominance of physiological communications (that is, voice or handwriting as opposed to electronics or print). The Vietcong in South Vietnam were, for example, able to make quite a show out of "Stop Taylor!" signs in remote rural areas which had never been exposed to repetitive signs before.

In both Communist and commercial societies, however,

[6] An intellectual obituary on Whorf was pronounced—somewhat prematurely, let us hope—by an interesting symposium edited by Hoijer, Harry, *Language in Culture, Conference on the Interrelations of Language and Other Aspects of Culture* (Chicago: University of Chicago Press, 1954).

mass communications build up a large amount of "social noise." [7] The effect is to diminish the amount of attention paid to any form of mass communication, to make the individual more indifferent to mass communications as a whole and more selective in his processes of choosing the particular items to which he wishes to pay self-conscious attention. Emergent societies are usually served by newspapers which have learned the sensationalism of the West without learning its professional traditions of honest, systematic reportage. All news becomes crisis, all events horrendous, and consecutiveness in understanding public affairs becomes well-nigh impossible. It is significant that the Communist press, though much more distorted than ours in the handling of news, tends to be more sober *in tone* than the non-Communist press.

When mass communications saturate cities like Singapore and Manila, the individuals learn to duplicate the communications processes of city dwellers in the advanced nations. They reject all communications ab initio, and learn to employ some kind of scanning system (itself rooted in their individual temperaments and living habits) by which to ignore most of the print or electronic communication within their area of attention, and to select out of that bulk only the particular things in which they have a personal, emotional, or operational interest.

From the American point of view, it is sometimes forgotten that an increase in the total social noise does not necessarily redound to our benefit or to the advantage of democracy. The Communists try much more bravely than does the West, in their initial propaganda assaults, to reach subdivisions of the public such as youth, women, peace groups, farmers, the professions, and so forth, but the Communists often fail because their propaganda to the specialized groups

[7] With the term "social noise," the authors refer to communications which any individual receives with low or subliminal attention, accompanied with rejection, because his preliminary scanning shows the material to be undesirable for himself at that particular time.

turns out to be nothing more than propaganda (manipulative communication), and because their biased semantics do not leave enough room for the *operational* communications which such specialized groups seek and desire. Magazines for women from the Communist side do not have enough recipes, patterns, etc., while even Argentine magazines make their appearance in Southeast Asia because of the excellent, simple, and varied women's fashions which they portray.

The communications advantages of a pluralistic society, whether democratic or merely traditional, lie in its pluralistic linkages to those other societies to whom it appeals, almost always from one subgroup to another; the communications advantages of a coordinated society like Russia or mainland China lie in startlement and reiteration, at the cost of the quieter operational appeals. Both forms of advanced society risk becoming involved in social noise which everyone hears but to which no one listens; yet the risks they take are different, and the Western output can be reinsured against failure by concurrent, mutually irrelevant, and even contradictory appeals while the bloc output has no sure safeguard.

The free world propagandist has the handicaps and blessings of trying to reconcile an unpredictable output of relevant communication (relevant, that is, to the nation, group, or individuals in question) coming from both official and private sources in his own home country; he may be able to influence what the USIA will send him, but he cannot control a Senator Ellender or a Senator Morse, much less a source like *The New York Times*.[8] The bloc propagandist, on the other hand, must go back through cumbersome, rigid, and complicated channels to make the home

[8] A recent thoughtful study of Burmese foreign policy by Johnstone, William C., *Burma's Foreign Policy, A Study in Neutralism* (Cambridge: Harvard University Press, 1963), p. 284, shows that the term "neutralism" was virtually forced on certain Asian states by the private Western press.

output fit the local situation; sometimes, like the Chinese Communists in India, bloc communicators come close to giving up and merely tell their addressees that the addressees are all wrong.

Renzo Sereno has repeatedly made the realistic point that no propaganda is addressed first of all to the audience: it is addressed to the propagandist's boss or to his budget-maker, because the propagandist, like anyone else, wants to keep his job and to maintain his function in his own society. This is something that he will not do if the propaganda satisfies the audience at the price of alienating his own superiors in the originating government.

COMMUNICATION AS POWER

Most of the political theory written about "power" under one definition or another refers either to military and legal command or to direct political influence of an unmistakable kind, such as the shouting legions at Nazi Nuremberg or Maoist Peking, the silent pedestrians on Stalin's streets, the rioters or counterrioters in many of the world's cities. What is widely overlooked is the fact that *all* language has a manipulative effect.

All cultures have rules concerning the manipulative role of ordinary language, thus far stated only in preliminary and inadequate form by the anthropological literature available on Southeast Asia. An excess of manipulation is almost everywhere rejected; an incomprehensible manipulation (for example, the American saying, "let's *all* be prompt next time!") is dismissed as mere noise; while recognized manipulation, of a familiar kind, is accepted as a familiar, playful challenge, to be met, understood, and replied to in kind.

Language is not only a power instrument between any two people; it is a *normative* factor as well. The behavioralist loads his qualifications with values merely by selecting this or that to measure; yet values which cease to be explicit merely become implicit[9] and continue to lurk behind the scenes. Negative language produces negative values, that is, weak or concealed ones; it does not produce objectivity, which can be found only if *all* significant premises are stated, recognized, and then allowed as variables in the attempt to make a communications or political relationship into a scientifically describable series of happenings.[10]

Quite apart from the referential value of language, well described forty years ago by C. K. Ogden and I. A. Richards in their classic monograph, *The Meaning of Meaning*, language serves a concurrent and often-hidden role in every communications situation. It serves to *identify* both the speaker and the addressee. Such simple statements as "This is a pencil," "Stop that car!" or "Rice is 45.50 a catty, local currency," serve to identify not only the subjects being discussed; they also identify the communicators, both the utterer and the recipient. The recipients above, for example, are quite obviously the pupil, the passer-by, and the purchaser.

Both the bloc propagandists and the American information programmers slip frequently on the "identification of the recipient." In each case a "propaganda man"[11] of some kind is set up to give the propaganda office a general idea of how to write, but the condescension shows through just the same. People who work in mass media are usually convinced of their own superiority to their hearers or readers; when this is multiplied by the factors of international distance, the helplessness of the consumer who cannot even nonbuy a program, and the translation from one language

[9] See the fascinating commentary on this line of thought presented by Waelder, Robert, "Protest and Revolution against Western Societies," in Kaplan, Morton A., ed., *The Revolution in World Politics* (New York: Wiley, 1962), especially pp. 4–8 and 13–20.
[10] See how this problem is met by Pye, Lucian, *Politics, Personality and National Building: Burma's Search for Identity* (New Haven: Yale University Press, 1962), especially pp. xv–xix and 295–301.
[11] For the technical description of the "propaganda man," see Linebarger, Paul M. A., *Psychological Warfare* (New York: Duell, Sloane & Pearce, 1956), pp. 153–155.

and one situation into another, the recipient often gets the net communication that somebody on the outside looks down on him and wants to do something with him, letting the rest of the content slip away into social noise.

SOME POLICY SUGGESTIONS

Information programs have become governmentalized and conventionalized on both sides. Where they appeal to action audiences, they retain a certain amount of freshness, because the communicator has a test—the behavior of his audience—which shows him the effect of what he is doing. Where they are merely communicated for the sake of communication, they are forestalling actions which do no harm and may do some good.

Fresh developments in the information field require a great deal of basic research into the theory of applied communications and into the nature of the societies and subgroups with which we are communicating. (The intake of communication—that is, the artificial stimulation of the importation of Southeast Asian communications into the United States, so that the utterers could know that they were heard and deemed important by the great American people—is still a largely unresolved problem.)

The second part of this essay gives a summary of the current state of affairs in the information field in Southeast Asia. In the over-all view, one must remember that it is not what we do to them (whoever "they" may be at any moment) which matters to a foreign audience; it is what we do to ourselves.

The world has momentarily come to a rather bleak and unproductive period. American democracy is not doing anything very new at home. Communist China is a disappointment, even as an enemy.

The communication which matters most of all is the one which the recipient wishes to hear—real news, about historically important people, concerning acts or decisions which affect mankind. War can always provide these, and the cold war can sham them. Perhaps one of the things which real communications effectiveness requires is this: an actual acceptance of peace, the peace we have had and are having, the peace we intend to keep. If the emphasis of both leadership and propaganda is directed away from the endless braggadocio of minor power-plays in this corner of the world or that, and if people accept the simple fact that they cannot count on a thermonuclear war to relieve them of all responsibilities of everyday living, it may be possible for information policies to use ordinary life and real human affairs as sources for a better persuasiveness.

It is difficult for the United States to lead Southeast Asia somewhere if the United States does not itself know where it is going, or why.

In our domestic political and economic developments, in our eventual escape from the now-obsolete clichés of the 1930's, there lies the best hope that our information programs will reach real audiences—not because the information techniques are clever but because we Americans, here at home, have made the world friendly and inquisitive about ourselves. This is a task for the scholar, the official, and the citizen in this country—for the citizen most of all. It is too complex to be handled by specialists. Political hope and political innovation are like styles and fashions in other aspects of human culture, essentially noncausable and usually unpredictable. We cannot make America do much of anything, but we can see to it that, if we begin going somewhere ourselves, the world shall know of it, fairly, fully, and interestingly.

Within the limits of our present position and the kind of leadership we have had for the past decade, we have done professionally very well in the information field. Information supplements reality, unless it falsifies it. Since only the worst of crises justifies falsification, American information programs will continue to depend, as they have in the past, on domestic developments to give them vitality and appeal. As citizens and as taxpayers, we should not be penny-wise and pound-foolish, spending billions on weapons systems while grudging each of the information media the few million dollars it needs for Southeast Asia, but we must never expect the information officer to make up for the things which the President and the citizens are not doing at home. If we have a New Deal or a Real Step Forward, the world will want to hear of it, but it will be our actions and not our slogans that will exercise the ultimate appeal.

THE CURRENT OPERATIONAL SITUATION

There are a number of intangible factors in the operations of information agencies and other psychological instruments of policy.[12] Government specialists are unanimous in their statements that the most important factor in any information program is the effect of the personalities involved. In many cases, the interrelationships of the American personnel with that of the citizens of the countries to which they are sent are impossible to assess ahead of time. For example, a young Negro secretary sent to one United States Information Service (USIS) post in a Southeast Asian country was the most popular member of the American team with the natives of the country. In another neighboring country, a Negro employee was not even allowed to demonstrate efficiency or

[12] The material for this section was gathered by extensive interviews with USIA in Washington and with its branch offices, called USIS (United States Information Service) in the field. The writer has called in person at the offices in Djakarta, Singapore, Kuala Lumpur, Rangoon, Bangkok, Saigon, Vientiane and Manila. In Washington, USIA was very helpful, and so were officials of AID and HEW. Recent documentation for 1961–1963 included an evaluation of the binational centers, a summary of recent trends on technical education in Indonesia, a summary of special presentations for 1962 in the Far East, and the "fact books" prepared on these countries for USIA's own use. Sources from the information services of Malaya, Indonesia, Singapore, Burma, the Philippines, Laos, Hongkong and the Republic of China were also consulted, either through personal visits or through correspondence.

empathy; the government of that country demanded his removal on the grounds that the United States was demonstrating contempt for that country by sending a Negro.

No matter how potentially good an information program might be, if the persons chosen to go to the field are unable, for one reason or another, to be accepted, or if they cannot demonstrate sympathy with and understanding of the indigenous population, the program has little chance of success. Conversely, persons possessing the psychological acumen and attunement which make native populations, both elites and villagers, feel that here is a person who *understands* them and their problems, are able to accomplish virtual miracles with very little to work from. Ideally, of course, both the attuned personnel and the materials and program with which to work should be present, but the most important single factor is the individual. In some senses, such programs as Medico and the Peace Corps, or individuals such as American students and tourists, may be the most effective—although unmeasurable—instruments of American policy.

Another element difficult to measure is that of informal communications: gossip, rumor, family relations, custom, travelers and merchants, meetings at market, and the penetration of other organizations (teachers, religious leaders, trade union leaders, village headmen, and the like), as well as political parties and other groups theoretically without a primary communications goal. Much of the population of Southeast Asia is rural (Indonesia's population is, for example, almost 85 per cent rural), and in many of these areas informal communication is more effective than formal communication, both because of the ease of transmission and because direct oral communication is more likely to be believed as coming from a known source than is an impersonal communication. Cambodia and Laos have two of the least developed mass media systems in Southeast Asia, as shown in Table 1. Newspapers are few, ephemeral, and urban; there are almost no periodicals; library facilities are extremely limited; and the literacy rate is low. In Laos, even radio broadcasting is not considered particularly effective because of the dearth of radio sets. In Cambodia, on the other hand, radio is probably the most effective means of mass communications; there were estimated to be about 28,000 sets in Cambodia in 1962. Government-sponsored information halls incorporating radio speakers and film projectors in large villages have not met with marked success in terms of participation and use.

Pressure groups, elites, political parties, and many other factors affect communications patterns. It is impossible even to skim the surface of all these potential influences in a brief essay. This part of the essay, therefore, is confined to a discussion of such (theoretically) measurable means of communication and information as newspapers, periodicals, books, information centers, and radio. Data concerning film and audio-visual presentation, unfortunately, are for the most part not available.

Attendance figures at USIS centers and libraries are subject to various interpretations. Although there are figures available concerning total attendance in any one year, or total circulation of books, there is no way of knowing whether these figures represent repeated attendance by a relatively small group or infrequent attendance by a large percentage of the population. (In Moulmein, Burma, for example, with a population of 107,250, attendance at USIS centers in 1962 was 232,643. Did the entire population of Moulmein average attendance of more than twice during the year, or did a relatively small group attend repeatedly?) Initial attendance might indicate nothing more than curiosity; repeated visits might indicate a greater degree of interest. In one Southeast Asian country a few years ago, USIS was flattered by the vast number of requests for a certain booklet, until it was discovered that the Communist party was deliberately collecting and destroying the booklets to prevent their falling into the hands of the general population. Frequent attendance by a small group might

TABLE 1

COMMUNICATIONS IN SOUTHEAST ASIA

	Burma	Cambodia	Indonesia	Laos	Malaya	Philippines	Singapore	Thailand	South Vietnam
Population	21 million	4.95 million	88 million	est. 2.5 million	6.3 million	27.5 million	1.63 million	26 million	13.2 million
Literacy	55–60%	35–40%	40–50%	very low	25% Malay 35% Chinese	65% English or Tagalog	62% Malay 46% Chinese	60%	40–60% in Vietnamese
Indigenous Newspapers	34	21	114	2 or 3	15	125	8	19	29
Indigenous Periodicals	10	12	497	—	—	783	—	165	65
Book Publication: New Titles	442	—	652	—	147	250 est.	47	200	—
Radio Stations	one (4 transmitters)	one (5 transmitters)	one (29 transmitters)	—	one (7 transmitters)	50	one (3 transmitters)	80	one (3 channels)
Radio Sets	110,000	28,000	ca. 1 million	very few	273,000; 251,600 redifusion	750,000	190,000; 150,000 redifusion	3 million	ca. 300,000
Urban Population	6.35 million	792,000	14 million	130,000	2.35 million	9.3 million	993,700	3+ million	3.96 million
Rural Population	14.65 million	4.16 million	74 million	2+ million	3.23 million	18.2 million	587,900	22.5 million	9+ million
USIS									
Attendance at Centers	610,530	67,431	414,332	53,580	463,845	776,353	256,443	318,174	552,365
U.S. Books in English	56,298	5,746	64,073	2,788	23,619	31,998	14,452	26,086	17,656
U.S. Books in Translation	1,179	2,142	5,198	1,311	3	3	3,695	2,953	3,833
Periodicals	1,173	61	1,731	117	286	478	275	405	315
Book Circulation	280,970	19,748	173,833	2,326	122,168	204,533	45,930	131,337	1,107,243
VOA									
Weekly Hours in English (regional)	10.30	10.30	10.30	10.30	10.30	10.30	10.30	10.30	10.30
Hours in Cantonese	21	21	21	21	21	21	21	21	21
Hours in Mandarin	7	7	7	7	7	7	7	7	7
Hours in Indigenous Language	14 Burmese	7 Khmer	14 Indonesian	7 Lao 7 Thai	14 Amoy 14 Indonesian	—	14 Amoy 14 Indonesian	7 Thai	14 Amoy 14 Vietnamese

This table is based primarily on the "fact books" prepared by USIA for its own use, though the author has used her own judgment in checking basic data against other sources. Of special value, in this connection, were technical reports from the Philippine Department of Commerce and Industry and of the Thai Central Statistical Office.

also indicate that materials were not chosen to meet the needs and interests of the larger group, or perhaps that the center was catering almost exclusively to a small pro-American nucleus without attracting any new participants. Sometimes such selective attendance indicates nothing more than a low literacy rate.

One of the relatively measurable comparisons is the availability of other news sources to the population. In some countries of Southeast Asia, news is almost completely government-controlled. During 1962, for example, free world press coverage in Indonesia was in an extremely unfavorable position because the merger of Antara, the pro-leftest government news agency, with the PIA (Persbiro Indonesia) a non-Communist independent agency, had the effect of sharply reducing independent news sources and free world access to news channels in Indonesia. The Communist world had a relative advantage here in that at least eleven Communist-front and fellow-traveling newspapers accounted for well over one-third of all Indonesia's newspaper circulation. In South Vietnam, also, there is only one domestic news agency, the Vietnam Press, which operates under the auspices of the Department of Information. News is censored, most newspapers are pro-American; none is pro-Communist. Although news channels are closed to the Communists, they are not completely open to the West either.

In Laos, newspapers are almost nonexistent. During 19 the mimeographed daily Lao-Presse, published by the Ministry of Information, and the Bulletin de Nouvelles, issued by the French embassy (both in the French language) probably formed the chief source of news for the elites addition, some 10,000 copies of Thai newspapers and periodicals were said to be distributed daily. Of the few, transitory Cambodian newspapers, only one was definitely Western, most being pro-Communist or neutralist. Almost all news sources have relative freedom of access to Burmese newspapers, but the papers themselves are ephemeral rapidly appearing or disappearing with the splintering various political parties.

Thai newspapers have a generally rather low credibility among the population as a whole, but although the nominal circulation is low, readership is high, with each individual copy of a newspaper having an estimated 20 to 25 readers. In both Burma and Thailand, Buddhist priests, village headmen, or teachers read and interpret the news to the villagers. In both Burma and Thailand, there is a certain irresponsibility and sensationalism which tends to discredit belief, although entertainment value remains high. There is, nevertheless, some serious press, particularly in Burma, but Thai newspapers tend to emphasize entertainment.

In Malaya and Singapore, although news sources are accessible to all, there has been since independence increasing left-wing Chinese pressure placed upon the more conservative newspapers. In order to retain circulation within Malaya, however, many newspapers have been constrained not to go to leftist extremes. The Philippines probably has the communications system least controlled by the government of any of the Southeast Asian nations. About 125 newspapers are published in the Philippines, with an official circulation of 1.33 million but a probable readership of 4 million.

Periodicals also vary greatly from country to country. Very few periodicals are published in Cambodia or Laos; a vast number are published in Indonesia and the Philippines. One of the most popular of the Indonesian periodicals is the USIS publication *Aneka America* ("Many-sided" or "Variegated" America), a monthly with a circulation of 140,000, the largest circulation of any single magazine in Indonesia. The publication issued by the Soviet Embassy, *Negeri Soviet* (Soviet Country) has a circulation of 80,000, which ranks it fourth or fifth among the magazines of Indonesia. The magazine published by USIS in Indonesia is the only USIS magazine issued in any of the countries of Southeast Asia. Since there is a dearth of periodicals in Burma, this would appear to be a favorable country in which to issue an American periodical. Many periodicals are imported in Malaya and Singapore.

USIS centers and reading rooms are scattered throughout Southeast Asia. These serve for special exhibits, and contain in addition a library of books in translation and in English, and of periodicals. There is a center in each capital city, and one or more centers or reading rooms in other cities of each country. Attendance varies greatly from country to country, not always in any discernible relationship to the political coloration of the country. Indonesia and parts of Burma, for example, although not particularly pro-American, have a relatively high attendance rate at the centers; Laos, considering the literacy rate, has an extremely high attendance; South Vietnam, however, with a presumably strongly pro-American sentiment, has one of the lowest attendance rates. At Saigon, for example, the ratio of attendance to population in 1962 was one in sixty. Thailand also had a relatively low attendance record for a pro-Western country (about one in nine), but considering the general Thai apathy toward books, this is not inconsiderable. A curious aspect of the USIS centers in Thailand is the fact that, although USIS rates the English-language facility of the Thai as low, it nevertheless had some 27,000 books in English with less than 3,000 in Thai. Book circulation figures indicate, however, that either USIS erred in its rating of English-language reading ability or that the books in translation were in almost constant circulation. Songkhla, for example, with about 2,400 books, had a circulation of well over 12,000.

Radio appears to be one of the best and most effective means of reaching much of the scattered rural population of Southeast Asia. In several countries (Indonesia, Thailand, and the Philippines) there are village radio sets, sometimes privately owned, sometimes provided by the government to the headman of the village, around which the people gather to listen in the evenings. In some places, particularly Indonesia and Thailand, verbal communication has a much higher credibility rating than the written word, probably in great part because of illiteracy. The Voice of America (VOA) broadcasts regularly to the Far East. Weekly there are 77 hours of English audible in the area, of which over 10 hours are regionalized English (that is, directly beamed to the area and having a local application). VOA also broadcasts in Chinese, as well as in Burmese, Cambodian, Indonesian, Lao, Thai, and Vietnamese. (See Table 1.) Reportedly one of the most popular programs throughout the world in 1962 was the VOA report of the Telstar operations. It seems evident that VOA radio programs are potentially one of the most effective means of reaching the peoples of Southeast Asia.

Figures on USIS films and audio-visual presentations are not available, but in radio-starved Laos a number of USIS films were reportedly very popular. Films have also been very popular in Thailand and serve as an important means of communication. In 1962, USIS showed the film "Friendship Seven," about American astronauts, to 28 schools in 62 showings for 15,546 students. All showings were at the request of the schools in response to a letter of inquiry from USIS. As an aftermath, several hundred students then enrolled at the USIS libraries as new members.

Another VOA program that has had unprecedented popularity in several of the countries in which it was used is the Let's Learn English program. In Cambodia, American books were used for the first time in Cambodian classrooms in conjunction with this program. In Thailand, the program resulted in the sale of 10,000 copies of the accompanying manual, something of a record for book-apathetic Thailand.

In 1962, television was available in Bangkok, Thailand, and the Manila area of the Philippines. It does not as yet play a major part in the communications pattern of Southeast Asia.

The presentation program of USIS (that is, presenting books and subscriptions of certain American periodicals to certain leaders of countries) has also elicited favorable comment from many of the Southeast Asian governments. These books are carefully selected so as not to convey an obvious propaganda aspect, and this fact is one of the reasons for their popularity. For example, 150 copies of the *World Almanac, 1962* were given to newspaper editors and information officers in Burma; 6 subscriptions to *Art in America* were presented to Cambodian artists; 15 copies of *Webster's New Collegiate Dictionary* were given to university students. These are only a few examples.

In Burma, USIS has been of particularly effective help in inaugurating a library training program (conducted under the auspices of the Rangoon and Mandalay USIS centers). Twenty-five people were trained, including reading room assistants, teachers, and youth leaders; as a result of this program, school libraries were being established for the first time in some of the high schools outside of Rangoon.

From the above brief description, it should be obvious that, although American information programs are undoubtedly not at maximum efficiency, they provide a potentially useful psychological instrument of policy as a means of influencing youths and leaders. In many instances (Indonesia, Cambodia, and Laos, for example), the information programs appear the best, if not the only, means of portraying the American viewpoint, of projecting a good American image, or even of serving as a source for free world news. In countries with large newspaper circulation and radio coverage, when there is relative openness of news channels (such as in the Philippines), while retaining importance as a means of communication, information programs lose some of their value as psychological instruments of policy.

In some countries there appears to be an insufficient number of books in translation for use in USIS libraries; VOA is also broadcasting for a relatively short time to some areas which have an adequate number of radio receivers. To judge by experience in Laos and Thailand, USIS motion pictures have great popularity and could perhaps be put to greater use than at present. American publication of periodicals and comic books, perhaps for budgetary reasons, is relatively low, although this type of publication has had demonstrated popularity.

The most frequent complaint on the part of countries in which USIS operates in Southeast Asia has been the rather obvious propaganda aspect of some USIS activities. One Asian told the writers that he always listened to the Armed Forces radio dictation-speed English, directed to other American forces, rather than the VOA programs, because he felt he could trust the Americans to tell each other the truth, but did not trust broadcasts which he knew to be directed specifically toward him. Most appreciated items in presentation programs and in USIS libraries have been works describing American life in the same terms in which the material would be presented to Americans, and books that have demonstrated American understanding and appreciation of some aspect of the Southeast Asian country to which the books have been sent. Works obviously aimed at proclaiming America's greatness, superiority, or glory to Southeast Asians were most disliked, and at times even had a counterproductive effect. Vindictive polemics against Communist countries were also disliked, although objective presentations of facts about Communist operations were acceptable.

It seems self-evident that the information programs are of great importance in much of the area, that USIS in general is doing a fairly good job, and that there is room for improvement. It is to be hoped that a realization of the importance of such programs will lead to larger budgets, which in turn would lead to the improvements indicated. It is also possible that greater effort put into the study of intangibles would indicate means by which information programs may be made a more effective psychological instrument of policy.

11

SOME REFLECTIONS ON
UNITED STATES POLICY
IN SOUTHEAST ASIA

{ornament}

WILLIAM HENDERSON

I

One of the most frequent criticisms voiced about United States foreign policy, especially with respect to Asia, is that we really do not have a policy but rather a sad mélange of improvisations and stopgap measures, often working at cross purposes and serving no clear objectives. The intent of this brief concluding essay is to examine the validity of this criticism as it applies to American policy in Southeast Asia, and beyond this to provide a framework for the critical evaluation of policy toward the region.

The United States was slow to become intimately involved in the concerns of Southeast Asia after the end of World War II. Not until 1950, when the Communist Chinese completed their conquest of the mainland and entrenched Communist power along the whole periphery of Southeast

Asia, did our involvement in the region take on serious dimensions. Faced with the perceived threat of Communist expansion in Southeast Asia, Washington thereafter gradually adapted for application to the region the same basic concept of containment that had served so well in dealing with a comparable threat to Western Europe. The overriding objective of policy was to safeguard the independence, whether actual or incipient (for we recognized that the day of colonialism was drawing to a close), of the countries of Southeast Asia against the imminent danger of Communist absorption, either overtly in consequence of external aggression or covertly as the result of internal subversion. From the beginning this was viewed as primarily a military problem, at least in the first instance. The principal American effort was therefore directed to safeguarding the military security of the Southeast Asian countries against the Communists, both by strengthening in so far as seemed feasible their own military establishments and by extending the mantle of American military power over the region. But United States policy was also aware of the close relationship between the Communist threat to Southeast Asia and the profound political, economic, and social problems besetting the region. Hence behind the protective barrier thus thrown up (a Southeast Asian salient of the "wall of containment," to apply Secretary Acheson's term), we also strove within the limits of available resources to ameliorate these problems in order to lessen the appeals of communism within the region and to strengthen the Southeast Asian countries so that they could themselves contribute more effectively to their own defense against Communist aggression and subversion.

Of course, specific containment policies originally developed for Western Europe could not be applied automatically to Southeast Asia. The nature of the problem here was much different. These were weak, impoverished, underdeveloped countries just emerging from Western colonial domination. All of them were beset at every turn by the processes of profound revolutionary change set in motion by their irrevocable and progressively more intimate involvement with the civilization of the West. Policies appropriate to the highly industrialized and politically advanced nations of Western Europe, which were possessed of great inherent military capacity and which shared a common appreciation of the Communist danger, were hardly applicable to the countries of Southeast Asia. This is, indeed, one of the reasons for the uncertainties and ambiguities that have often appeared in the implementation of Southeast Asian policy over the past decade and more. The courses of action required to give substance to containment in Western Europe, however difficult and complex they seemed at the time, were simplicity itself in comparison with those required in the almost totally different and infinitely more challenging environment of present-day Southeast Asia.

In consequence, United States actions in Southeast Asia have often appeared ill-advised, inadequate, and occasionally downright foolhardy. Something, a great many things, obviously went terribly wrong with our policy in Laos in the years following the 1954 Geneva settlement. After almost a decade of massive effort in South Vietnam, we are still on the edge of the precipice. The main instrument of our alliance policy, SEATO, has often seemed to divide and disrupt the region as much as to unite it in the common defense. Much of our economic assistance appears to have fallen on fallow ground. And so on.

But, leaving entirely aside the question whether such criticism takes adequate account of the severe limits to what foreign policy may hope to accomplish anywhere, it is simply wrong to go on from there and conclude that we do not have a Southeast Asian policy in any real sense. If one means by policy a conceptual framework for the guidance of concrete actions toward the accomplishment of comprehensible goals, we have had a fairly clear Southeast Asian policy for a good many years. The concept, to repeat, is to safeguard the independence of the Southeast Asian countries against the menace of Communist aggression and subversion, first and foremost by strengthening their military security, and secondly, by encouraging their political, economic, and social development in freedom behind the secure barrier of containment.

Some would argue (the author is not among them) that the underlying concept of containment in Southeast Asia is itself short-sighted and misconstrues the main problems with which we must deal in the region, particularly by unnecessarily injecting "cold war calculations" into the Southeast Asian environment and by its emphasis on military policy. Whatever the merits of this line of criticism, the point to be made here is that we have at least had an approach, a fairly clear idea of what we are trying to do—in short, a policy. It has given purpose and a considerable measure of coherence to United States actions in Southeast Asia for more than a decade.

II

The great weakness of United States policy in Southeast Asia since the 1950's, which indeed may ultimately prove a fatal defect, is that we have never been quite sure how serious we are about the whole business. Are our interests in Southeast Asia really *vital* national interests? Despite our rapidly increasing participation in the affairs of Southeast Asia, especially since the Communist take-over on the Chinese mainland, we have never quite been able to accept without serious question, as we have for the most part (it is hazardous to generalize too precisely about national attitudes) with respect to Western Europe, that the independence of Southeast Asia is a literally vital national interest of the United States. In consequence, American policy toward the region has usually lacked dynamism, a sense of urgency and crisis commensurate with the dimensions of the Communist threat to the region. Nor has there ever been much popular interest in, or active support for, the steadily increasing involvement of the United States in Southeast Asian affairs. Hence, when the going gets really tough, as for example in Laos in 1961 or South Vietnam in 1963, one hears growing doubts and questionings. Why should we strive to help the Laotians when their own army won't fight the Communists? Why must Americans die for Ngo Dinh Diem?

Such things can hardly be measured, but it is the author's conviction that whatever the material or strategic importance of the region for the United States, its loss (or the loss of any comparable area, such as South Asia or tropical Africa) to the Communists would be an irreparable blow to the cause of freedom everywhere in the world and would fatally undermine confidence in our determination and ability to lead that cause successfully. While the situation in Laos since 1954 has been muddied at best and while one may endlessly argue the wisdom of such a course, the failure of the United States to vindicate its moral commitment to come to the defense of the royal government in 1961 when beset by a Communist-led insurrection has already compromised our claim to leadership, at least in Southeast Asia. My own view is that we shall ultimately fail to secure the basic objectives of policy in Southeast Asia until our commitment to the region becomes unlimited, and it has not been up till now. This does not mean simply that we must be prepared to fight for Southeast Asia, if necessary, although it certainly means that at a minimum. Beyond this is involved a much greater commitment of our resources, our knowledge, and our whole national effort than we have hitherto been prepared to make, in order effectively to influence the political, economic, and social development of these countries along fruitful paths.

Such a commitment will come, if at all, only in response to sustained and persuasive governmental, that is to say presidential, leadership and guidance. We have not had such guidance on Southeast Asian policy by any administration in Washington since the end of World War II: not by President Truman, although his administration began the process of intimate American involvement in the affairs of the region; not under President Eisenhower, despite the far-reaching commitments of the Manila pact; and not (yet) from President Kennedy, whose military ambivalence in Laos has not been wholly compensated for by military determination in Thailand and South Vietnam. All three administrations have done much to broaden and deepen the American involvement in Southeast Asia; all have contributed creatively and constructively to the formulation of policy toward the region. But through all of their actions have run an unmistakable reticence and restraint, an unwillingness to go the whole way, to make the final commitment and to carry the public with them. And this has probably been because, by and large, senior foreign policy officials have themselves, like the general public, remained unconvinced that the region is a truly vital interest of the United States.

III

This doubt and ambiguity in Southeast Asian policy is perhaps best illustrated by the evolution of United States military policy toward the region.

The military or security emphasis of United States policy in Southeast Asia has been widely criticized, and it is difficult to understand exactly why. For if the security of the Southeast Asian countries is not safeguarded in the face of threatened Communist internal and external aggression, all other aspects of policy are futile and the other objectives of United States policy in the region become by definition unattainable. First things must come first, and in Southeast Asia security is the prerequisite for progress in the political, economic, and social fields. There is, of course, an intimate interrelationship among these problems. Since World War II the Southeast Asian countries have afforded innumerable demonstrations of the truth that the single-minded pursuit of security, without reference to the amelioration of conditions of political tyranny, economic backwardness, and social injustice, is doomed to failure. But United States policy *has* been aware of this, and a substantial proportion of our attention and aid has always gone for nonmilitary purposes. No doubt the balance of policy, the "mix" as between military and nonmilitary purposes, and still more the content and implementation of policies in specific instances, may be heavily criticized. But the underlying concept of policy and the ordering of relative priorities have been sound.

A proper test of policy is performance. How effectively has United States military policy helped to preserve the security of Southeast Asia against Communist aggression and subversion? With respect to large-scale, overt Communist aggression of the Korean type, there has been none. Much of the credit for this may reasonably be assigned to the American commitment, extended primarily through the SEATO alliance system, forcibly to oppose Communist aggression in the region. To be sure, we cannot be certain that such aggression would have occurred in the absence of American involvement; but the Communist, especially the Chinese Communist, record elsewhere in Asia is highly suggestive. Whether SEATO was the best vehicle for extension of the main American guarantee is much more open to doubt. In 1954 there may, indeed, have been wiser approaches to the problem of security in Southeast Asia; but once established, it is difficult for the author to see how SEATO could be dismantled without disastrous political and psychological consequences.

The record in dealing with internal subversion, particularly in the form of Communist-instigated guerilla warfare or insurgency, has been less impressive. There are three aspects of this problem to be touched on. In the first place, we have not yet demonstrated beyond cavil that we know how to develop in Southeast Asian countries, through the provision of modern arms on a large scale and extensive military training and advice, indigenous military forces capable of dealing effectively with Communist-led guerilla movements. Perhaps we have been too disheartened by our lamentable failure to make much out of the royal army in Laos. But the problem here was probably more one of morale and motivation than of technical military capability. In South Vietnam, by contrast, we have apparently made real progress (especially since 1961) in improving the capacity of the South Vietnamese military for coping with the Vietcong insurgency. Further, the largely American-equipped and American-trained Philippine armed forces successfully suppressed the Hukbalahap movement; and the Thai military, also partly American-trained, is reported to have a substantial antiguerilla capability. There would appear to be no technical or military reason why the United States could not, if given sufficient time, assist interested Southeast Asian countries to develop effective antiguerilla forces.

Second, in this general area the inadequacy of military policy *by itself* as an approach to the problems of Southeast Asia is clearly apparent. Guerilla warfare feeds on political, economic, and social discontent in the Southeast Asian countries, and a narrowly military solution to the challenge of Communist-led insurgency is virtually impossible. Nor will indigenous armies fight to suppress such insurgency, which invariably does battle in the name of reform, unless adequately motivated by hope for a better life. The point is only touched on here, since it should be obvious, although it sometimes seems to be lost sight of in the implementation of United States policy in the region. An effective military policy is simply the essential *precondition* for the achievement of over-all United States objectives in Southeast Asia. But military policy cannot be effective, nor the larger objectives of policy secured, unless at the same time the United States finds ways and means to assist, cajole, guide, and even coerce the countries of the region to measures of reform which offer promise for substantial improvement in living standards and in the political and social fabric of the state.

There will be times, however, when the local armed forces will prove inadequate to the task, however well trained, competently led, and highly motivated they may be. In such circumstances, the only alternative to ultimate Communist take-over is forcible intervention by the United States, with whatever elements of power may be necessary to swing the balance. Succor cannot be expected from any other Western great power that might conceivably have the means to intervene effectively (with the exception of the United Kingdom in relation to Malaysia), for their interests and responsibilities in Southeast Asia have substantially attenuated since the end of World War II. The United Nations offers no plausible protection. Nor does "neutralization" of the threatened country, as with Laos at the Geneva Conference in 1962, offer a realistic alternative. For the Communists, this represents simply a temporary halfway house of policy, a tactical pause to be honored only so long as necessity or expediency dictates and meanwhile to be exploited as opportunity affords. Given the unlimited nature of Communist ambitions, there can be no permanent accommodation between the countries of Southeast Asia, on the one hand, and their indigenous Communist movements or the Communist bloc countries, on the other.

Hence only the United States can make up the difference. This has posed a real dilemma for American policy in the region. The case would not be so difficult in the event of direct, overt Communist aggression against a Southeast Asian country—that is, an open and undisguised invasion by the regular armed forces of Communist China, for example, or North Vietnam, which the indigenous armies of Southeast Asia will probably never be strong enough to contain. The United States could hardly fail to respond to such a challenge to its position and commitments in Southeast Asia, to its world-wide prestige and leadership, and to the security of the region as a whole, with whatever force might be necessary; and we would almost certainly carry the war to the heartland of the aggressor in such circumstances and employ nuclear weapons as necessary. But it is precisely because the United States response to overt aggression in Southeast Asia is almost (but not quite) certain that such aggression has so far not taken place.

The situation would be much more obscure in the event of a Communist-led guerilla movement that threatened a complete take-over, to say nothing of a successful Communist coup d'état or victory at the polls. But such eventualities are much more likely than overt Communist aggression in Southeast Asia. Here it is by no means certain just how the United States would respond; the record of somewhat comparable cases over the past decade is ambiguous. The United States decided against military intervention in the Indochinese civil war in 1954 in face of imminent French military disaster, although we joined in diplomatic efforts to limit the extent of Communist take-over to North Vietnam and two provinces of northeastern Laos; covert, half-hearted, and on the whole rather absurd intervention in Indonesia in and after 1958 on the side of anti-Communist rebels against Sukarno's government proved an utter fiasco and highly counterproductive; in Laos, in 1960–1962, we declined to intervene militarily, although employing diplomacy and the threat of possible military intervention to slow down the pace of Communist take-over; Washington sent troops to Thailand during the same crisis to demonstrate our determination with respect to that country; and in South Vietnam after 1961, we undertook a limited intervention, in face of a rapidly deteriorating military situation, which has been enormously helpful in stabilizing the military balance as against the Vietcong, at least for the time being, but which has not provided the margin for victory over the Communists. Who can tell what the United States might do in the next comparable circumstance? To be sure, the United States since 1961 has greatly increased its capability for waging limited and guerilla wars, and this is to the good. But will we really use our "special forces" when the next bell rings?

The reasons for this uncertainty are readily understandable. Guerilla warfare in the jungles of Southeast Asia is messy and difficult to win. We may become bogged down in interminable, indecisive conflict, which would be politically highly unpopular at home, to say nothing of the reaction in many Southeast Asian quarters as well. Should we not preserve our military strength and moral stamina for the main event? Moreover, intervention might provoke counterintervention, the war could quickly escalate and touch off the very thermonuclear holocaust we have striven so mightily to prevent. Is the game worth the candle? Is Southeast Asia *really* vital to the national interests of the United States?

While there are obvious political and military advantages to maintaining ambiguity of response to less-than-overt challenges in Southeast Asia, such uncertainty in the kinds of circumstances discussed here also has strong countervailing disadvantages. For one thing it reduces the credibility of the prospect that the United States will in fact respond in any given circumstance, and by the same token it encourages military and other adventurism on the part of the Communists. But most of all, it must undermine the will and vitiate the determination of the local governments to stand against Communist subversion and civil war. The problem here is not so much that a Southeast Asian regime, having fought bravely and well but confronted with overwhelming odds, would be left to fend for itself in the moment of supreme crisis by a suddenly pusillanimous America. It is rather that, lacking the certainty of all-out American support in the first place, the Southeast Asian government might oppose the Communists halfheartedly, ineffectively, or not at all. The assurance of American backing in face of *all* likely Communist challenges is a prerequisite for the maintenance of Southeast Asian effort and morale in protracted struggle with the Communists.

IV

If one of the main purposes of military policy in Southeast Asia is to buy time, this is no guarantee that the time will be wisely used. How effectively has the United States employed its power and influence to promote meaningful political, economic, and social reform in the region? The record seems to show that here, too, the United States has been strong on concept but much weaker in the elaboration of specific policies than in the security field. Our painful shortcomings in these broad areas have given the critics a field day, and rightly so. It may be helpful, therefore, to place these weaknesses of policy, which are very serious indeed, in proper perspective.

We *have* grasped the larger outlines of the historic tasks confronting us in the Southeast Asian countries. We have understood, in general terms, that these countries are passing through a protracted period of revolutionary transformation, engendered primarily by the impact of the West on the autochthonous civilizations of the region. The twilight of Western colonial domination has been a major turning point in this long historical process but not the end of the road. Quite the reverse; if anything, the modernization of Southeast Asia has rapidly accelerated since the end of colonial rule. Great turmoil and unrest have been an inevitable concomitant of this process, even if communism had never been invented to complicate the situation and to cloud the minds of men as to the staggering underlying problems involved. (On the other hand, many commentators on United States policy in Southeast Asia, especially those who for some reason resent our overriding concern with the threat of communism, seem to forget that communism *does* vastly complicate the situation and make the resolution of these basic problems infinitely more difficult.) We have realized, finally, that it is to the interest of the United States to assist these countries in the achievement of a new cultural synthesis which hopefully would bring an end to revolutionary ferment in Southeast Asia; and we have further realized that this new synthesis should include as major components not only stable and effective government but also a liberal political and social environment and a dynamic, growing economy. No doubt these goals of United States policy have derived primarily from calculations of national interest in the context of the cold war, as has already been suggested. But we needlessly belittle ourselves not to concede that they reflect also, at least to some extent, more generous and humane motives as well.

Yet I wonder whether we have taken the full measure of these historic tasks. They are, in short, nothing less than to assist purposefully and constructively in the processes of modern nation building in Southeast Asia, to deflect the course of a fundamental revolution into channels compatible with the long range interests of the United States. They place upon our foreign policy demands of a wholly new dimension, of a kind that we have not had to cope with hitherto. They demand a degree of involvement in the affairs of Southeast Asia that few could possibly have imagined even a decade ago. They call for a new diplomacy.

There is no space here to discuss what would be required of the United States in order to practice successfully the new diplomacy of nation building in Southeast Asia. At a minimum, it would require a greater commitment of material resources. But this has not been the principal shortfall to date. There is a limit to the external material aid which the countries of Southeast Asia can prudently put to use. The difference between what has thus far been available and what could be wisely employed, although large, would not be an unmanageable demand upon the United States.

Much more critical is the inadequacy of our human resources with which to pursue a manipulative, constructive diplomacy among the modernizing countries of Southeast Asia (and, indeed, in the other underdeveloped regions of the world). Our knowledge is pitifully inadequate; we do not have the people to teach us; and we do not have the practitioners to act upon that knowledge. If the United States is to play its proper role in the development of Southeast Asia, perhaps the most immediate call upon our energies and industry must be to enlarge the body of expertise and the corps of specialists, both in the government and in the academic community, without whom we can never hope to conduct a resourceful diplomacy in the region.

We must greatly speed up our research and experimentation in the alternatives of action available to us in Southeast Asia. A good deal has already been done in the science of economic development, although even here we are still beginners in the field. Vastly more awaits doing with respect to guiding and assisting the processes of political and social modernization.

At the same time, we must always keep in the forefront of our perspective the limits of a constructive diplomacy. There are at least two aspects to this. In the first place, while the horizons of the new diplomacy must be energetically explored in order to capitalize on all possibilities for influencing the development of the Southeast Asian countries, we must realize that there are inevitably severe limits to even the most creative policy. The art of a constructive diplomacy will be to discern the bounds of the possible in the exercise of constructive influence, to approach them but not to transgress them. Secondly, while the horizons of the new diplomacy greatly augment the possibilities of constructive action, they will place a corresponding premium on subtlety and delicacy of touch. To be sure, one can coerce with a bludgeon, and very occasionally this may be necessary. But in the long run, the gentler techniques of persuasion and cajolement are infinitely to be preferred.

Most of all, successful practice of a constructive diplomacy in Southeast Asia requires that we surmount a great psychological barrier. The new diplomacy is frankly interventionist, and we must recognize that it goes counter to all the traditional conventions of diplomatic usage. To be sure, even traditional diplomacy was interventionist in practice far more often than the publicists would care to admit. And our own diplomacy has increasingly intervened in the internal affairs of the Southeast Asian countries ever since the end of World War II—but almost always hesitatingly, surreptitiously, as it were, guiltily. For the old dogma persists in strength. One must readily confess, too, that departure from its comfortable canons poses the most profound moral problem for policy. Do we have the moral right to interfere in the properly autonomous affairs of others? For myself, I justify my affirmation in terms of the dictates of necessity arising out of the Communist threat in Southeast Asia, not only to our own interests but to the countries of the region as well. Others must deal with the dilemma as they will. But whatever the justification, we must at least frankly recognize what it is that we are trying to do. It is to prosecute a constructive, manipulative diplomacy in the interests of nation building. To pretend that the new diplomacy is less than interventionist is not only hypocritical but imposes a psychological inhibition that may prove disastrous to the elaboration of successful policy.

Once we frankly accept the role we have cast for ourselves, we can throw off one of the great millstones of United States policy in Southeast Asia since the end of World War II, namely, that it is narrowly and negatively anti-Communist in content. Instead we may take on the more positive goals of nation building for modernity. In truth, we seek only the well-being of the Southeast Asian nations themselves, to help and guide them into the twentieth century with freedom.

INDEX